AFTER THE
POST—COLD WAR

SINOTHEORY

A series edited by Carlos Rojas and Eileen Cheng-yin Chow

AFTER THE
POST–COLD WAR

THE FUTURE OF CHINESE HISTORY

DAI JINHUA

*Edited and with an
Introduction by Lisa Rofel*

DUKE UNIVERSITY PRESS *Durham and London* 2018

© 2018 Duke University Press
All rights reserved
Printed and bound by CPI Group (UK) Ltd, Croydon, CR0 4YY

Designed by Amy Ruth Buchanan
Typeset in Minion by Copperline Book Services

Library of Congress Cataloging-in-Publication Data
Names: Dai, Jinhua, [date] author. | Rofel, Lisa, [date] editor.
Title: After the post–cold war: the future of Chinese history /
Dai Jinhua ; edited and with an introduction by Lisa Rofel.
Description: Durham : Duke University Press, 2018. | Series:
Sinotheory | Includes bibliographical references and index.
Identifiers: LCCN 2018007280 (print)
LCCN 2018008408 (ebook)
ISBN 9781478002208 (ebook)
ISBN 9781478000389 (hardcover : alk. paper)
ISBN 9781478000518 (pbk. : alk. paper)
Subjects: LCSH: China—Civilization—21st century. |
China—History—2002– | Motion pictures—China—
History. | Motion pictures and history.
Classification: LCC DS779.43 (ebook) |
LCC DS779.43 .D35 2018 (print) | DDC 951.06—dc23
LC record available at https://lccn.loc.gov/2018007280

Cover art: Jacqueline Humphries, *Untitled*, 2013.
Oil and enamel on linen, 72 × 76 in. Courtesy of the
artist and Greene Naftali, New York.

CONTENTS

CARLOS ROJAS

As Dai Jinhua notes in her discussion of Zhang Yimou's 2003 film *Hero* in this volume, the work contains two pivotal scenes in which the swordsman known as Broken Sword is seen writing Chinese characters. In the first, he uses a brush dipped in bright red ink to write an enormous version of the character 劍 (*jian*, "sword") on a sheet of paper or fabric, while in the second, he uses his sketch to write the two characters 天下 (*tianxia*, "all under heaven") in the desert sand (see accompanying images).

In the first instance, the visual image of Broken Sword's calligraphic rendering of jian comes to have an iconic significance in the film. Hung in the palace behind the king of Qin, the text comes to symbolize the military might that would permit the king to conquer the rival states in the region and establish a unified dynasty. By contrast, in the second instance all we observe is what Dai Jinhua describes as Broken Sword's "fluttering-sleeved, sword waving posture" (chapter 2, this volume) as he inscribes the two characters in the sand, and we never see the written characters themselves. Instead, we learn the content of his short inscription when the assassin Nameless (who observed Broken Sword writing the two characters in question) relays the contents of this short message to the king of Qin, who takes it as an affirmation of his political goals. Equally importantly, the same message also helps convince Nameless to abandon his own plans to assassinate the Qin king, precisely so that the king might then be able to realize his ambitions to establish a unified empire.

The notion of tianxia is, as Dai Jinhua observes, central to Zhang Yimou's reimagination of the events leading up to the founding of China's first unified dynasty, the Qin (221–206 BCE), which viewed itself as ruling over "all under heaven." Literally meaning "all land under heaven" (in the subtitles prepared for the U.S. version of Zhang's film, the term is rendered simply as "our land"), the concept of tianxia designates an ethnoculturally

Images from Zhang Yimou's *Hero* (2003).

grounded understanding of universality, and historically it has been used to articulate a vision of sociopolitical order within a specifically Chinese frame of reference.[1] Zhang's film was controversial when it was released in 2003, because it was seen by viewers as offering an apologia for China's history of imperial conquest, and as an indirect commentary on the political aspirations of the contemporary Chinese state. Part of that controversy resonates with a set of parallel discussions of attempts to reappropriate a traditional notion of tianxia in relation to the contemporary world.

At the same time, this concept of tianxia also metaphorically captures a central objective of the present volume as a whole, in that as a detailed and theoretically informed critical engagement with the sociopolitical configuration of modern China, the volume constitutes an attempt to map a sociocultural space onto a conceptual order that is both intrinsically part of that space but at the same time ontologically outside of it (somewhat like the paradoxes that emerge from Borges's parable of the "map of the Empire whose size was that of the Empire, and which coincided point for point with it").[2] More specifically, this volume is concerned with an analysis of Chinese film, and in her discussion of the desert calligraphy scene, Dai notes that "cinema as a genre bases its true text on the image. That which is not visible, then, lacks signification" (chapter 2). In her own analysis throughout the volume, Dai similarly attends to the visual specificities of cinematic works, but at the same time is equally interested in the works' erasures and blind spots. Her goal, in other words, is to make legible the works' occluded sociopolitical and ideological implications in order to consider how the films' focus on history offers a commentary on a contemporary process of historical amnesia.

Although it is true that written characters for tianxia remain invisible in Zhang's film, we are nevertheless shown a thirty-second sequence of Broken Sword sketching the characters in the sand, in a series of elaborate dramatic arm motions that appear to correspond to several long, curved written strokes. In fact, the writing sequence is so elaborate that many viewers have speculated that Broken Sword may not have been sketching the relatively simple characters for tianxia, but rather something different altogether. Moreover, even if Broken Sword was indeed writing the characters for tianxia, as is subsequently reported by Nameless, it is nevertheless unclear which version of the Chinese script Broken Sword is presumed to have been using in the first place. Before the king of Qin founded the Qin dynasty in 221 BCE, many different versions of the Chinese writing system were in use in the region that is now China. One of the first things that the king did upon becoming emperor was to oversee the systematic standardization of the Chinese script. The Chinese writing system has been reformed many times since then, most recently in the 1950s under Mao Zedong, during which over two thousand different characters were simplified (though the previous traditional forms of the characters continue to be used in Hong Kong, Taiwan, and other overseas Chinese communities). When Broken Sword writes the character for *sword* in the film, accordingly, he uses not the version of the character in use today (劍), but rather a version that closely resembles one preserved in the early dictionary *Shuowen jiezi* (Explanation of simple and compound graphs), in which the character is rendered as 劒. Similarly, although the contemporary version of the binome *tianxia* consists of a mere seven nearly straight strokes, 天下, the rendering of the same two characters in the *Shuowen jiezi*, 兲 下, is significantly more curvy, and would appear to match more closely what we observe of Broken Sword's arm motions as he writes the two characters in the sand.

On the other hand, even if the characters preserved in the *Shuowen jiezi* are indeed presumed to be the model, in Zhang Yimou's film, for both Broken Sword's (visible) rendering of the character for *sword* and, possibly, his (invisible) rendering of the binome "all under heaven," this nevertheless underscores a fundamental ambiguity within the film itself—which is that the work is set during the period immediately preceding both the establishment of the Qin dynasty and the ensuing standardization of the Chinese writing system that was the basis for the compilation of the *Shuowen jiezi* three centuries later. The fact of the matter is, we have no real idea what precisely the Chinese characters written by a historical figure during this immediate pre-Qin period would have looked like, and by projecting a vision of the post-Qin script back onto the pre-Qin era, the film is in effect reproducing in miniature its more general attempt to take a post-Qin (and, indeed, contemporary) understanding of tianxia and the Chinese state, and project it back onto a pre-Qin moment.

The resulting temporal chiasmus, meanwhile, is the focus not only of Dai Jinhua's chapter on Zhang's *Hero*, but also of this volume as a whole. Through a series of incisive analyses of contemporary films dealing with periods ranging from the pre-Qin to the contemporary moment, Dai considers the ways in which these works view the past through the lens of the present, and in the process she argues that they comment ironically on how the post–Cold War present is constituted through a process of strategically eliding critical elements of its own past.

ACKNOWLEDGMENTS

Dai Jinhua and Lisa Rofel would like to thank first and foremost the translators of the essays in this volume. We appreciate that translation work is never simple; there is no straightforward correspondence between words in different languages, especially the kinds of theoretical terms prevalent in this book. Each term carries a whole cultural history with it. Dai Jinhua's dense, creative, and challenging prose makes the translation work all the more admirable. Thank you all. We would also like to thank the reviewers of this volume for the care they took in reading carefully through the essays. Angela Zito, as one of them, conceived a brilliant reordering of the chapters. Yizhou Guo did the selected bibliography; she and Caroline Kao helped with final copyediting questions. Karen Fisher carried out graceful editing. Finally, we would like to thank Ken Wissoker and Elizabeth Ault for their persistent care in getting this book to publication.

LISA ROFEL

Dai Jinhua is the equivalent of a rock star in China. Students, intellectuals, and the general public flock to hear her searing, radical insights into the enormous transformations in contemporary life—and the injustices and ills they have wrought. For over two decades she has brought her feminist Marxism—framed through film theory, psychoanalysis, poststructuralism, and cultural studies—to bear as a prescient public intellectual of and for our times. Her works have become celebrated classics of the academic studies of Chinese cinema. While she locates herself in China—a deliberate, self-conscious choice—Dai is equally in dialogue with cultural theorists from Europe, the United States, Asia, Latin America, and Africa. Dai Jinhua and Meng Yue were the first to initiate post-Mao feminist literary criticism in China with their renowned *Emerging from the Horizon of History*. She also founded the first film theory specialization at the Beijing Film Academy and established the Institute for Film and Cultural Studies—the first in China—at the premier Beijing University. Finally, Dai has participated in numerous global activist organizations, including the Third World Forum, World Social Forum, and the initiative to nominate one thousand women for the Nobel Peace Prize, as well as rural women's organizations in China.

This collection of her recent essays focuses on questions of history, memory, and the historical revisionism of the new millennium. As a film theorist, Dai uses a specific film in each essay as a touchstone for a broader discussion of China as it exists today within global capitalism. As she has stated elsewhere, she departs from approaches that treat film as a text internal to itself, instead placing each film within a broader cultural discourse and sociopolitical context.[1] Far more than a film critic, Dai is penetrating and illuminating in addressing the forces, contexts, and incidents in the imbrication of national and transnational scenarios. This volume follows on the previous English-language translation of Dai's essays, *Cinema and Desire*, edited by Jing Wang and Tani E. Barlow, published over a decade ago.

If, in that earlier collection, Dai analyzed the 1980s in China—what in retrospect we would call the beginning of the postsocialist era—as a moment when "history experienced reconstruction,"[2] then in this set of essays she diagnoses symptomatically the first decade of the new millennium, under the hegemony of neoliberal capitalism, as a moment when history experiences its own disappearance. Dai is both reading and writing allegories of our contemporary moment, as in her discussion in her introduction of a discarded, rusty advertising sign with Marxist political pop she found in the trash heap behind a newly built suburb for the international, cosmopolitan middle class of Beijing. As she asks in that essay, "Communism was once a specter from the future floating over the present. Today, is Marxism a phantom from the past that now and then emerges and takes shape in the present?"

In all of the films she addresses in this volume with the exception of two, socialist subjectivity has been hollowed out and forgotten in favor of global, depoliticized images. The war films and epic narratives, for all their historical sweep and invocations of memory, display the signs of the erasure of collective politics and social movements that constituted the alternative narrative of modern China. Dai finds instead the reduction of collective history into an individual story of trauma, as clearly delineated in films such as Lu Chuan's *The City of Life and Death* (*Nanjing! Nanjing!* 南京! 南京!), which celebrates the universal image of the human, and among filmmakers influenced by Bertolucci's *The Last Emperor* (discussed in the finale).

One of Dai's central arguments in this volume is that the erasure of the past simultaneously forecloses imagining the future. Dai's abiding concern is that this disappearance of history leaves us with no hope of moving beyond the degradations of the present into a future that might offer us a socially just world. With an equal dose of pessimism and passion, Dai serves up an incisive indictment of our times and calls for a return to utopian thinking. She urges us to do so by way of the past: to not forget the important socialist-inspired utopian thinking that tried to present us a true alternative to capitalism. Her goal is not a return to socialism—and certainly not an embrace of Maoism—so much as an excavation of the urge to find that alternative.

The title of this collection, *After the Post–Cold War*, points toward this erasure of history. Dai contends that with neoliberal globalization, we have moved beyond the post–Cold War era. This post-post–Cold War development refers to the forgetting of the previous ideological and political tensions between China's socialist path and Euro-American modernization. The end of the Cold War gave the impression that this conflict had been replaced by economic globalization, the end of modern history, and the closure of the political imagination of an alternative future. Yet the global scramble for supremacy means that a complex mixture of old and new ideological forces has created the new era of the post-post–Cold War. Dai is able to see and diagnose these contradictory forces in the textual detail of film.

This post-post–Cold War era begins, in her view, with the U.S. war on terror, which she argues provides new grounds for globalization. A key year is 2008, with the financial tsunami; the Sichuan earthquake, which enabled the visible emergence of China's new middle class (through its do-nations and volunteer efforts); the Olympic games held in China; and China's emergence as the United States' greatest creditor. Indeed, she contends that the Cold War has been readily forgotten in this era of global capital-ism, as if it were part of a misty past, or an ancient "scary fairy tale" (see Dai's introduction). At the same time, she recalls the legacies of the Cold War. From the positionality of China, Dai reminds us that the Cold War was never just a binary. After 1960, China was neither in the camp of the Soviet Union nor in that of the U.S. Instead, it created an alternative third world position and set of alliances. From that neither-nor position, China offered an alternative development path for formerly colonized countries. Radical intellectuals and movement revolutionaries around the world were inspired by some forms of Maoist thought. But Dai, in her fearless quest for (at least contingent) truth, and her ability to think dialectically without totalities, goes on to deconstruct that very path, arguing that a dream of modernization is also part of the problem, not least because of the environ-mental nightmares it has wrought.

Dai is uncanny in her sense of how to craft a genealogy of the present. One could say, following Stefano Harney and Fred Moten, that her unique vision finds its inspiration in the undercommons.[3] While Dai positions herself from within a leftist perspective, she deconstructs the well-worn de-bates by and about the so-called New Left and the neoliberals in China. Dai is not so easily pigeonholed. In her introduction, for example, she analyzes their shared nostalgic melancholia for a lost past (albeit different), which creates blurred thinking about the present. While some would accuse the left in China of giving the Chinese state a pass, Dai, as shown in these essays, clearly implicates the Chinese state in the conditions wrought by neoliberal capitalism. Throughout, she also deconstructs the relation of China to the West, reminding us of a history when these relations were otherwise—that is, China's alliances within the third world. Finally, she analyzes global anxieties about the so-called rise of China, as well as the manner in which China has entered into the fold (borrowing from Deleuze) of neoliberal capitalism.

Indeed, Dai Jinhua exemplifies the quintessential Deleuzian thinker—always in motion, restlessly seeking possibilities for impossible thinking. Her ability to self-consciously interpret the political unconscious of her generation of intellectuals is unparalleled. Dai has honed these intellectual tools since her undergraduate days. Dai was in the cohort of 1978—the first generation of students after the Cultural Revolution who entered college based on the revival of entrance exams, when a full decade of young people vied in the competition (see my interview with Dai in this volume).[4] The seeds of her feminist thinking began, however, in the previous decade during the Cultural Revolution. On the one hand, she truly felt that women and men were treated equally—she was a student cadre and leader of the group that went together to the countryside during that era. On the other, she had contradictory experiences for which there was no language.

One of Dai's first set of explicit conflicts was with the masculinist critique of Maoist socialism that started just as she entered Beijing University as an undergraduate student. The dominant voices were all from this masculinist perspective—how Maoist socialism had emasculated men and masculinized women.[5] These voices then ridiculed women with the admonishing prescription "marriage should be your only business," as many workplaces in the 1980s laid off urban women in the name of economic efficiency and growth.

"What is a woman?" became a guiding question Dai pursued in her studies of literature and later film. For Dai, women's rights (*nüquan zhuyi*) is not the main problem; the main problem is *nüxing zhuyi*, that is, women's consciousness or gender ideology. In China, women had a great deal of legal rights—at least until the revision of the constitution in the 1980s.

What was needed was a consciousness of the way women experience a patriarchal injunction as well as an understanding of the naturalization of gender discrimination that came with post-Mao reforms.

During this period (the 1990s), Dai became increasingly disturbed with both the growing difference between rich and poor and the way the rhetoric of gender was used to cover over these seismic social shifts by making these problems seem small (i.e., they were only about women). She began to write about this new kind of violence: the redistribution of wealth, which also sacrificed women's lives in the process. Dissatisfied with the way women's studies programs addressed women in the new middle class and used feminist theories for those who benefited from the reforms but not for those who were exploited, Dai turned to reanalyzing class. Thus, while Dai's feminism may seem oblique in this volume, she brings from feminism an understanding of how to analyze the naturalization of power, difference, and inequality.

As Dai explains in my interview with her (this volume), given the wholesale rejection of Maoist socialism, there was no way in the 1990s to talk about class, even as a great deal of violence was perpetrated through growing class inequalities. The language of class was rejected, although the theory of class subtending this language (i.e., Marxist-inspired theories) was exactly what was needed. However, as Dai states, those theories originally inspired by Marx also had their lacunae that needed to be addressed: the conflicts between the countryside and the city and between different regions of the country; the relations between middle-class women and the rural domestic servants they hire, displacing their own oppression onto these women; and the displacement of dispossession onto gender relations. Thus, one sees in the essays presented here Dai's inventive and capacious approach to class inequalities that takes into account how class is shaped in and through capital's originary and uneven accumulation strategies, which include gender relations, nationalism, and regional disparities.

Dai has also turned for inspiration to third-world movements and the theories that subtend them, from Samir Amin's Third World Forum to Subcomandante Marcos's Zapatista Army of National Liberation, from global environmental movements (she served on the first board of Greenpeace in China) to China's new rural collective movements. Over the last fifteen years, then, Dai has brought an assemblage of theoretical tools to bear on questions about history and memory as they intersect with global capitalism and nationalism, most importantly because of the manner in which China has become imbricated with the global capitalist world.

Dai's leftist cultural critique in these essays comes after the rapid privatization and profitization of China's economy were well under way and after the discourse about the rise of China became pervasive. Rather than drawing a division between domestic affairs and global ones, these essays delineate how China is in the global capitalist world and, equally, how that world is in China. If, in her earlier work, she was concerned with the orientalizing gaze of the West and the uncritical adoption of Western theories by Chinese intellectuals, in these essays she builds on those earlier insights, examining the impossibility of separating the local from the global while simultaneously insisting on the specificity of Chinese historical experience. She develops these insights by analyzing contemporary life and ideology in China while never losing sight of the mutual imbrication of China and global capitalism. In critiquing China's global capitalist developments, Dai repeatedly reminds us of the productive and heuristic potential of the earlier political imagination of China's twentieth-century history. In refusing to forget, she cautions against the alignment of the Chinese middle class with the global financial elites at the expense of the working people, whose liberation, mobilization, and newfound subjectivity constitute the essence of China's past revolutionary culture. If the middle class has its way, China's touted rise will amount to adding a new player in the global scramble for wealth, power, and supremacy.

In these essays, Dai brings to bear her mastery of film's visual techniques along with her theoretically innovative approach to the interpretation of contemporary cultural life. While she takes off from a particular film, she locates in filmic scenes, cinematography, and visual signifiers the political unconscious of contemporary Chinese life. She has a masterful command of film language and film technique to interpret contemporary ideas, sentiments, and contradictions. In each essay, she further demonstrates the underlying links and echoes among multiple texts, including video games and popular novels, that seem at first glance far removed from one another.

Dai thus reads and diagnoses the signs of our times—in film, but also in material objects and structures of feeling. This is a locational reading of China, but readers would be misinterpreting Dai's arguments if they concluded she is merely doing a study of her country. Rather, she is reading the contemporary global moment as it manifests in and through and out of China. Dai thus analyzes the national/political/cultural struggles enmeshed in film both visually and in terms of content. In these essays, she emphasizes how these struggles shape the erasure of history. At the same time, she excavates history in the aporia of these erasures. She does so in order to task us with the reconstruction of memories otherwise from those we have been fed in the years after the post–Cold War. She gains insight from globally circulating theories while challenging their pretension to universality from no location. Her abiding questions are the following: In this age of "after theory," how do we define a new and effective social criticism? Do we need a new historical subject (*zhuti*)? How do we avoid a grand narrative? How do we avoid using the kind of historical subject such as the proletariat but then still think about capitalists? Do we need utopia?

In Part I, "Trauma, Evacuated Memories, and Inverted Histories," Dai offers cinematic analysis that lays out one of her most important arguments in the book: that China's current situation is the imbrication of unresolved contradictions: the world (i.e., the global capitalist world dominated by the West) is always already within China, even as China grapples with its own self-image in relation to that world. Chapter 1, "I Want to Be Human: A Story of China and the Human," discusses the film *City of Life and Death* (*Nanjing! Nanjing!*), directed by Lu Chuan, a tale of the Nanjing Massacre by the Japanese during World War II. Dai lays out the dense contextualization of the ambiguous status of the Nanjing Massacre (not Hiroshima, not the Holocaust, never recognized as a human catastrophe) and thereby helps us to grasp how "China's" (Dai deliberately uses quotation marks to signify its contingent narrative status) modern relationship to its own history is always already seen through a global gaze.[6] Dai views the massacre as the kind of suspended, shared, open trauma whose displaced memory causes the evacuated subjectivity of the post-post–Cold War that China suffers from today. This is the kind of terrible space in which Dai wishes to dwell in this book. The film is a recuperation of universal humanity through a portrayal of the Japanese soldier's Christian humanism purged of blood and death. The Chinese characters in the film, however, do not get placed in this universal humanity. But by casting the film in this light, Dai also slyly makes legible that Lu Chuan's heavily criticized choice to cast as his protagonist a sympathetic Japanese soldier was useful in the way it ventriloquized, through one of its perpetrators, a regret for the massacre that the Japanese government has, to this day, been reluctant to express. This first essay also introduces the important contradiction of the rising middle class and its role in a concomitant rise of nationalist/culturalist sentiment.

This sets the stage for chapter 2, "*Hero* and the Invisible *Tianxia*." Dai argues that, like *City of Life and Death*, Zhang Yimou's *Hero* (英雄) mines history but similarly evacuates it of any meaning that could be used to envision a future for China. It does so by inverting the story of the assassins of the first emperor, Qin Shihuang, from how to assassinate the king to how not to assassinate him. The film relies heavily on the term tianxia, or "all under heaven," to make this historical inversion appear logical. Tracing the contemporary use of tianxia by bringing in popular culture sources beyond the film (video games and fantasy novels), Dai argues that tianxia, instead of being a space of all under heaven in today's China, is now associated with power, conquerors, and hegemony—the "private property of the victors." Dai delineates how this new meaning replaces its usage not just in the imperial past but also under Maoist socialism, thus opening a key theme in this collection of essays: that the visitations into pre-twentieth-century history are done in the service of outflanking and forgetting China's revolutionary history of the twentieth century. Tianxia in the film represents an aporia, or evacuation, of meaning. The social symptomaticity of this aporia is reflected in the way the film empties out the alternative possibilities (alternatives to modernity and capitalism) that had been contained in the term, turning it into merely an empty signifier of China. Yet along with this pessimistic assessment, Dai continually urges us to find resources for imagining a more just future. Thus, she ends this essay with the query: in what sense, from which angles, and to what extent can China serve as a method to sketch an alternative world imaginary?

Part II, "Class, Still Lives, and Masculinity," offers a close interpretation of the past, present, and possible future of class in China. There are two filmmakers, both of whom got their start in independent art cinema, whom Dai praises for their ability to break through what she calls the "delirium and aphasia" of ahistorical histories. They do so by consistently portraying the lives of China's subaltern classes experiencing capitalism's intensive exploitations and marginalizations. Jia Zhangke is one of them, and Zhang Meng is the other. Chapter 3, "Temporality, *Nature Morte*, and the Filmmaker: A Reconsideration of *Still Life*," discusses one of the most important films to come out of China in years. Jia Zhangke's *Still Life* (三峡好人) addresses the controversial Three Gorges dam project and the precarious lives of China's internal migratory classes. The Three Gorges reservoir, the largest hydro-engineering project in Chinese history and the largest water conservation project in the world, led to a massive forced migration. Dai analyzes how Jia Zhangke moves aside the grand images at the heart of mainstream depictions that glorify modernization projects such as the Three Gorges dam to show us the so-called insignificant people behind the canvas. She reads the film as a contemporary Chinese parable about rebuilding or drowning, creation or destruction, remembering or repressing. She puts this film in conversation with documentaries and art installations about the Three Gorges project and, more generally, about exploitation and violence. Thus, it is temporality, or the development projects carried out in the name of progress, that, as Dai states, "sweeps away historical and natural spaces like a hurricane and rewrites them."

Chapter 4, "*The Piano in a Factory*: Class, in the Name of the Father," discusses the way the director Zhang Meng breaks through the amnesia about the socialist past. Here, in a more optimistic vein, Dai argues that this is almost the only feature film that counters the erasures of history to depict the tremendous upheavals in the lives of millions of people in China over the last thirty years. *The Piano in a Factory* (钢的琴) depicts the lives of factory workers laid off under the 1980s economic reforms that closed many bankrupt state-run enterprises. But rather than a melodrama, this film is full of black humor, including music and dance sequences, as one of the main characters rallies his former fellow workers—many of whom have been forced to turn to a variety of illegal activities—to build a piano for his daughter, as part of his fight to retain custody of her. Dai's in-depth analysis of the film's cinematography leads her to conclude that what she calls Zhang Meng's "anticinematic" idiom fits with the black humor approach to the heavy theme of the abandonment of workers in the postsocialist era. But the film's formal language also signifies the theme of dignity in labor and creation. In this sense, the film is a paean to socialist culture's efforts to create new human beings, even as it also highlights the lost masculinity— as "masters of the country"—of the former working class.

In Part III, "The Spy Genre," Dai takes up the spy as a pretext for a film genre that was popular during the Cold War and that has recently been revived. In its historical genre, Dai interprets the spy as a brilliant figure through which to apprehend the sufferings and failings in the struggles for personal and political identity under the pressures of the socialist experiment and its bruising campaigns. In its more recent recasting, Dai sees a genuine anxiety over identity. In chapter 5, "The Spy-Film Legacy: A Preliminary Cultural Analysis of the Spy Film," Dai argues that, in true spy-film genre, the spy film itself is not what it seems. Dai first reviews the Cold War history of the spy film, finding that despite the mutual isolation of enemies from each other's cultures, the spy-film narrative subgenre is distinctive in being the only type of film, nearly without exception, to cross Cold War boundaries and antagonisms. Moreover, China made spy films as well, despite its lack of attachment to either side of the Cold War binary. Dai further argues that the spy film departs from other popular films in its treatment of gender. Chinese films from the 1950s to the 1970s made illegitimate the scopic desire of the male subject; not so the spy film, in which the treacherous female is in fact the activator of scopic dynamism. Dai then addresses the film's current popular revival, arguing that the current spy films, unlike Cold War–era spy films, exude hesitation and self-doubt about identity. In Dai's view, the spy films in the post–Cold War era address the abyss that has opened up between society and memory. They portray a world split with cracks and fissures, as they continue to address unresolved questions around the basic nature of the nation-state itself, and of personal and national identity. In this essay, rather than analyze one film in depth, Dai offers an overview of the breadth of spy films from the 1940s to the present, both nationally and internationally.

Chapter 6, "In Vogue: Politics and the Nation-State in *Lust, Caution* and the *Lust, Caution* Phenomenon in China," interprets Ang Lee's film *Lust, Caution* (色·戒)—a hit throughout the Chinese-speaking world—as resolving the contradiction between the legitimacy of a communist regime dependent on socialist ideology and the reality of class division with China's full turn to capitalism. The film addresses patriotic resistance to Japanese military rule in the period leading up to World War II. The film avoids previous interpretations of this history, which highlighted the struggles between communists and nationalists, and their quite different forms of resistance. Instead, it addresses a group of elite students who infiltrate the Chinese government installed by the Japanese military regime. Dai argues that the film presents a depoliticized history of the twentieth century, framed within a patriotism that enables the evasion of history and politics. Dai further argues that *Lust, Caution*'s popular, and somewhat controversial, reception delineates a genealogy of China's new middle class and its cosmopolitanism. Dai concludes that the film has constructed a floating stage detached from history in an age of globalization. In the two films presented in this part, Dai thus develops her uncompromising analysis of the formation of the subject and subjectivity in relation to global politics, history, and memory.

The "Finale," "History, Memory, and the Politics of Representation," takes off from Bertolucci's *The Last Emperor* and its influence on the fifth generation of Chinese filmmakers to reflect on the transformations in historical writing in the last half of the twentieth century and the first decade of the twenty-first century. Dai argues that Bertolucci used the individual (in the person of the last emperor of the Qing dynasty [1644–1911], who became a puppet emperor under Japanese colonialism) to erase the history of modern China by using space and stereotypical historical background settings to de-historicize historical events. She argues that Chinese films have adopted his approach, similarly using space to erase time or the temporality of twentieth-century struggles for alternatives to capitalist modernity. Since the beginning of economic reforms, Dai contends, historical writing has deconstructed mass memory by using individual experience and memory so as to call into question any critique of the past. At the same time, paradoxically, there has been a deep self-awareness of the significance of history for politics and culture. Dai argues that China has seen what she calls the "reversal of the reversal," that is, a rejection of the socialist history of China's past and a restoration of the mainstream logic of the modern world. Dai diagnoses a current sociopolitical difficulty that China faces: the continuation of Communist Party rule along with an economic and political rupture with the past. This tension produces dilemmas for interpretations of the past: is there a continuation of past ideologies or the construction of new ones? The result has been what she calls ahistorical histories.

Finally, I have also included a brief interview I conducted with Dai in the summer of 2014 as well as a selected bibliography of her books.

These lucid, inspiring essays together offer a scathing indictment of the way global capitalism has eviscerated hopes of a better world. In a talk entitled "A Cultural Landscape without Coordinates" that Dai delivered at the University of California, Santa Cruz, she spoke of how cultural critics in China have lost the means to describe the realities of the present. She diagnoses our current ills with uncompromising insight, while she goads us not to give up on dreams of a better world. True to her uncompromising commitment to refuse the cynicism of the current moment, Dai ended her talk by invoking a popular slogan from the May 1968 uprisings in Paris: "All Power to the Imagination."

INTRODUCTION

TRANSLATED BY JIE LI

Prologue

In 2009, I went to Beijing's satellite city, the new district of Wangjing, to visit a German curator who was living in an avant-garde artist's studio. The neighborhood of my destination did not have a Chinese name. Its English name was Class.

My taxi driver used to be a farmer in the Beijing suburbs and had only recently begun this not-so-easy livelihood of the taxi business. He got completely lost in this brand-new, nameless urban labyrinth.

On the streets of this new phantasmic district, we could see only the flying dust in the afternoon sunshine over the recently cleared grounds that had yet to be laid with grass. Apart from construction trucks and migrant workers, the streets were eerily silent and unlike Beijing—as if nobody lived there.

On the margins of this new neighborhood were crumbling old neighborhoods constructed in the 1970s and '80s that were still bustling with activity. But when passersby were asked about Class, they looked only bewildered by the English word.

The enormous new district looked not so much like the little town in *The Truman Show* as a deserted city in one of Michelangelo Antonioni's films. When we finally located the so-called Class neighborhood with the help of the taxi company's customer service, I realized that we had passed by this stretch of buildings many times. The huge letters of the word "Class" towered over the skyscrapers that formed part of the skyline.

The buildings exuded an aura of classy residence. Their automated doors were tightly shut; there were gentle hills and lawns, birds and flowers, children with different skin colors playing soccer—the scenery of an international middle class.

The nondescript bronze plaque next to the gate stated something to the effect of "private residence; no solicitations." There were two security guards in uniform—one was taking great pains to interrogate a visitor before me, and the other had stopped a delivery van and was confirming his comings and goings with his walkie-talkie. Neither had time to pay any attention to me.

Since I was early, I walked around the outer walls of the compound and found myself at the end of a back wall beyond the reach of the sun. Next to a pile of construction garbage, I found a cast iron structure or a piece of urban sculpture. I thought perhaps it was made by the architecture firm, with the signature of the designer. It looked quite grand. I went up for a closer look. Written in German and Chinese were the words: "Base determines superstructure.—Karl Marx."

Like all cast iron, it was rusty where rainwater had soaked it. It was as if the traces of rust told a tale of the etching and decay of time. I stood there amazed. I knew that it used to be quite a fad to use the rhetoric of political pop for Beijing's real estate commercials and that cast iron was an international architectural fashion. Yet this work still stunned me for a moment, as if I had walked into an anachronistic world and encountered an allegory of contemporary China.

It seemed as if I had found a boundary stone of history at the end of history, and the reality of class in a place at the city's edge literally named Class. In today's China, questions of class are no longer explicitly named as such in political science or sociology. Sometimes people euphemistically talk about social strata or obscurely about differences. The most direct expressions are about the rich and the poor (their polarization, the Gini coefficient, the nouveau riche versus the nouveau poor, the elite versus the subaltern, the entrepreneurs versus the weak). For me, this chance encounter revealed the landscape of contemporary urban China; it became a possible entry to reflect on and evaluate China, and perhaps the world and its contemporary culture.

The Cold War, this most important, endlessly long era of global twentieth-century history, seems to have vanished without a trace, as if it were a short-lived illusion far beyond reach, like a nightmare in an ancient, hard-to-recall, and somewhat scary fairy tale. Before my encounter with Class in Beijing, I was invited to visit Freie Universität Berlin. The open-air book-stalls and bookstores featured a magazine with a portrait of Marx on its cover, which looked quite striking in the Berlin cityscape. My German friend told me it was a special issue on the financial tsunami, and that the title of the story read, "He Said It Long Ago."

Marx or Marxism: a totally discarded and forgotten history? A continuing present? Or a future still to be anticipated? Such a familiar signifier appeared in this sudden and bizarre way, intimating a new international order. In *The Communist Manifesto*, communism was once a specter from the future floating over the present. Today, is Marxism a phantom from the past that now and then emerges and takes shape in the present?

China: Cold War, Post–Cold War, Displaced Time

Needless to say, the most prominent transformation in twenty-first-century China is its emergence as a nation-state within the system of global capitalism. Beyond that, we could speak of the desires and anxieties in various international discourses attendant upon China as a potential new empire.

The Cold War order was once the basic parameter defining China's position: a forefront socialist nation that faced off against the Western world, as well as an oddity that rejected the Soviet bloc. Surrounded by strong enemies on the international front, China's tenacious survival as well as its political, economic, and cultural practices made it appear to be a special case. Yet what stands out even more is its distinctive status as a representative of the third world.

One could say that it was precisely the political and economic experiments of the 1960s and '70s in China that turned Mao Zedong Thought or Maoism into an intellectual resource for Europe and the United States, turning the Chinese revolutionary path into a topic of relevance for the world.

Yet if China of the Cold War era used third worldism to break through the isolation and embargo imposed on it (as if it were an extra chess piece in a binary order), then these efforts to crack the iciness not only shattered the pattern of the Cold War order, but also provided an alternative model for the transformation of the socialist path into a zigzagging route to modernization, affirming political sovereignty, encouraging industrialization, and standing tall within the world of nations. Thus temporal narratives and modernist apprehensions that filled China's twentieth-century era repeatedly surfaced and were repeatedly displaced.

One could say that the 1911 revolution began China's history as a modern nation. The Western calendar replaced the agricultural and dynastic calendars and signified that "China" had finally gained a sense of "time"—world history or so-called linear historical time.

Then the founding of the People's Republic of China seemed to proclaim once again that Time had begun, with 1949 as Year One, implying China's entrance into world history as an independent and sovereign nation. It also signified a form of red or political periodization, suggesting that the People's Republic had entered into Marxist-Leninist (people's) historical time that marched toward the future promise of a classless society.

Or we could say that the Sino-U.S. Joint Communiqué in 1972 was another turning point, with Deng Xiaoping's reform and opening beginning a post–Cold War era within the socialist camp even before the end of the Cold War. Time itself was foreshortened, displaced from communist utopian processes into global capitalist time. This time-space enunciated the idea that China was (once again) marching toward the world. Within an imaginary of stagnation, China was forever chasing after the West.

World revolution became a distant memory. By the 1970s, China's vision of itself as a world revolutionary leader began to fade. By the 1980s, this landscape became inverted and critically judged.

An interesting fact is that China's prosperous New Era was not accidentally synchronous with the rise of global neoliberalism. By the end of the 1970s, as the entire Chinese society settled accounts with itself, if it wasn't merely reciting the neoliberal canons that originated in the West, then it was at least adding an effective footnote. China's transformation also contributed to the reorientation of continental and especially French political thought that was settling accounts with European leftist intellectuals.

Without a doubt, the turning point and event in China with international implications was the 1989 Tiananmen movement. Threatening the regime for the first time since 1949 and tragically crushed with brutal military force, this citizens' resistance movement nevertheless helped the collapse or implosion of the socialist camp. One can see it as the first domino in a global domino effect. Yet ironically, as these changes led to the end of the Cold War and a redrawing of the world geopolitical map, China became the last infallible socialist giant, falling into a post–Cold War cold war.

Hence China Time became disjointed from world historical time once again. And it was misrecognized from both sides. On the one side, the party line insisted on Chinese characteristics to strategically emphasize China's historical time. The other side saw China as a socialist totalitarian nation.[1] Neither view took into account the degree to which China was implicated in globalization.

Even more strangely, in the last ten years of the twentieth century, the world that had witnessed Tiananmen (and had previously not had a shared enemy) united against the Chinese government as humanity's common enemy.

Meanwhile, the violent conclusion of the Tiananmen protests totally destroyed and purged socialism's spiritual legacy and mobilization potential that had once hindered the path of Chinese capitalism. The Chinese regime began pushing for capitalism with unprecedented energy.

Before ridding itself of its international crisis, China had already emerged at the forefront of global capitalism.

In the last ten years of the twentieth century, the post–Cold War era, the self-recognized victors redrew the map of the world. First, the U.S. empire came to be seen as the sole, unshakeable leader of the world. Neoliberalism or the Washington Consensus became the belief that there is no alternative and even ended history.

The flood of capital passed over the barriers dividing the two sides of the Cold War and rushed into the wide region of what was previously the Eastern camp. Large numbers of legal and illegal immigrants crossed former Cold War boundaries and embarked on the reverse journey of third-world immigrants toward the heart of darkness.

The second, and perhaps an even more important, new international reality was the emergence of the European Union. As one of the victors of the Cold War, Western Europe took as its booty Eastern Europe's huge, precapitalist real economy, its latent consumer market, and its army of cheap labor. This helped to alleviate the political, economic, and military conflicts of interest between various Western European countries that had lasted for several hundred years.

At the same time, as a dynamic zone within the global capitalist map, China remains caught in rather bizarre cultural-political circumstances. In the last decade of the twentieth century, Chinese society and culture were consistently mired within the delirium and aphasia of multiple ideological discourses.

The post–Cold War cold war atmosphere enveloped China and the globe. In order to give legitimacy to its rule in the midst of crisis (after Tiananmen), the Chinese government continued to use the name of the Chinese Communist Party (CCP) and the ideological discourse of socialism. Even if they have become vacuous soliloquies, their endless repetition obscures the meaning of these enormous contemporary transformations.

Even more peculiar, this ideology that has exposed itself as a lie shares the ideological cynicism of the postrevolutionary, globalized world. Yet, in the vast territory of China, socialism/communism remains the core conviction of certain people, including grassroots officials. Some regions have even maintained features of socialism in their social organization.

While ironically highlighting China's process of pursuing capitalism, such meaningless chatter can still return like a specter to which one has made sacrifices. Its vocabulary can still be used to interrogate and oppose the government.

But in reality, an important component of the post–Cold War cold war situation is the pervasive dissemination of a cold war ideology that inverts the subject while blocking the delirium and aphasia that conceal and contain a double legitimation crisis.

On one side is the remnant authority and political repression remaining from the Tiananmen massacre. The government was in a position to smash quickly the resistance of the entire society in order to complete its violent destruction of collective ownership. Large-scale wealth redistribution has meant the exploitation of both urban and rural laborers and the small number of haves quickly plundering and hoarding what used to be collective wealth.

On the other side, the polarization of classes, social suffering, and despair produced by the pursuit of capitalism are again displaced onto world historical time and misdirected into anger and outrage toward the Communist Party (though not the so-called communist political regime of the present) and socialism (though not the so-called socialist system of the present). Such displacement and misrecognition have made resisters give up the legal, intellectual, and discursive resources still at their disposal. Hence they do not recognize the restoration of capitalism or the peaceful evolution toward capitalism that surrounds them.

As a result, these resisters resort to riots or uprisings (that are the condition of this aphasia), or they might helplessly and uselessly appeal to the law to protect their rights, or they are forced to share in the government's so-called hardships.

This subject-inverting Cold War logic renewed the imaginary of institutional fetishism. A direct transformation occurred from the notion that only socialism can save China to a belief in the capitalist system as represented by the omnipotence of the free market. This further enabled the progress of Chinese capitalist development.

Hence in the second half of the 1990s, the consensus over classical liberalism in the Chinese intellectual world split into a conflict between the liberals and the New Left. Their core differences focus on their different understandings of the nature of Chinese society. Is everything happening in China the inevitable result of the tyranny of the Communist Party and socialism? Are the multiparty system, representative democracy, total privatization, and opening up the market to the Western world the ultimate solutions to China's problems? Or is a new round of social conflict and suffering the very result of accelerated capitalism? The exchange of power and money between the regime and multinational and domestic capital is violently polarizing the rich and poor classes in China.

Hence exposing and investigating the social suffering of China's lower classes clearly shows by contrast the social justice of a distributive system. Discussion of public wealth and the property rights of workers, accounting for the historical legacies and debts of socialism, and implementing democracy on the basis of socialism (not necessarily the past of actually existing socialism)—these became the concerns of the New Left.

Yet because the debate on the nature of Chinese society or its most important problems directly points to the core issue and dilemma of the ruling regime, so-called liberals and the New Left never engaged in a real intellectual dialogue but instead got entangled in the contestation for the imaginary moral high ground of opposing the regime. The latent deep differences between the two could not surface but instead became another labyrinth and quagmire of this strange and displaced Cold War style of thinking.

If the sorrow of the leftists and the nostalgia of the rightists are cultural political expressions, then the despair of China's neoliberals about the tyranny of the CCP and the indignation of the New Left over the sufferings of the subaltern share something extraordinary, namely a politics of melancholia. The neoliberals express imagined loss for the days before the revolution, focusing on 1930s Shanghai, whereas the New Left yearns for and defends the yonder days of the Maoist era from the 1950s to the '70s. They present a precise enunciation of mutually antagonistic nostalgia.

An interesting symptom: "nostalgia" is translated in mainland China as longing for the past. In Taiwan and Hong Kong, however, it is translated as a yearning for origins or one's hometown or native place. This seems to indicate that within mainland China's twentieth-century cultural logic, a utopian imaginary placed in the future has negated the notion of hometown or native place.

An imaginary space, an origin of where we come from, a site of the heart's belonging. Nostalgia is only a way of looking back in time. But at the turn of the twenty-first century, the diametrically shared nostalgia of the Chinese liberals and the New Left further exposed the symptoms of social and cultural crisis.

The heterogeneous historical narratives that arose from the binary cultural logic of the Cold War thus fought for the ownership and narrative of history and time. Whether they lament or celebrate the end of the Cold War, whether they regard the socialist experiment as a huge loss or the end of history, these discourses have closed off visions of the future. They pronounce the promise of future justice to be a mere illusion, erasing the depth and breadth of history. They use the eternal and locked present to seal off any space for imagining the future.

Hence, in the post–Cold War, the continuation and stabilization of the CCP's power created a deep sense of sorrow among Chinese liberals, a sorrow that usually belongs to the left. Meanwhile the obstruction of any future vision has led China's New Left to feel a lingering melancholy.

After the Post–Cold War: The Beginning of Time?

At the beginning of the twenty-first century, the waves of globalization and the turbulent tides of antiglobalization, as Antonio Negri and Michael Hardt sketched out, namely, the hegemony of the American Empire (X + America) and the multitude resisting this hegemony, constitute the primary landscape of the world.[2] Yet this landscape is also gradually being displaced as it emerges.

Without a doubt, the September 11 attack on U.S. American territory has accelerated the renewed militarization of American imperial hegemony. As a result, terrorism and antiterrorism not only became the United States' new political strategy, but also quickly became the guiding ideology of globalization.

If the binary opposition between democracy and authoritarianism began to replace the binary of capitalism versus communism and is gradually rewriting the ideological imaginary of the Cold War, the antiterrorist campaigns led by the U.S. unexpectedly began a new era after the post–Cold War. Continuous international military interventions—Kosovo, Afghanistan, Iraq, Libya—have time and again negated the twentieth century, such as the miracle of the Cuban Revolution, and keep on flaunting the unassailable logical connection between political-military hegemony and domination over the financial empire.

If that is the case, then continued military interventions (especially the swamp of American involvement in Iraq for over a decade) seem to be proving American imperial hegemony while consuming its overall strength. Just as Samir Amin once said, global capitalism seems to have turned into a three-headed monster led by the U.S., the EU, and Japan.[3]

Yet unexpectedly in 2008, Wall Street, the heart of the financial empire, became the tipping point. Suddenly all was panic and paranoia. The crisis then spread into other developed countries, especially dragging the European Union into the quagmire of disaster.

The year of the financial tsunami turned out coincidentally (and not by theatrical design) to be China's year of the Olympics. In fact, the 2011 HBO film *Too Big to Fail*, based on a *New York Times* best-selling book, included a scene that used as its background the fireworks of the Beijing Olympics opening ceremony. In this scene, the American secretary of the treasury reluctantly held onto a Chinese flag while he spoke to a nameless Chinese official about the financial crisis. Even though Wall Street had not yet reached the depth of its crisis, the domino effect was already beginning to show through.

Ironically, the huge disaster of the Sichuan earthquake at the beginning of 2008 became the stage for the debut of China's new middle class: the donation of money and goods, blood donors lining up in the rain in big cities, and various volunteer rescue groups descending into the disaster zone.

All of these became an opportunity for the new Chinese middle class to self-consciously display their sizeable presence, even if they did not constitute a large percentage of China's enormous population. Rather suddenly, what emerged on the landscape of the disaster was an effective collective imagination led by the new middle class, a national identification autonomously summoned by the once powerless mass media.

Within international discourse, however, the Wall Street financial tsunami and the global stock market disaster unexpectedly gave rise to the fact or myth of China's rise. Although the statistics that are batted about supporting China's rise do not constitute news, the continued growth of the GDP has quickly raised China to the second largest economy in the world. Yet the financial tsunami fully displayed or perhaps we should say reversed the meaning of this phenomenon.

Previously, what helped the Chinese economy take off were the rows upon rows of giant processing plants and sweatshops along the southeastern coast, constituting the typical third-world landscape in the age of globalization.

Yet China has followed the example of other developed northeastern Asian countries by building a number of megacities adjacent to the processing plants, featuring leviathan, brand-new postmodern architecture designed by star international architects and hosting luxury consumer goods—China's young middle class has been born here. They also arose from a transition in property ownership from state-run to state-owned—from collective ownership to state ownership. On the basis of the large-scale industrialization of a nationally planned economy, the state-owned enterprises reorganized and expanded to create a central regime with solid financial strength.

Government projects since the new century began (such as developing the Great Northwest, renewing the northeastern industrial zones, and infrastructure construction in the countryside) have opened up giant reservoirs of capital, leading capital from the coast inland. When the financial tsunami hit and led to the decline of the coastal processing plants, the inland areas became a bulwark alongside national monetary sovereignty.

Paradoxically, this economic order under the state's leadership and monopoly has given China great vitality in the midst of the global crisis.

Most ironically, Chinese-style primitive capital accumulation and industrial development from the 1950s to the 1970s (through the replacement of capital by labor) was usurped through the transfer of ownership in the 1990s, such that the real economy was quickly monetized and capitalized into enormous state wealth by the turn of the century.

This economy had no choice but to be converted into dollars and U.S. Treasury bonds. Yet following the financial tsunami, the gold and silver earned through the real economy had to be donated to the U.S. financial market to fill in the enormous gaps resulting from the dollar's financial bubble. They led to the conversion of China's status into America's greatest creditor. This contribution was even seen as China's financial atomic bomb.

The amount of American Treasury bonds held by the Chinese government shows the extent to which the U.S. is interior to China. (This is deeply imbricated with Chinese mainstream culture's stubborn love and imagination of America, though this imbrication is not recognized.) While it conversely also demonstrates the extent to which China is interior to America as well as the depth of globalization, it simultaneously reflects the visibility of China's emergence on the world economic and cultural map, even if this image is full of the mirages of Cold War ideology.

Yet when the financial tsunami persisted and expanded into a European debt crisis, China's creditor status doubtless raised its negotiating power in international affairs. Hence in 2010, in the Hollywood disaster film called *2012*, China was merely a giant empty space. The world's sweatshops were not visible in scenes where the fate of humankind was decided. Yet *Too Big to Fail*, the American nonfiction drama about U.S. power, prominently featured China. Even though China in the film appears as somewhat of a caricature, it's not quite the classic Cold War scenario.

In fact, accompanying the high-speed growth of the Chinese economy was China's growing need for energy and resources. Hence China became active again in the Asian, African, and Latin American third world, but this time playing a very different role. On the one hand are the open and hidden international wrestling matches between China and the U.S. and China and Europe, which are altogether different from before.

On the other hand, on the map of the global capitalist political economy, China became an important parameter, or perhaps we should say variable. Is China then replacing Japan as a head in the three-headed monster? Has it rewritten Negri and Hardt's formula? Has the world political economy become X + America (Europe) + China? This author cannot make such an optimistic confirmation.

We can confirm that after 9/11, after the financial tsunami and China's associated rise, the post–Cold War era ended. We are now living in an era after the post–Cold War. Or, rather than characterize it as the end of the Cold War or prophesy unilateral control by the American empire, perhaps Subcomandante Marcos of the Zapatista National Liberation Army in Mexico put it best: "The Fourth World War has begun."[4]

Of course, different from the incitement of its literal meaning—just as he defined the Cold War as the third world war—the fourth world war refers to another round of competition for domination between empires, a war for resources and energy, or a battle for the crown of financial hegemony. Perhaps we could borrow the titles of the popular twenty-first-century Russian science fiction trilogy *Twilight Watch* to say we are now living in "Nobody's Time, Nobody's Space, and Nobody's Power." In other words, the lack of a dominant power only indicates the current instability of identity and the global scramble for supremacy.

Returning to China, if in 2008, the reality of the post-post–Cold War within world discourse seemed to emerge precipitously in China, perhaps it was merely the result of a sociopolitical process that had begun much earlier.

The year 2003 was undoubtedly an important turning point for China. That year, the CCP proclaimed its transition from a revolutionary party to a ruling party. Before that, they had already called their principles of governance the Three Representatives—that is, promising less than even the Social Democratic Party.[5] Meanwhile, they also encouraged entrepreneurs to join the CCP. The revision of the constitution added the protection of private property.[6] The significance of this revision lies in the fact that the Chinese regime finally struggled free of its embarrassing ideological dilemma. Moreover, it is trying to free itself of its double legitimation crisis. At a constitutional and legal level, this completes the transfer of ownership from state-run to state-owned, from public to private.

If the discussion of the nature of Chinese society was the latent focal point of intellectual debates in the 1990s, then today the nature of Chinese society has become a self-evident fact, despite labels inherited from its past. A small episode provides a footnote to this enormous transition: in 2003, the government declared the official merging of the Chinese History Museum and the Chinese Revolutionary Museum on the politically symbolic Tiananmen Square. It was renamed the China National Museum, and Jiang Zemin, then the top leader of the country, inscribed its dedication.

This is another allegory: the history of the Chinese revolution and the socialist alternative to global capitalism have disappeared inside the memory hole that is called history. Not only did it bid farewell to revolution, but it has also wiped out all traces of revolutionary history. In the last twenty years of the twentieth century, under the reference framework of China as a nation-state, Chinese history, torn apart by heterogeneous narratives and logics, finally closed up and healed. The era from the 1950s to the 1970s—an era edited out through historical as well as ideological montage—was again recycled into the historical logic of China's zigzagging path toward modernization. This era no longer floats above the current moment like a homeless specter nor brings out the threat of subversion.

So once again, Time begins. China is no longer a piece that cannot be fitted into the jigsaw puzzle of the world. It is no longer out of joint with Time. Conversely, it has finally entered into the time corridor of world history or Euro-American Western history. As an indication of this successful transition, since 2000 contemporary Chinese history, once a political minefield, has not only become an academic hotspot but, more strikingly, it has become a consumer fad in popular culture.

In the post–Cold War era, the popular culture industries tried, not entirely successfully, to fill in the blanks of China's ideological vacuum. They attempted to construct a new cultural hegemony, furthering the consumerist carnival from an unconstrained position. This time, rather than mass culture joining to construct hegemony, one might say that mass culture only exposes or confirms the new sociocultural hegemony. Just as with popular imagination and writing in the 1990s about 1930s Shanghai, depoliticized and romanticized legends of the 1950s to the 1970s became the material of popular novels, TV soap operas, and films. They became the shared gossip of elite and commoners alike.

Previously, using personal memory to counter official history was the double-edged sword of elite writing. Today, the flood of historical writings in the name of memory has successfully blocked off and covered up memory, that is, the memory of the spiritual legacies of socialist history. Needless to say, an analogous narrative logic (i.e., modernization and capitalism) once again achieved the continuity and coherence of Chinese twentieth-century history. It became the basis for the regime's legitimacy. This depoliticized narrative strangely and successfully fulfilled its political intentions.

In the story of the harmonious reconciliation between the various Cold War opponents, the party, the class, and the subject of the People's Republic of China erased itself and realized the displacement or inversion of the subject. The strangest logic in the historical narrative: the "successful losers" (of the Sino-Japanese War, the 1947–49 Chinese civil war, and the Cold War) are reacknowledging China's rank in global capitalism, eliminating the logic used by socialist China during the Cold War. If this is true, this logic can continue to triumph after China's rise. Hence the humility and self-effacement of its historical narrative became a powerful defense of Chinese capitalist development and fulfilled the imagination of China as savior or leader of the capitalist world.

After this transition in 2007–8, a new social hegemonic discourse was established in China. Most prominent within this discourse are developmentalism, consumerism, the market, and fetishism-filled capitalism. Important evidence of its establishment is how the new hegemonic discourse successfully absorbed and reconciled Chinese liberals and the New Left. From the 1990s to the present, clashes between China's important liberals and New Leftists did not produce any winners or losers. Rather, both lost. The only winner is big capitalism, that is, bureaucratic monopoly and entrepreneurial interest groups.

The new hegemonic discourse is further supported by a piece of superficial evidence: the prominent emergence of the young middle class in Chinese cities. While much hope both within and beyond China (among those who referenced the East Asian model) had been placed in the Chinese middle class as the force to push forward Chinese democracy, the debut of this class was in fact the identification with the nation-state and with the regime.

Even though national identity is very unstable even as it permeates the fetishistic imaginary of capitalist systems (adoration of the U.S. and hatred for Japan are frequent symptoms), the worship of abstract power or the deep respect toward the victors remains a basic parameter for the establishment of national identification.

From another perspective, when the financial tsunami broke out and expanded into the EU debt crisis, China became the last bulwark to shore up the value of financial capital. It immediately turned into a magnet for international hot money. A huge amount of international capital has flooded into China through both legal and underground means. The Chinese government used an old trick to protect the safety of its currency: its corresponding distribution of RMB created inflation that burdened the livelihoods of those at the bottom of the social hierarchy. Meanwhile, it also created an unprecedented scene of flowing money. In 2009, a sarcastic popular phrase in China was, "I don't lack money." Hence, like other modernizing countries whose economies took off belatedly, the RMB was forced to appreciate, making it possible for a small percentage of Chinese (though large in absolute numbers) to engage in the fashion of international travel.

Travel abroad may well be the typical activity in the era of globalization, but let us momentarily put aside its ideological implications. If the nouveaux riches born out of the commerce between power and money have raised China's status to number one in international luxury travel and in the consumption of international luxury goods (the most luxurious consumer brands have all established flagship stores in Shanghai), then throughout the world, especially in brand-name shops in Euro-American Western cities, omnipresent Chinese tourists seem like a minor but prominent detail that validates China's rise.

For this author, the so-called rise of China is the most important sign that the world has entered an era after the post–Cold War. One no longer need beat around the bush and evade the open secret of China's total entrance into capitalism and its role as the most active and lively player in a global capitalism in crisis. It also signifies that the curtains have finally dropped on the Cold War (as well as on the cold war situation after the Cold War, or the persistence of cold war after the Cold War). Compared to the previous socialist camp, capitalism has become the ultimate victor.

China Time or a Future Imaginary?

When China finally joined world time and world history, when the reestablished hegemonic discourse once again displayed the depth of China's long and winding historical minefield, it simultaneously also experienced the foggy barriers or even the disappearance of time and future. This is another displacement of time: when China finally entered the grand road of capitalism, with its seemingly brilliant prospects, the entire capitalist world sank into a systemic crisis.

Even if this crisis passes, the crisis of resources and environment has already stopped the unlimited expansion promised by developmentalism.

Any solution proposed within the current logic will only further or deepen the crisis. For example, the biofuel proposed by the European Union to replace petroleum as a renewable clean energy is already reducing or compromising the safety of African food. Or we could just call it famine. In 2011, after the March 11 Tohoku earthquake and tsunami, the crisis of the Fukushima nuclear power plant continued to evolve and deepen the global ecological disaster.

For a century, the history and self-image of China as a nation-state subject kept on postponing utopia to the other end of time—promising the future to posterity, endlessly trying to surpass the West and to make the new into the beautiful and the good. Today, China seems to have realized its dream of ranking among the advanced nations of the world, enriching the state and strengthening its military. But what of the future?

At this point, we might pause to consider the following events. In 2009, when General Motors filed for bankruptcy protection from the U.S. federal government, General Motors China broke its annual profit record. A private company in Sichuan bought Hummer from GM, making headlines throughout China. Meanwhile, the Hollywood blockbuster *Transformers 2*, which serves as a commercial for GM, broke summer box office records; China's box office was second only to North America's. Shortly after, in 2011, when the 3D movie *Transformers 3* again swept the globe, its product placement advertisements were all Chinese brands, even though this latent fact outside of the film's diegesis provoked very complex feelings among both North American and Chinese audiences. The ongoing logic of surpassing or continuing is recognizable. Ironically, this logic's model of emulation is a failed player in the quagmire of capitalism.

When China is no longer an oddity in the capitalist world but a regular member, when China's rise means the sinking of Cold War echoes and their epilogue, then it not only means the failure and disappearance of socialism as an alternative to global capitalism, but it also means the fading or evaporation of China's path—which refers to China's revolutionary path, China as a third-world country that freed itself from the global capitalist system, and China as an independent, sovereign, and self-sufficient nation.

Once, the real or imaginary Chinese path inspired and encouraged critical thinkers in the West and opened up other future imaginations in the third world. Today, is the meaning of China simply what the British foreign minister said in jest ("In 1989, capitalism saved China; today, China will save capitalism")? If capitalism saved China, then we must ask: Which China? Whose China? If China should save capitalism, then how? And with what?

Will China use its foreign currency reserves (the largest in the world), created and earned with its real economy (i.e., the labor of state-owned factories and sweatshops), to fill the deep gullies of the financial empire after its bubble burst, so as to begin a new round of games—just like those online and electronic games that won't let you quit until you lose? Or should we follow the proposals of some of China's political scientists and economists and begin China's Marshall Plan to save the EU and thereby lay the foundations of China's imperial position?

Two further significant illustrations: the late American leftist critic Giovanni Arrighi sketched out a vision of China guiding the global economy in his book *Adam Smith in Beijing*; Francis Fukuyama, who had proclaimed the end of the Cold War and hence the end of history, is now praising the Chinese century and Chinese model. Similar to the distorted and fantastical reflections in the global reactions to Tiananmen (even though the departure point and focus are quite different), but with regard to the present and the foreseeable future, leftist and rightist thinkers have again reached an amazing consensus over China's place in the world.

If such optimistic or terrifying imaginings (according to which subjectivized positions are distinguished) have realistic possibilities, then what is the true meaning of the Chinese model? How is the world led by China different from where it is heading anyway? Using the fact of China's rise (in terms of GDP, foreign currency reserves, ranking in the world economy) to inversely deduce China's special characteristics (the Chinese model) will only achieve a new version of the same old story of winner takes all, except that in the new story, the powerful central government is no longer the source of all evil as in the orientalist authoritarian story, but instead becomes the model for low systemic costs and high management efficiency.

China's own historical schema, the premodern Chinese empire that gave birth to a modern China within its borders; the Chinese revolutions of the twentieth century (which included almost every kind of revolution); the primitive accumulation and industrialization in the socialist era; China's identification with the third world and its resistance against the historical destiny of third world nations—all this has vanished without a trace.

As a previous historical legacy, twentieth-century Chinese and world history might still hold some resources and significance for the Chinese path today. In fact, much discussion about China's rise and the Chinese model has to do with Chinese cultural or historical tradition. Within China, what accompanies the heated debates about China's rise is China's cultural self-awareness. Even if we temporarily set aside the soft power or core values of the government-led culture, similar discussions among intellectuals have rarely dealt with some basic premises.

First, for Fei Xiaotong, who proposed the concept of cultural self-awareness, the premise and context for the discussion of cultural self-awareness was the nativist China or the Chinese countryside.[7] Today's China still has a vast countryside, with 900 million farmers according to household registration. But even if we don't mention how a hundred years of modernization and revolution destroyed traditional rural society, the current cultural self-awareness that accompanies the theory of China's rise focuses not on the countryside but on modern urban societies.

Second, the cultural traditions of the Chinese countryside belong to a totally different episteme than modern capitalism. Even though tradition versus modernity remains the basic ideological binary of the twentieth century, the modernization of traditional culture keeps emerging as the most pressing conventional issue of Chinese society. Yet there is rarely progress—not to mention resolution—on this issue. Apart from social and historical factors, epistemic difference and geographical segmentation might be the foremost intrinsic explanation. Hence in the context of contemporary capitalist political economy, it is only wishful thinking, albeit well intended, to use traditional Chinese culture as the subject or basis to create a new cultural self-awareness, to make China into an alternative to Western global capitalism. Again, what remains most prominent for me is the present-day revival of discussions about cultural self-awareness and its promotion. This doesn't mean the beginning of a Chinese cultural renaissance. In fact, this only clearly reflects the hollowness and paucity of Chinese cultural identity and subjectivity.

I have pointed out elsewhere that the beginning of modern Chinese culture—the May Fourth Movement with its twinned themes of antifeudalism and anti-imperialism—created a subjectivity with a hollow interiority that takes an enemy, namely imperialist powers, as the structure of its own Lacanian mirror image.[8] If this is precisely the general social cultural fact of the third world and late-developing world, then China's difference is that from the very start, Chinese intellectuals already realized that no matter how sincerely they wished it, China could not possibly repeat the Western path of modernization. The modernizing efforts of twentieth-century China thus often sought other paths, went elsewhere, and looked for other kinds of people.

Yet a hundred years have passed. At the turn of the century, a China that has completed its own inversion in the post–Cold War order needs to erase alternative social memories of subjectivity and social practice from its mainstream account. Hence Chinese cultural subjectivity experienced another hollowing out from within, multiplying and deepening the historical ruptures of the May Fourth Movement.

A film provides an illustration. Zhang Yimou's *Hero* did very well at the international box office. Throughout the film, one can see the blood-red word "sword" that symbolizes absolute power and violent struggle. It becomes a prominent background for the film. Yet the keyword of premodern Chinese culture and of the film's plot, tianxia or all under heaven, was never visible in the film.

Even more interesting is the domestic picture *Assembly* (2007), which is almost a direct piece of evidence for the post-post–Cold War. This film is about communist soldiers in the Chinese Civil War between the communists and nationalists. It was a blockbuster throughout East Asia and won the Golden Horse Award in Taiwan. But the symptomatic significance of the film lies in the scenario created by the director Feng Xiaogang and screenwriter (and well-known author) Liu Hengji: as soon as the CCP members changed into the Nationalist Party's German-style uniform and took up their American equipment, the film's characters took on the figures of international soldiers. The film re-created the spectacle and editing rhythm of Hollywood films, thereby successfully displacing or covering up the historical meanings of this special war: land reform, political mobilization, the politicization of the army, and the popular support of the people through the fact that the weak overcame the strong—that is to say, the outcome of the war manifested the people's choice of China's destiny and path.

If mainstream scholars have cut short the extension of twentieth-century Chinese history, then we obviously cannot inversely deduce a Chinese model from China's rise. Rather, this model can only become the latest case or footnote of global capitalism. It cannot draw from or transform the cultural and social debts, legacies, and resources of twentieth-century

Chinese history. It also cannot begin to imagine or implement a different and hopeful new world on account of China's intervention. To the contrary, if China's rise only means a new player in the global scramble for supremacy, then it could only signify the approach of an even greater global disaster.

Of course, China has not yet committed the same crimes or created the same disasters as the originators of capitalism, whether it is in terms of social injustice, exploitation, internal and external colonization, the crisis in energy resources, or ecological disasters. Yet if China cannot choose and demonstrate a different path, then its intervention will only replay and aggravate these existing disasters. Hence, so-called Chinese cultural self-awareness cannot originate from traditional cultural resources. To the contrary, it must be an awareness of the hollowness of its subjectivity on multiple levels. Moreover, traditional culture as a different episteme can only be revived in an alternative imagination of the future than that of modern capitalist logic and practice.

Yet in the aftermath of the post–Cold War, the international communist movement's alternative vision to counter the capitalist world has totally failed. The most important resulting change (and global phenomenon) is the disappearance or sealing off of a future vision. In the twentieth century, the utopian vision of Marxism was to end capitalism, obliterate class differences, and achieve the liberation of humankind. Its implementation and promotion, however, evolved into totalitarianism and bloody violence, finally causing a self-generated implosion. It lost without a fight.

The trial of global communism did not end without the arrogance of the victor's justice. It became a total negation of an alternative future other than capitalism. Hence the question became how to deal with the crisis of capitalism instead of how to deal with capitalism in crisis.

If a Chinese model exists, then it seems to be inevitably a capitalist model and not an alternative to capitalism. American AMC movie theaters imported and distributed the CCP propaganda film commemorating the ninetieth anniversary of the CCP's founding, titled *Beginning of the Great Revival*, and screened it in five American cities simultaneously. Despite the poor box office, it still demonstrates that the Cold War is far away in the past and communism is no longer any kind of meaningful threat.

Even in China, Marx or Marxism lies in a corner where the sun never shines—a piece of dispensable political pop. Of course, Marxism is not all about communism's utopian ideals. That's not even the most important aspect at times. But the significance of Marxism for social practice is that it promises a form of future justice. Only the imagination and promise of an alternative future allow historical and present suffering to emerge and speak. Only this can give meaning to past and present victims. For me, this includes the victims and sacrifices of twentieth-century communist movements. And only a nonteleological future vision can free history and time from the custody of power and violence.

At the turn of the century, the deep nostalgia that surrounds both left-wing and right-wing Chinese intellectuals not only reflects their powerlessness but also unexpectedly enacts Freudian mourning. Pay homage to and then forget the sufferings and the dead of capitalism and socialism, because there is no future that can give us back justice. There are only nation-states or empires, economic winners and losers. There is no choice for the sheep, only for lions with the ability and motivation to protect their own food sources. This might be why the late Jacques Derrida kept on reiterating memory and rejecting mourning. Thus he chose to salute the specter of Marx that has lost its flesh and blood.

Indeed, it doesn't have to be Marxism or communism, but it has to be the imagination and promise of an alternative future—a promise that will be kept, a promise along with an assumption of responsibility, a promise along with the performance of that promise. To act on one's promise seems to be the most ordinary yet most religious manifestation of premodern Chinese culture. Perhaps we can say that after the post–Cold War both the tidal movements of antiglobalization and the work of critical intellectuals, both directly and indirectly, contain the elements to reinvigorate a new utopian imagination and demand something of the future: the motto of the World Social Forum, Another World Is Possible; or the dream of Subcomandante Marcos, a world that can contain many other worlds; or Alan Badiou's *Communist Hypothesis*, as well as the return to communist theory among many scholars. Perhaps only in multiple future visions can we define and interrogate the meanings of nation, politics, revolution, democracy, and freedom. Only then can we debate the new historical subject and the possibility for its renaming. Only then can we draw on the resources of diverse histories rather than merely summoning ghosts.

Under the mask of a film character, V (in *V for Vendetta*, 2005), Occupy Wall Street unexpectedly broke out in New York and spread to the whole world. Just as eye-catching as the V mask was a self-referential slogan: We are the 99 percent. Yet in China, we see the opposite: class conflicts frequently explode in clashes between different ethnicities and regions. In other words, the crisis of capitalism is already awakening or creating other futures and possibilities. The imagination of an alternative future is already under way. For China, this topic is especially urgent, because China must be a China of the future, or there will be no future.

PART I

Trauma, Evacuated Memories, and Inverted Histories

I Want to Be Human

A Story of China and the Human

TRANSLATED BY SHUANG SHEN

In 2009, a Chinese blockbuster, *City of Life and Death* (*Nanjing! Nanjing!* 南京! 南京!, dir. Lu Chuan), unexpectedly managed to become a symptomatic representation of contemporary Chinese society. It did so by constructing an allegory of China and the human.

The movie represents the horrendous tragedy of the 1937 Nanjing Massacre, the mass murder of 300,000 Chinese within a matter of six weeks.[1] It has a distinct visual style: wide screen, black and white with a brownish hue, shallow focus throughout. It transposes human figures in near and medium shots onto an expansive and depthless canvas, exposing the traces of some unselfconscious allegorical construction. The human is projected against the historical backdrop of China, but exactly where the human is located in relation to history lacks clarity or depth. Considering the fact that the film was a state-sponsored project through and through (approved directly by the central government, funded entirely by the China Film Corporation) and its main objective, according to Lu Chuan, the director, was to present a "Chinese style of resistance," the choice of narrative (the Nanjing Massacre) as well as the film's style of narration appear to be at once nonsensical and thought provoking.[2]

The discourse of China and the human presented in this movie reflects the historical entanglement and tension of those two key terms in twentieth-century Chinese cultural criticism. The movie also directly engages with issues of historical trauma (the Nanjing Massacre in particular), the politics of memory, and the recuperation of humanity in the Chinese context. What is unique and important about the Nanjing Massacre is that this historical incident, along with its existing representations, positions the China and the human problematic not just along the China-West axis but also in an intra-Asian regional context. The Nanjing Massacre narrated by this movie and other narratives (*The Good Man of Nanking: The Diaries of John Rabe* and *The Rape of Nanking: The Forgotten Holocaust of World War II*, for instance) testifies to the intricate power relations revolving around the human as a concept with a history of unequal and non-equivalent distribution regionally and globally. In this essay, I analyze *City of Life and Death* as a text that illustrates this nexus of power, which has shaped the narration of China in history and the contemporary moment. I also argue that the movie articulates the desire for the universal human among the emerging new Chinese middle class, which has proved itself to be a formidable force in cultural and ideological production in contemporary China.

Discourses of the Human in Modern China

First, I would like to discuss the historical discourses of the human in Chinese intellectual and cultural histories of the twentieth century. The narrative trajectory of China and the human in *City of Life and Death* is neither new nor original. It resonates in a belated and anachronistic fashion as the leitmotif of twentieth-century Chinese social criticism. At the turn of the twentieth century, the discourses of modernity and social criticism were constructed upon an alignment between the human and a modern China and an opposition between the human and the real China. The genesis of the modern human is coterminous with the birth of modern China, but the historical and real China represents everything that is inhuman or antihuman.

This is why Lu Xun wrote in "A Madman's Diary" (1918), "I tried to look this up, but my history has no chronology, and scrawled all over each page are the words: 'Confucian Virtue and Morality.' Since I could not sleep anyway, I read intently half the night, until I began to see words between the lines. The whole book was filled with the two words—'Eat people.'"[3] Alternatively, we can think of the often-cited incident that has virtually gained the status of a representative case in modern Chinese history: "Lu Xun and the Slide Show."[4] A slide show at a Japanese university where Lu Xun was studying medicine depicted the beheading of some Chinese spies, along with expressionless Chinese spectators looking from the sidelines. Lu Xun's Japanese classmates, who frame the incident, cheered as they watched the propaganda film in the classroom. This is what led Lu Xun, the most important Chinese thinker of the twentieth century, to make up his mind to give up a career in medicine, return to China, and pursue literature instead as a way to save the spirit of the Chinese.[5]

In most discussions of this widely known event, it is conventionally understood that the killer references the Japanese as the forerunners of Asian modernity, and the spectators symbolize the real China (the imperial China of the Qing dynasty) at the time. However, the true objects of violence at the center of the picture—the beheaded spies—seldom get much attention. In a way, it is this silent center that exposes the hidden connection between this incident and some important characteristics of the self-narration of twentieth-century China. That is, much noise surrounds and reinforces a silent center, a silent object, and this is the location of China and the human.

The subject that is dead—slaughtered and silenced—identifies a site of hopelessness but also a site where hope resides. In the intellectual tradition of the early twentieth century, the human is thus figured both as a bloody corpse and as a fetus waiting to be born. These narratives position the human and a new China against the horizon of the future. The discourse of the human in China is thus a utopian discourse that articulates both the desperation about our condition of existence and the desperate need to resist this sense of desperation.

Even though it is a shared characteristic among many belatedly modern societies and third-world nations to engage in self-criticism and self-negation as a way of jump-starting their entry into modernity, the fact that Chinese intellectuals relied on a deeply felt sense of trauma to define their self-identity and to launch a project of constructing modern Chinese culture configures them as a rather singular case. This has to do with a history of rapid transformation from an ancient empire—the center of world civilization and global commerce—to a battered target of the fast boats and strong cannons of Western imperialism, all within the last hundred years. This transition has produced a trauma of disparity and the psychology of China as the "sick man of East Asia."

What needs to be pointed out is that absolute self-negation and debasement have left the subject of modern China—as well as the human subject of modern China—empty and undefined. The two motifs of Chinese modernity, anti-imperialism and antifeudalism, are not only mutually connected but also contradictory toward one another in profound ways. While anti-imperialism seeks the reaffirmation of the Chinese self through programs of "national salvation in pursuit of survival," antifeudalism implies the total and drastic negation of traditional Chinese culture and articulates a yearning for Westernization throughout the past century. As an invention of modern Europe and a capitalist society, the human is dangled above China, signifying a promise and signified as an object of desire.

The Repression and Return of the Human in Contemporary China

This discourse of the so-called Chinese national character (*guominxing* 国民性) was fundamentally transformed by World War II, of which the Sino-Japanese War in 1937 formed a part.[6] It took yet another turn after the establishment of the People's Republic of China. If the emergent demands of national salvation during the Sino-Japanese War enabled the formation of China as an imagined community, then the founding of the People's Republic gained for the new China the rights of self-representation even before the Communist Party defeated the Nationalist government's army. Thus, it has been widely believed that, with the founding of the People's Republic in 1949, the Chinese people stood up and that if "the old society turned humans into ghosts, the new society [would] transform ghosts back into humans."[7]

Nevertheless, this radical transformation also implied a suspension of discussions over issues of China and the human, since the category of the people now replaced the human as a keyword for the new society. In other words, the Marxian ideology of class struggle replaced bourgeois humanism to become the centerpiece of a new hegemonic narrative. Unexpectedly, this substitution exposed a central dilemma in socialist ideology, a dilemma caused by two sets of intersecting criteria: one aligning the modern with China and socialism; the other connecting the modern with universal notions of the liberal human and humanity. Between these two sets of criteria, a provocative history that plays with the alignment of as well as the contradictions between China and the human is bound to recur repeatedly.

We can see this history manifested in the 1970s and 1980s, when China had just ended its Cultural Revolution and was about to embark on a new era. It was at this moment of transition from the Mao era to the Deng era that the ten years of the Cultural Revolution, along with the entire socialist period, were deemed to be "inhuman," judged from some preconceived standard of the (universal) human. It was also at this moment that a rhetoric of the human replaced the discourse of class struggle in the critical discourses of various intellectual communities. The humanism of the young Marx replaced the Marx of political economy. These shifts effectively launched a series of social-political practices that, while effective, were depoliticizing. At the same time, we witnessed in the literary arts—more specifically, in the "scar" novels and films—the genesis of a term that does not make much sense in the ideographic system of written Chinese: "the human writ large."[8]

The human writ large stands in opposition to the real condition of the human in China. It is a utopian construction poised above the horizon of the future, one promising the materialization of some kind of universal value. The relationship between the notion of the human writ large and that of the new person of socialism is of course a relationship of the universal versus the particular, but the former also mutates to underwrite the person writ small as the natural condition of human beings to desire profit and to avoid danger.

Furthermore, the discourse of the human at the end of the 1970s and the beginning of the 1980s is associated with death or the dead. However, death here is no longer related to conditions of torture and pillage, as in the early twentieth century and as embodied in the Nanjing Massacre. Rather, death is chosen voluntarily in connection with some determined faith or higher expectations for the promise of the future. In the 1979 short story titled "Who Am I" ("Wo shi shui" 我是谁) by the female writer Zong Pu, the protagonist becomes obsessed with the philosophical question "Who am I?" after enduring much political persecution and psychological torment.[9] When she looks up to the sky one day, she sees a line of geese flying by, creating a pattern that resembles the Chinese character ren, or human (人). In a sudden flash of light, she becomes aware of the dignity of the human, and she makes a willful choice of death as a protest against political violence—as a strategy to defend her own humanity.

In the same year, 1979, the film script *Bitter Love* (*Ku lian* 苦恋), also known as *The Sun and the Human* (*Tai yang yu ren* 太阳与人), managed to generate a great deal of controversy, becoming a social and political event indicative of a new era.[10] This movie presents a highly dramatic, vivid depiction of the death of its protagonist, a principled and upright intellectual who returns home from overseas. This scene shows the dying man crawling his way across an expansive snow-covered plain, under the blazing sun and through howling wind. With his body, he inscribes the giant figure of "ren" on the exposed black earth. In the transition from the late 1970s to the early 1980s, Chinese society and culture repeatedly inscribed the character meaning the human over sky and earth, as if it were a dying wish, a will to mandate utopian expectations for a future generation.

At this historical juncture, what was unique about this particular evocation of the human was its presentation against the backdrop of Chinese social tragedy, in opposition to political violence as well as the violence of the state, but not in opposition to "China." This acceptance of China came from a highly naturalized and depoliticized concept of the homeland—a discourse of China as the homeland. In my view, instead of considering this homeland-China narrative as the emergence of a nationalist sentiment, it is more productive to think of it as the reappearance of early twentieth-century cultural complexes: love for homeland is bitter love, entangled with certain globalist sentiments and imagination as well as with multiple inversions and transpositions of self and other, homeland and alien lands.

In the late 1970s and early 1980s, the human not only provided an emotionally charged term of protest against political violence but also served as a metonymic figure of internal subversion within socialist ideology. Thus, the discourse of the human writ large is a specific landmark in world history. It testifies to China's participation in launching a project of post–Cold War globalization—indeed, with nearly the same eagerness and pace as those political leaders in Washington, DC, during the last decade of the Cold War (1979–89).

However, when a communist regime starts a process of wholesale capitalism, there are bound to be disruptions that threaten the continuity of party principles and power as well as rifts within social structure and ideology. A crisis of legitimacy is bound to occur. Thus, the originally apolitical rhetoric surrounding China and the human, patriotism and cosmopolitanism, was bound to be tolerated, if not appropriated, by reformers within the Communist Party. This is how a discourse of China and the human today has come to occupy a space shared between Communist Party reformers and intellectuals. In the last two decades of the twentieth century, the notion of the human became the seam as well as the fissure of Chinese social culture. After the Tiananmen Square massacre of June 4, 1989, when political ideology collapsed, discourses of the human became a foundation for the reconstruction of mainstream ideology.[11] The discourse of the human writ large has become a symptomatic figure for Chinese society because, whereas this discourse invites self-criticism and a negation of Chinese society and culture (since adopting the perspective of humanity is tantamount to an unexamined identification with the West), what called this figure into existence in the first place was a great anxiety concerning China's position on the global stage.

City of Life and Death

This history of twentieth-century discourses of China and the human informs the narrative of *City of Life and Death* by placing China and the human in a complex international context, where the two concepts are often at odds with each other. The film tries to resolve this difficulty through fictional means by constructing a representation of a historical trauma—the Nanjing Massacre. Even though the film is supposed to be about China, or Nanjing, in 1937, the dominant figure of the human represented by the film's main protagonist is not Chinese but rather a young and handsome Japanese soldier, the invading conqueror Kadokawa. The film begins with a shot taken from the perspective of the attacking Japanese army looking up toward Nanjing, the former capital of Republican China. It ends with a Japanese ceremony celebrating the seizure of the city. In what might perhaps be considered a grand concluding gesture, the Japanese military, clad in native costume, march in perfect unison to the beat of a taiko drum through a city that has just been reduced to near-total ruin. Interestingly enough, according to initial plans of the director, two sets of parallel perspectives were supposed to contrast with one another in this representation of the city of life and death: one provided by the young Japanese military officer, Kadokawa, and the other by the young Chinese officer Lu Jianxiong (played by the tall, handsome film star Liu Ye).

Originally, the film's main narrative strand was going to be the story of this Chinese officer in the resisting army; moreover, it was supposed to be a love story in the manner of *Titanic*.[12] But during shooting, the director unsurprisingly could not create a credible form to construct and anchor this romantic story line. Ultimately, Lu Chuan had to kill off one of his two protagonists: Lu Jianxiong expires one-third of the way into the film. In the current version of the movie, Lu Jianxiong, fully aware of the fate lying before him, faces the guns calmly and dies, just like millions of prisoners of war before him, slaughtered by the Japanese army. This major change in the film's plot shows that, even though the director managed to turn this character into a symbol of Chinese resistance, placing him at the center of the film's promotional posters, Lu Chuan could not finally salvage a believable narrative logic for this failed resister, which also suggests that he could not salvage his humanity. Thus, the Chinese resister has no choice but to be slaughtered, just like countless others who also failed in their efforts of resistance.

After the implicit Chinese perspective of the film is terminated midway, the point of view of the young Japanese officer takes over. A story about the Nanjing Massacre is thus transformed into one about the recuperation of Japanese humanity against this historical backdrop.[13] According to Lu Chuan, it was his deliberate choice to represent the Nanjing Massacre from the point of view of a Japanese solider. Lu admitted that this was a "risky" move. However, he felt it was the "only narrative trajectory" available to him, "the only way" for China to tell its story about the Nanjing Massacre to the world.[14]

In one of the final, emotional scenes of the film, the young and innocent Kadokawa finds himself unable to bear the atrocities of war. After releasing two Chinese prisoners, he shoots himself. This narrative sequence is constructed through a series of contrasting images: after Kadokawa calmly releases two older prisoners, he bids farewell to his friend. Then we see the prisoners running for their lives, as we hear a few crisp and clear gunshots in the background. The terrified prisoners try to find out whether it is they who have been shot. When they discover they are still alive, they turn around to see a boundless plain of yellow dandelions, into which Kadokawa's body has fallen and been buried. The camera then pans to the happy smiles of the two surviving Chinese prisoners, depicting expressions that reveal no trace of shock, sadness, or misery—despite the fact that the two have just witnessed horrible atrocities of urban slaughter, ones that they themselves have survived.

With severed ropes still dangling from their bodies, the two prisoners walk away with yellow flowers stuck behind their ears. Blowing dandelion into the air, they are apparently jubilant about being alive. The underlying message of the film could not be more explicit: on the one hand, we have a dignified (Japanese) death that enables the human to be animate and redeemed; on the other hand, the undignified (Chinese) live on, vividly represented by the two older prisoners running for their lives out of a sheer instinct for survival.

Indeed, all that the older prisoners of war seem to do in this film is run for their lives, without any strategic regard whatsoever. When the Chinese army, vastly outnumbered, has given up resisting the invading Japanese army, we see one of these older soldiers in a long shot screaming hysterically, tearing away and abandoning his uniform. His shameless cry for help in another scene results in the exposure and killing of the film's female protagonist, Miss Jiang, a teacher at a local missionary school. During the Japanese army's celebration of the occupation of Nanjing, we see this prisoner's face behind barbed wire in the midst of many other stunned faces of prisoners of war. To drag out an ignoble existence and to look on passively: these are the stereotypical images of China in the Euro-American imagination. Ironically, they are now also the stereotypical images of self-representation in twentieth-century Chinese cultural production as well.

The Nanjing Massacre in Regional and Global Contexts

Although it is not uncommon for war movies to propagate humanistic values, what is unique about *City of Life and Death* is the conjunction of the naming and narration of the human with the historical incident of the 1937 Nanjing Massacre, an incident whose cruelty almost completely destroyed our faith in humanism and left the foundations of modern, bourgeois civilization in shambles. The Nanjing Massacre is a singular and unique episode in the history of World War II, compared with other atrocities of the time. Although Auschwitz, Nanjing, and Hiroshima all bespeak the greatest cruelties of twentieth-century civilization, their difference resides not in scope and degree but in status—the fact that the Nanjing Massacre still remains a nameless and even ambiguous incident today. The massacre has been enveloped in uncertainty and vagueness, with many of the basic facts of this event still hotly debated in Japan and worldwide. Although on January 9, 1946, the Far Eastern International Court confirmed the occurrence of the Nanjing Massacre, some Japanese right-wing politicians, political organizations, historians, and compilers of middle-school text-books still claim that the massacre is a lie manufactured by the Chinese.[15] Those who oppose this view, including Japanese left-wing political groups, in their attempt to prove the occurrence of the massacre, have been mired in an endless debate themselves on the actual number of the murdered (is it 140,000, 210,000, 340,000, or 420,000?).

Although debates over the occurrence of the Nanjing Massacre have consistently been one of the pressure points in Sino-Japanese diplomatic relations and political exchange since the end of World War II, particularly after 1949, the massacre has attracted little, if any, attention from the international community. In other words, although World War II is recognized as a global catastrophe, the atrocious deeds of the Japanese military invasion, exemplified by incidents such as the Nanjing Massacre or the germ warfare experiments carried out by Unit 731, are but insignificant regional incidents and topics. The emergence of the Nanjing Massacre as a unique case of traumatic memory in the disaster-laden history of twentieth-century China stems exactly from such erasure on the global level.

In contrast to the ambiguous status of the Nanjing Massacre in the global context, the World War II atrocities of Europe have aroused much public attention and propelled the international community to engage in investigations and self-reflection. While the Holocaust has become the emblem of crimes against humanity, the international anonymity of the Nanjing Massacre has denied the name and status of the human to its Chinese victims and foreclosed any reflection on the Japanese military's brutality. While the victims of the nuclear bombs at Hiroshima and Nagasaki are memorialized, and Japan thus gains its place in reflections on the meaning of the human during World War II, the trauma and anxieties of the Chinese over the nonrecognition of the Nanjing Massacre are intensified. The grotesque historical wound of the massacre is reopened whenever the Chinese and Japanese governments dispute the facts of the atrocity. Moreover, whenever the West and the rest of the world reflect in the name of history and remembrance on the memory of Auschwitz and the Holocaust, on the brutalities of World War II, and on their crisis of witness bearing, or whenever international courts convict Nazi war criminals for their crimes against humanity, or whenever the German (for a while West German) government memorializes or apologizes in various forms to the Jewish victims, this inexpressible anguish and hopelessness are once again induced among the Chinese.

The discourses surrounding this historical incident—including whether China should seek reparations from Japan—have also been inextricably entangled with the ideological oppositions of Cold War politics. Moreover, the Nanjing Massacre has been viewed as an incident internal to Asia—a dim corner in the history of World War II, where Europe and America played the leading roles. In the second half of the twentieth century, the massacre became an "unsolved case," suspended between fact and fiction, war atrocities, and Cold War politics. As such, it became a pivotal phrase, frequently invoked, hijacked, and detonated in the realms of Sino-Japanese political, diplomatic, and economic collaboration and competition. Because of its suspended nature, the Nanjing Massacre is repeatedly invoked at the turn of this century, as if a wound still open, ripped, and oozing blood.

Between Iris Chang and John Rabe

In the genealogy of modern Chinese film, there is a history of cinema concerning anti-Japanese militancy, including a long list of movies that deal with the specific subject of the Nanjing Massacre. However, Lu's *City of Life and Death* does not seek to continue this domestic narrative trajectory but rather maintains an intertextual relation with the book *The Rape of Nanking* by the Chinese American author Iris Chang. To be precise, the 1997 publication of this book in the United States and a series of international political and cultural incidents resulting from its publication, up to the tragic death of the author in 2004 at the young age of thirty-six, form the social and cultural pretext of *City of Life and Death*. When *The Rape of Nanking* was first published, it unexpectedly garnered such enthusiastic responses in the English-speaking world that it remained on the best-seller list of the *New York Times* for over fourteen weeks, selling over a million copies. Another fact relating to this book is Chang's discovery of historical documents that led to the publication in China of *La Bei Riji* (The diaries of Rabe), which subsequently appeared in the United States as *The Good Man of Nanking: The Diaries of John Rabe*.[16]

While China occupied both the center and the margin of the cultural event of *The Rape of Nanking*, it responded to it in a provocatively displaced manner. Even though the Chinese media initially welcomed Chang and her book with great enthusiasm and praise, subsequent reactions to its publication reflected complex and mixed emotions that blended pleasure with sadness and joy with anger. In the Chinese-language world, the success of Chang and her book in the English-language world reopened the never-healing wound of the Nanjing Massacre and stirred up sad memories. The book created a perfect maelstrom, registering the great anxieties and complex emotions that China has toward the world as well as the confluence of a new form of nationalism and cosmopolitanism in the formation of mainstream ideology. What made China elated is that "we" (China) finally managed to provoke the world to come to terms with this historical incident. That is why many news reports as well as Internet coverage of the book heralded Chang as a national hero, a "woman warrior."

Nonetheless, people had an even stronger and more effusive reaction to *La Bei Riji*. The Chinese translation of Rabe's diaries was first published in 1997, whereas the Chinese translation of Chang's book did not appear until 2005. Comparing these publication dates suggests that the diaries were considered a more authentic document by a real onlooker, promising absolute objectivity and testifying to our desire for such an act of historical witnessing—a desire that indeed precedes our knowledge of the existence of Rabe's diaries. Rabe was an outsider to China, a German national who happened to be working in China as the regional leader of the Nazi Party, and thus he belonged to the enemy camp. In today's global context, his race and gender gave him additional power. The fact that his diaries offer an eyewitness account written in German by a white European male lends them more credence than any similar account by a Chinese witness, the testimony of such a witness, or even the detailed historical research of a Chinese American female.

Rabe's diaries have been used not only to confirm that the Nanjing Massacre indeed happened but also to provide the basis for making a connection between this massacre and genocide more broadly (in particular, the Nazis' killing of the Jews). Being able to secure this connection elevates the Nanjing Massacre to the level of crimes against humanity and the suffering of humanity. Thus, the Nanking Massacre is no longer just an ordinary incident in a region considered by the West as a repeated site of disaster, mass murder, and war. In fact, this elevation of the massacre into world history was the objective and impetus of Chang's scholarship.

However, the enthusiasm exhibited toward *La Bei Riji* by the Chinese media was not so much a reflection of the historical trauma or memory of the Nanjing Massacre as a response to Steven Spielberg's 1993 movie *Schindler's List*. In the Chinese media, Rabe is frequently referred to as the "Chinese Schindler." In mainstream Chinese opinion, the existence of Rabe as a human witness not only enables China's gradual ascent up the steps of power and significance (China, Japan, Europe) but also testifies to the existence of our humanity. Thus, Rabe also belongs to us. It is for these reasons that "we the Chinese" embrace the Chinese Schindler, also known as the "living Buddha of Nanjing." The figure of Rabe allowed Chinese mainstream culture to see a gleam of light above the bloody darkness of the massacre, finally to recover Chinese humanity through a kind of historical knowledge that bridges the gap between there (Europe) and here (China), the present and the future.

In the United States, *The Rape of Nanking* enabled Nanjing to appear frequently in Hollywood cultural representations and in American popular culture. Nanjing has become a new historical backdrop for mainstream dramas. In the Chinese context, by contrast, the recently revived Chinese film industry has made many attempts to incorporate into their representations Rabe and the recuperation of the human in Chinese history. The figure of Rabe enables the Chinese film industry to make direct connections with the non-Chinese world, largely meaning Europe and America. Both Xie Jin, a leading mainstream director in the Chinese film industry for over sixty years, and Zhang Yimou, the newly crowned cinematic representative of the Chinese nation, have sought to adapt Rabe's diaries for film. But it was not until 2009 that the character of Rabe finally appeared on the Chinese screen, with the release of *City of Life and Death* as well as a Chinese-German coproduction simply called *John Rabe* (dir. Florian Gallenberger, 2009; produced by Huayi Brothers Film Investment Corporation, a major private Chinese enterprise).

Politics of Memory in an Age of Development

Although Rabe is not the protagonist of *City of Life and Death*, his diaries can be considered an important subtext of Lu's film for two reasons. First, Rabe's diaries provide the historical evidence for the existence of refugee camps set up and managed by European or American expatriates in Nanjing. This detail lends credibility to an otherwise historically flawed narrative such as we find in *City of Life and Death*. Second, and more important, the fact that contemporary China welcomed and embraced the historical figure of Rabe prepared the ground for *City of Life and Death* to garner public support for the historical representation in the film.

According to the director, an objective of his film was to debunk some of the existing stereotypical representations of both China and Japan.[17] Placing this comment in conversation with the actual film, we can see Lu's attempt as radically one-sided. It is an amazing accomplishment that the film has succeeded in getting rid of some of the stereotypes by which Chinese culture represents Japan—or the invading Japanese army, to be more precise. It does away with the standard "hateful Japanese devil," for instance. But the film simultaneously reconfirms and underscores another set of stereotypes about the Chinese themselves. That is, this effort to debunk (Japanese) stereotypes is also a process of reinforcing another set of (Chinese) stereotypes.

In spite of the many subtle and emotionally convincing details in *City of Life and Death*, it is not exactly the case that the stereotypes of the Japanese invading army get rewritten but rather that these stereotypes have disappeared and evaporated from the text, displaced by representations of the (Japanese) human and humanity, which fill in this gap. From the beginning of the film, a set of traits is assigned to Kadokawa through his dominant narrational perspective. He is a student turned soldier with a missionary school background. This background happens to be shared with the female protagonist, Jiang. If these identity codes have supplied the empirical basis for the couple's ability to communicate with each other in English (language and communication have rich cultural significance beyond the unfolding of events in this film), the symbolic significance of their shared background does not stop at their exchange of "human glances" right before the slaughtering of the human is about to commence. What has been exchanged between Kadokawa and Jiang is not humanity in abstraction, but specifically a necklace—one with a cross attached to it.

This exchange is one of the most important scenes of the movie. It takes place in the refugee camp managed by the well-known Nazi Rabe and several other European and American nationals who remained in Nanjing. (In fact, most scenes involving Chinese characters take place in this refugee camp, the exceptions being the death of the Chinese officer and the two final survivors of the film.) In the most significant scene of *City of Life and Death*, the Japanese army demands that the camp release a number of female refugees to serve as comfort women. After a tearful explanation by Rabe and Jiang, one hundred women willingly stand and give up their lives to save the majority of the camp. This scene takes place in the symbolically charged location of a Christian church. The light that shines through the church's tall windows gives the setting the semblance of an oil painting with a religious motif. Thus, transcendence in the religious realm, as a matter of Christian faith, provides the framing for the definition of the human and humanity and serves as the criterion by which to judge these values.

Indeed, although the director has repeatedly argued that this movie is meant to establish the Chinese subject, the narration embedded in a Japanese point of view facilitates the absence of China and the amnesia of Chinese history relating to the Nanjing Massacre. Furthermore, what fills this void is a giant figure of the human projected against the backdrop of Christianity. The setting of the Christian church as the site of the human can be read as a trace of a political unconscious, or its symptomatic manifestation—one suggesting that the human resides elsewhere, outside "China," in a location that belongs to the higher end of the global capitalistic order (Germany/Japan).

What is missing from Lu's film are the actual atrocities of the Nanjing Massacre committed by the Japanese army toward ordinary civilians— atrocities carefully documented by Chang. In *City of Life and Death*, there are only a few representations of Japanese violence toward Chinese civilians, and these are inaccurate or idealized.[18] Most violence against women in the film, for example, takes place inside the comfort stations. This is a rather different representation from the gang rapes of civilian women that have been documented elsewhere. With Kadokawa's point of view becoming the only available perspective for the film's narration, the audience is encouraged not so much to identify with Chinese civilians in a fallen city but rather to experience the Japanese fear of penetrating the capital of an enemy nation. It is fear that makes Kadokawa shoot blindly at a set of swinging doors after he is ordered to look for Chinese army resisters inside the refugee camps. (The fact that these doors open onto the confessional is in itself a symbolic detail.) As a result of his random act, several girls die, their bodies rolling out from behind the doors, and this incident becomes the foundation for Kadokawa's trauma and sense of sin.[19]

Even if we resist comparing this movie with classic stereotypical representations of the Japanese devil or with representations of the Japanese soldiers in Japanese propaganda movies—even if we resist comparing this movie with Chang's book or Rabe's diaries—*City of Life and Death* still cannot be considered a representation of the Nanjing Massacre, but instead the erasure of its history. This movie does not trace the evisceration of the human or restore our faith in humanism after murder, blood, and blade. It renders the Nanjing Massacre a vague reference, a war that takes place in an unspecified location. This film is not a return to the traumas of the war. It actually blocks the intrusion of reality—the return of the repressed—through its construction of the illusion of the (Japanese/ German) human.[20]

The books and films about the Nanjing Massacre have become what Gilles Deleuze has called a "folding": they do not merely represent the horrible atrocities of civilization, an ugly face of the many faces of modernity; they explicitly represent a deep crisis of witnessing and the continuous trauma that accompanies the impossibility of naming these atrocities. Wrapped inside this folding also lies the continuous historical entanglement of Sino-Japanese relations, especially the rise of modern Japan in the past century and the shock and injury that two Sino-Japanese wars have wrought upon the Chinese people.[21] There is, in addition, the factor of the significant reversal of the hierarchy between Japan and China today, after China weathered the shock of Anglo-American modernity, not to say imperialism. It is against this historical background that the Nanjing Massacre, or the Japanese invasion of China, becomes atypical, the hard core of a wound that is repeatedly refreshed yet cannot be dissolved by a new Chinese nationalism and cosmopolitanism.

Because of this, what used to be a consensus in Chinese intellectual circles, and what later became the basis for a new ideological consciousness— namely, cosmopolitanism—ultimately reflects a certain kind of acquiescence and deep internalization of the hierarchical structures of global capitalism. The new economic neoliberalism at the turn of this century folds back upon a reversed logic of the Cold War, mutating into a new admiration for hegemonic power.

According to this logic, "China" (an entity made ambiguous by the partitions of the Cold War) defeated Japanese imperialism, yet the rapid economic development in postwar Japan and the esteemed position held today by Japan in the global economic order actually make China look like a failed victor. As a result, Japan becomes a wound, a complex, a mirror stage: the ambiguous status of the Nanjing Massacre becomes one permanently dislocated piece of the jigsaw puzzle of China's modern self-image in relation to the world and to humankind. Because of this dislocation, as well as the Chinese imaginary and envy of Euro-American cosmopolitanism, Japan and anti-Japanese sentiment become fissures, touch-and-go points, in the complex nexus of contemporary Chinese nationalism. It is against this larger historical canvas that *City of Life and Death* becomes a symptom: as it wraps itself around the wounded core of the Nanjing Massacre with allusions to the "human," the film consciously and unconsciously fixes a bloody and painful history to questions of cosmopolitanism and humanism in an age of development.

With *City of Life and Death*, Lu belatedly joins a global trend of post–Cold War amnesia, employing the mechanism of forgetting to erase traces of historical trauma. If we examine viewers' mixed and divided response to the film, the film can be considered either a huge success or a complete failure, depending on one's position in this politics of memory in an age of development. On the one hand, the film was a box-office success and received some overwhelming praise after its public release; on the other hand, the film touches some deeply felt anxieties and complexes that I discuss above, so much so that it invited angry denigrations and criticism from both print and new media. Some Chinese netizens labeled it the film by a traitor, and a small group of citizens of Nanjing filed a lawsuit against the National Film Bureau for allowing the film to be shown in public. Between the critics and the defenders of this film, we are presented with an impossible choice, caught in the middle of an opposition between angry and provincial nationalism on one side and the transcendent and vacuous discourse of cosmopolitanism and the human writ large on the other.

The New Middle Class and Chinese Nationalism

I have chosen this film as my object of discussion because the new lips that tell the old story of this film nonetheless bring insights about China. If we temporarily suspend the realities internal to Lu's film and consider instead film as a sort of reality, then what we discover here is an instance in which a supposed art-house production suffused with human compassion is, in actuality, a major blockbuster representing the perspectives of the authorities. (Indeed, when *City of Life and Death* was attacked by some Internet media organizations, the vice president of the National Film Bureau, the authoritative government film management and censorship organization, organized a press conference and defended the film by invoking the need to protect artistic freedom and creativity.)[22] The film has even become an educational movie for patriotism recommended for high school students.

It is worth mentioning that when the film premiered in 2009, China was also celebrating the sixtieth anniversary of the PRC's founding—sixty years being a Chinese century. Moreover, this was the year after the Olympics. If China's hosting of the 2008 Olympic Games offered the promise of "China's rise" on the international stage, then the public's various reactions toward the riots in Tibet, as well as their visible participation in the relief efforts during the Wenchuan earthquake in Sichuan, all occurring right before the start of the games, marked an important transition leading up to this anticipated ascent.

These public demonstrations conveyed the message that, after two centuries of turmoil, some kind of nationalist spirit was finally emerging in Chinese society, one that was generated not by overt political means or solely by the reaction toward a condition of crisis. The new middle class—the product as well as benefactor of rapid economic development in China—became the dominant voice in this expression of nationalism. In other words, all the debates about violence in Tibet, the groundswell of support for those suffering in Wenchuan, and the glamorous setup of the Olympic Games collectively prepared the stage for the arrival of the newly minted Chinese middle class. After three decades of reform and change, these performances suggest not only that Chinese middle-class consciousness has become the mainstream ideology but also that a new brand of nationalist identification has replaced older forms of self-deprecation and disgrace in Chinese self-identification.

Some external characteristics of this new middle class: they are mostly urban dwellers, rather well educated, relatively young (usually under forty), have mid- to high-level incomes, and play the role of intellectual, economic, or even political elites in society. While this group makes up only a small percentage of the entire population, it is already sizable enough that its patterns and powers of consumption can influence the Chinese cultural market.

Once again, China's change has not occurred in the ways in which we had anticipated: economic development in China has indeed produced miraculous growth in gross domestic product (GDP), but during the last two decades of the twentieth century the middle class and civil society did not become the forerunners of political reform in China, as expected. Rather, they have become the advocates of a new nationalist discourse.

We can think back to some recent self-representations of the intellectual elite who hardly had direct connections with the authorities—for instance, the television series *The Rise of the Great Nation* or the social-political commentary published as *China Is Not Pleased.*[23] These examples present a clearer picture of the emergence of the new Chinese middle class. The film *City of Life and Death*, considered against these other cultural productions, illustrates the absurdity of our contemporary situation: we must recognize this cultural production (like all productions) as a cultural act motivated by the nation-state, a recognition that might be substantiated by the director's claim that *City of Life and Death* represents a Chinese self-writing. But where exactly China is located in the film remains rather ambiguous and suspended, since all of the Chinese in this movie seem to be indistinguishable from one another and lacking likable personalities. In contrast, the Japanese soldier Kadokawa defines the human through his conscientious life and dignified death.

What is most notable here is the public's critical as well as enthusiastic reaction toward the film. On the one hand, many people have uploaded pictures and historical documents of the massacre from their own archives to the Internet to prove that Lu's film was a disgrace. On the other, the Chinese movie audience, comprising mostly urban youth, rushed to the theater to watch it. The box-office receipts for *City of Life and Death* swelled until they finally launched the director into the Billion Yuan Box-Office Club and into the company of directors such as Zhang Yimou and Feng Xiaogang. In addition, the movie was selected for screening at the San Sebastian Film Festival in Spain and won its major prize. It seems that the traditional three-way division in the Chinese movie industry between the political propaganda film (the major-theme movie), the entertainment movie, and the experimental art movie has been overcome entirely.

This three-way division in the Chinese movie industry has been but a microcosm of the intellectual differences and social conflicts in Chinese society of the past three decades. The major-theme movies represented the mainstream discourse of the state, which used to stand in opposition to both the marketized entertainment films and the art movies, the latter representing enlightened criticism. These three genres offer different responses to the future of China. However, the "happy ending" of *City of Life and Death* is deeply ironic in that it announces the failure of all three genres, with the winner being the logic of global capitalism.

When Lu attempted to respond to some of the criticism generated by the film, he emphasized repeatedly that the movie is designed to appeal not to a Chinese audience but rather to a global audience, a statement that underscores his familiarity with the tastes of the global middle class. In other words, *City of Life and Death* is not a cultural production in the vein of Chang's *The Rape of Nanking*. It is purely a Chinese version of *Schindler's List*. As a Christian, Kadokawa might as well not be considered a representative of the Japanese army, but more a Westerner located on a higher rung of the ladder of modern civilization. These misrepresentations and misrecognitions seem to be the only way that this film can be successful in the Chinese market yet share the profits of the global market at the same time. Here, the purpose of constructing the (Western) human writ large is to guarantee the economic viability of the (Chinese) human writ small. With the film being entirely funded by a government-owned production agency, this was the only way to ensure the safety of investment while at the same time ensuring that the film would not provoke public complaint and political trouble.

The case of *City of Life and Death* illustrates the changing role of the Chinese government. If China wants to push for regional economic collaboration with Northeast Asia, then Japanese army atrocities during World War II are both a memory block and a roadblock. Therefore, it is strategic to express one's regret (even if it remains unaccepted) and try to achieve some sort of redemption for both victim and victimizer by endowing the conquering invader with a human soul, one through which he is able to express the pain of regret.

The price one pays for such a huge box-office success as *City of Life and Death* is exactly what Foucault terms "a historical knowledge of struggles."[24] The debates raised by the film provoke the question of whether the power of capital is big enough to erase the social and psychic traumas of twentieth-century China. Returning to the film as social reality, we find that it proves to be not so much an experience of therapeutic psychological catharsis but rather a psychoanalytic case history still waiting to be treated.

As much as China's double-digit GDP growth is sufficient to support the myth of "China's rise," or the 2008 Olympic Games present to the world a holistic vision of China created through laser light shows, it is the bigger winner—*City of Life and Death*—that reminds us of the heavy debts of the twentieth century waiting to be settled. When people today attempt to invoke the subject of China, they find that the Chinese self is intrinsically empty and undefined. Thus, the subject position of China becomes a suspension of the subject, a performance of displacement and misrecognition of the self and the other, of home and the diaspora.

Two anecdotes provided by the director about this film are thought provoking. The first is the director's statement that the gun pointing at Kadokawa is almost like a gun pointing at himself.[25] The second is the director's explanation of his design for the ceremony celebrating the Japanese army's seizure of Nanjing. He noted that this glamorous scene emerged from a nightmare: when he was preparing for the film and browsing through materials about the Nanjing Massacre, he dreamed that a Japanese "devil" beating a drum was rushing toward him.[26]

It is not surprising that, when one attempts to turn Chinese history into a melodrama and continue the aesthetics of rituals that one witnesses so often in the aesthetics of fifth-generation Chinese cinema, the subject position of China and the Chinese as human cannot be tenable. The director can only identify with the Other, the hand of the enemy or the devil, an indispensable ingredient for any melodrama to complete its narration. In an absurd logic, Lu has transformed his own nightmare into a dream to be shared with the public. Depending on the different positions of the viewers, this drama unfolds as an unmitigated nightmare or a touching daydream. This story can be seen as either an exorcism or a ritual of calling back the spirit of the dead. It is not, however, a conscious interpretation of one's own dreams. It takes forgetting as its premise, and thus it will not help people come to terms with their memories.

This narrative, constructed according to the tastes of the global middle class, has been not only endorsed by the San Sebastian International Film Festival but also embraced by a specific consumer class in China—the new middle class. The Chinese new middle class, born out of high GDP and nurtured by the culture of consumption, has a very acute level of global awareness in terms of their self-identity. Their acceptance of this movie does not contradict new discourses of nationalism or their self-representations of their class position in social practice. The cheers accompanying China's global rise do not indicate the emergence of self-awareness of Chinese nationalism. Instead, they are cheers for the success of global capitalism in China.

We need to point out that this new Chinese middle class is segregated not only from Chinese history but also from China and the majority of the Chinese. But they are the ones who are the face of visible China on the global stage today. They are the legitimate citizens of the world defined by their purchasing power. At the beginning of the twenty-first century, forgetting has become the main theme of memory construction. It is this imperative to forget the sufferings and revolutions of the twentieth century that gives rise to the middle-class revolution and their subject position. Forgetting is a necessary step toward constructing the imaginary community of the nation. *City of Life and Death* is indeed a major-theme movie of China, but its propaganda also makes us reflect on the role of the Chinese nation-state in the process of globalization.

CHAPTER 2

Hero and the Invisible *Tianxia*

TRANSLATED BY YAJUN MO

In 2003, Zhang Yimou's epic period piece, *Hero*, unexpectedly became a global hit. Although *Hero* did not succeed in getting the hoped-for Oscar award (which undoubtedly would have been mere rhetorical flourish for Zhang Yimou), it managed to enter Hollywood's global distribution network, becoming the first Chinese film to profit from Hollywood's global box office. Via *Hero*, the Chinese film industry miraculously resuscitated itself and rapidly expanded its scale and range, as movie budgets in China competitively escalated.

Although *Hero* has surprisingly been characterized as cinematic realism, the film actually incorporates elements of Hong Kong cinema's fantasy and martial arts into the narrative structure of mainland Chinese cinema. Its visual style immeasurably amplifies the so-called fifth generation's aesthetics of ritual and color palette, as well as the "Chinese" signifying elements in Zhang Yimou's films. Its cinematic realism pales in comparison. Most intriguing in this postmodern version of the well-known story about the attempted assassination of Qin Shihuang (who at the time was still the king of the state of Qin) is that *tianxia*, or "all under heaven"—a relatively unfamiliar concept in new-millennium Chinese culture—plays a prominent role as the fragile linchpin of the film's narrative and as the pillar of its unconvincing plot reversals. Through the concept of tianxia, *Hero* has managed to partially reverse the narrative from how to assassinate the Qin king to how not to assassinate him. It has simultaneously changed the meaning of the original narrative: from a tale about the most steadfast opponent to one about the most resolute defender.

Adopting tianxia as a keyword, certain Chinese and East Asian scholars, as well as certain Sinologists and East Asianists in Euro-America, have used it as part of their constructivist theoretical efforts to reflect on Chinese and East Asian modernity and to mine the resources of traditional Chinese thinking. Given the dense interactions among the circles of art filmmakers, intelligentsia, and cultural producers in the 1980s and 1990s, one could conclude that the explanation for the use of the long-forgotten concept of tianxia as the crux of *Hero*'s narrative lies here. Yet from the perspective of the dramatic transformations in the structure of China's culture industries in the new millennium, *Hero*'s imaginative narration of tianxia is more likely derived from and opens up another context: namely the world of new media, Internet literature (historical, martial arts, and fantasy writings) written by the younger generation raised on popular culture from Hong Kong and Taiwan, and domestically produced online video games. In other words, the readoption of tianxia by both the intelligentsia and the culture industries is more of a coincidence. Albeit resonant with one another, their social and cultural contexts differ significantly. This contingent intersection, however, unintentionally exposes the fact that tianxia is a major concept in premodern Chinese intellectual and political thought, as well as a cultural imaginary linking the individual, the family, the country, and the world. Even as this enormously complex mutual imbrication and mutual antithesis emerged in the contemporary cultural context, a rich social and cultural symptomaticity also presented itself.

Appearing after *The Emperor's Shadow* (1996) and *The Emperor and the Assassin* (1998), *Hero* was the third film in as many years that based its plotline on the attempted assassination of the king of Qin. Its narrative distinctiveness is its evacuation of history or we could say the "MacGuffinication" of history. It is not even a popular history as is the convention in fantasy and martial arts films. Instead, it is purely and simply a story, a narrative enactment. The film's main narrative structure involves the assassin Nameless (Wuming) and the Qin king Ying Zheng sitting facing one another in the palace while interpreting the tales of three swordsmen/ assassins (all of whom had previously attempted to assassinate the Qin king): Long Sky (Changkong), Broken Sword (Canjian), and Flying Snow (Feixue). The film is thus divided into three sections—red, blue, and white (which includes a green part), signifying three different versions of the same story.

However, to resolve the "true" version, which is the white version, as recognized near the end of the film, the term "tianxia" appears, structuring the "surprising" reversal of the narrative and its signification. In this version, not only does Broken Sword abandon his mission to kill the Qin king just at the moment when he has almost succeeded, but he ventures to stop Nameless from carrying out the assassination as well. Without any explanation, Broken Sword's final words are, "The king should not be killed." When Nameless is determined to proceed, Broken Sword offers him two characters—tian xia—and walks away, leaving his sword behind. These two characters—tianxia—not only disrupt Nameless's will to murder, in the end they lead him to release the king and even willingly offer up his own life.

Presented as the logic behind the character Broken Sword, here tianxia undoubtedly signifies the proper ideals one should take to heart: to take tianxia, or "all under heaven," as one's own responsibility. It is the tianxia idealism captured by the Song dynasty poet Fan Zhongyan's famous verse: "Be the first to worry about the troubles across the land, the last to enjoy universal happiness."[1] In other words, the lesson here is to emulate the ancient role models who would gladly be the first to bear hardships before everybody else and the last to enjoy comforts. This tianxia idealism compels Nameless to transcend his own family enmity and righteous vengeance against the Qin as a subject of the Zhao kingdom (Nameless's family was killed by Qin soldiers, and the Zhao kingdom was defeated by the Qin). It drives him to abandon the raison d'être of a swordsman, namely to eliminate villains, remove despots, and bring peace to the people. If we examine the logic of the plot closely, however, Broken Sword's so-called tianxia spirit resembles a particular apprehension of the logic of history: if one yields and gives tianxia to someone truly capable of presiding over it, even a swordsman would not need to wander the world. He could just live out his days with the woman he loves in a place without swords and swordsmen, in a world with only one man and one woman.

This expansive interpretation of tianxia in the film means that Broken Sword need not retreat to that space of "self-cultivation" (*xiushen*) as in the old swordsmen tales.[2] When Nameless conveys Broken Sword's idea of tianxia to the Qin king, the king immediately breaks into tears. "With such a kindred spirit, one could die without regret," he exclaims. As conveyed by Nameless, Broken Sword's tianxia idealism can clearly be identified as directed toward the king: a deep appreciation and endorsement of the political ambitions of conquerors and the power of victors. The logic of his actions has here been turned upside down: owing to his comprehension of tianxia, Broken Sword desists from the vigilantism of swordsmen/assassins, that is, "going outside the social order to order society" and "using violence to end violence."[3] Believing that war can only be ended by war, he becomes convinced that letting the victor win is the only road to peace.

In fact, in Li Feng's original script, instead of killing Long Sky (to prevent him from assassinating the Qin king), Nameless only amputates one of his arms, since Long Sky's spear and arm are as one. And when Broken Sword tries to persuade Nameless to abandon his planned assassination, Broken Sword does not just discard his sword; he lops off one of his own arms. Citing Freud is probably unnecessary here, as the signification of self-castration is quite evident in this iteration. However, director Zhang Yimou, or better to say the finished film, does not include these actions. The name Broken Sword, albeit somewhat archaic, already metaphorically connotes being castrated or self-castration.

If we pursue this close reading further, one interesting detail is that in two different scenes the great swordsman Broken Sword appears and writes rough calligraphy. The first time is in the red section. Using cinnabar as ink, he writes the character "jian" (sword) eight feet high. Dripping red, it is clearly visible in this scene. Hung high in the palace, this character serves as the background to the king throughout the film.

The second time, Broken Sword uses his sword as a brush to write for Nameless the two characters "tianxia" in the windblown desert. However, this time only his fluttering-sleeved, sword-waving posture is visible, as well as, in a solemn reverse shot, Nameless and Moon (Ruyue) staring at the characters in the sand. We cannot see the characters Broken Sword has written; we only hear them spoken by Nameless. Cinema as a genre bases its true text on the image. That which is not visible, then, lacks signification. Therefore, even if we set aside the rather meaningful choice of writing on sand, tianxia is presented as an aporia, a completely emptied signifier, or a canard. The only visible thing is the sword (jian) and the palimpsest of sword and king. Implausibly, the film presents the king coming to the realization, through the red "sword" character written by Broken Sword, that (spoken in classical imperial language by the king) "the highest realm of swordsmanship" is "no sword in one's hand, no sword in one's heart, no killing, only peace." While Broken Sword's writing of tianxia had merely disturbed Nameless's will to murder, it is the king's epiphany about the character "sword" that propels Nameless to surrender allegiance whole-heartedly. In the film, Nameless leaves this absurd last testament: "The dead want you [the king] to remember this highest realm." That is, to en-trust life to slaughter, to place the hopes of peace in war, and to dedicate people's rights to the conqueror.

Rather than viewing the film as having a vicious cycle of self-entangle-ment, it would be better to interpret it as having an aporia that reveals a certain social symptomaticity and cultural predicament. The appearance of tianxia here has achieved the evacuation of the abundant meanings and alternative possibilities that had been carried by the word. What is ex-posed by this gap is "sword"—the symbol of force and violence. When Long Sky, Broken Sword, and Nameless successively discard their swords and when "sword" becomes associated with the king alone, it achieves a logic of power that is at once empty and fixed.

From the very beginning stages of production, the target market for *Hero* was set to share Hollywood's global box office and to garner an Oscar nomination by leveraging the global success of *Crouching Tiger, Hidden Dragon*. Hence, the cultural signification of *Hero* becomes more intriguing. In other words, the original ambition for *Hero* was not the domestic mar-ket, which was in a downturn at the time. Rather, it was the global market, primarily the North American market. (One telling anecdote is that when the September 11 attacks occurred, which was not too long after filming had begun, the film crew halted production for a short while to discuss whether a story of assassins/terrorists was appropriate.) Thus, like martial arts, Chinese *go* (chess), the sword, calligraphy, the Chinese zither, and postcard-like scenery, the application of tianxia is merely an empty signi-fier of China. When tianxia was translated into "our land" in the English subtitles, the word's semantics were lost, whereas the appreciation of and submission to the historical logic of power still held.

Although it was not made for the domestic market, surprisingly, after the dismal failure of *Crouching Tiger, Hidden Dragon* in mainland China, *Hero* reached an unprecedented box-office record, unforeseen in light of the ridicule it met. Moreover, it signaled the arrival of this simultaneously disparate and empty signifier, or better to say image, of tianxia on the main stage of commercial/consumerist culture. *Hero* thus opened up and established the general approach to the tianxia imaginary in the industrial production of popular culture. For the cosmopolitan, urban generation who emerged on the cultural scene in China with the new millennium, the most influential works in the cultural genealogy of their formative years were precisely the martial arts novels by authors like Jin Yong (a.k.a. Louis Cha) and Gu Long.[4] Historical classical literature, apolitical premodern Chinese history, and twentieth-century Euro-American literature were further supplements to an aporetic contemporary culture that is under erasure. Among them, the Taiwan version of modern literary history (which is actually copied from Cold War–era China studies in the U.S.) has replaced and created a palimpsest over the mainland Chinese version. Through the piracy market and the Internet, Hollywood films, as well as Japanese and Korean cartoons, online video games, and idol dramas, have constructed a globalized cultural/consumerist space in China. Hovering above this aporetic and uneven localism, then, tianxia has reemerged as a floating, nameless space, a space where "fire beacons are raised in the four corners of the world," "outstanding heroes fight for dominance," and "grand ambitions vie for supremacy."[5]

At the same time, so-called tianxia is also an abstract value, an object of contention among various sects, states, and nations. It is a trophy for the winner. Symptomatic in the film is the manner in which so-called tianxia—a premodern Chinese delineation of the world and its logic of order—is superimposed over and hybridized with *jianghu*—an outlaw world.[6] Knights errant, scholars, and thieves become crossover or trans-identities that one can arbitrarily assume. Or rather, here is an exemplar of the "*majia* phenomenon."[7] The strong always win, and the winner becomes king.

In fact, China's first independently developed Internet game is called Tianxia. (According to the statistics, its sequel, Tianxia II, had more than 300,000 registered players by 2010.) The world constructed in these games, called tianxia, is actually more like jianghu. The only roles or identities players can choose from are as members of various martial arts sects, each with its distinctive kung fu style and specific weapon. But unlike the so-called new school of martial arts novels and films from the 1950s and '60s, the ultimate goal of the game is not to contend for hegemony or to unify jianghu.[8] No matter which role one chooses to play, his or her mission is always the same: the elimination of evil (either demons, villains, or corrupt officials) and the rectification of the dynastic order. The game thus has echoes of the classical novel *Outlaws of the Marsh* (*Shuihu zhuan*), with its famous line: "Eliminate all the corrupt officials, restore the name of the Zhao royal family."[9]

Even more symptomatic is the first private self-named "native publishing business," Jiuzhou (Nine Provinces or Nine States), which was originally an Internet operation and later moved into print media (by associating with *Jiuzhou Fantasy* and *Jiuzhou Ambition* magazines).[10] Let us set aside for the moment the fact that *jiuzhou* is a Chinese fantasy world inspired by *The Lord of the Rings*. We will also set aside a discussion of the differences and similarities between jiuzhou and tianxia, both of which are premodern Chinese spatial (or geographical) concepts and imaginaries. The Jiuzhou media group has brought together more than sixty young writers with a background in Internet literature whose book series have created a brand effect in the publishing industry. Among them the most popular author is Jiang Nan, whose standout work is the six-volume series *Chronicle of the Misty Realm* (*Jiuzhou piaomiao lu*).[11] This series clearly reflects the imaginary of tianxia and its centrality in today's popular culture industries.

Composed in the form of a chronicle, this historical fantasy novel traces a struggle for hegemony in an imagined world. Allegedly, the author's infatuation with the histories of the Song dynasty and the Roman Empire left an imprint on the novel. Hence the setting throughout is a secret society the author playfully models as the Chinese "Knights Templar," called "Tianqu Wushi" or "the Order of Heavenly Warriors," which is supposed to represent the positive power in Jiang Nan's *Misty Realm*. Its members scatter as princes and renowned generals to different states, tribes, and ethnic groups. But their mission extends beyond any community, state, or tribe. Maintaining, upholding, and stabilizing the power structure of the Nine States is, above all else, their ultimate goal. They achieve this goal by ascertaining an existing or potential strongman, assisting him to victory, and helping him maintain his rule. One of the main characters explains the secret society's choices to its new members in the following manner: Which is the best master of a flock of sheep? A lion or a sheep? Unquestionably, the answer is lion, because he "has the ability and the motive to protect his own food source." This chilling statement can be seen as the best elaboration of and footnote to Broken Sword's unfathomable epiphany in *Hero*. It serves as an undisguised version of the film's repressed, unspoken main theme.

In a sense, this is a central theme of the historical narratives produced by these Chinese Internet writers and the contemporary culture industries, who are relative outsiders to the former state-controlled cultural system. In this narrative, tianxia as a space and as an object has become associated with power, conquerors, and hegemony. If we search for the keyword tianxia on the Internet, the prominent search results are phrases like *wangzhe tianxia* (the king's tianxia), *tianxia bachang* (the siren call of hegemons), and *yitong tianxia* (to unify tianxia). Conversely, rarely do we see terms such as *tianxia cangsheng* (all the common people under tianxia), *gan wei tianxia xian* (dare to be the first in the world), *jinhuai tianxia* (make tianxia your ideal), or *tianxia weigong* (tianxia belongs to all people). It seems that now tianxia is the private property of the victors. Apart from accepting the powerlessness, impermanence, and cruelty of fate, others can only acknowledge and endure this conqueror's logic. Anonymous yet effective, this new mainstream logic, evinced by *Hero* and *Chronicle of the Misty Realm*, reveals the situation of China in the postrevolutionary era of globalization, namely, if radical social change or revolution is impossible, if we urgently need to bid farewell to revolution once and for all, and if "there is no alternative" to this disaster-ridden reality, then the best choice in a choiceless world is to consent to or make an alliance with power. Cynicism is a certain stance or route through which to lead social consent toward a neoliberal global logic.

Tianxia is an unusual keyword in the Chinese language. Unlike words such as *yu/zhou* (universe), *li/shi* (history), or *ren/min* (people), tianxia was one of those rare terms in the construction of the modern cultural revolution that did not suffer the semantic displacement of modernization or, more precisely, Westernization in the substitution of modern vernacular Chinese for classical Chinese. In my view, although vernacular Chinese or what we now call modern Chinese has basically continued to use the same characters as those in classical Chinese, it should be viewed as a new language. For modern vernacular Chinese is by no means a natural continuation of the older vernacular. To the contrary, quite a few of its elements were completely novel creations. Moreover, at the same time as classical Chinese was being replaced by vernacular Chinese, a considerable number of philosophical concepts from Europe were entering Chinese language via the Chinese characters used in Japanese or by creating neologisms in Chinese. As they borrowed existing characters and phrases in classical Chinese, these neologisms thereby took root in Chinese language. In other words, compared to other processes, the creation of modern Chinese was a process of deep internalization of Westernization and modernization.

The term "tianxia," which held a specific concept, imaginary, and systemic paradigm, bore the brunt of the violence that opened modern Chinese history (especially in the early twentieth century). It was replaced by words such as "Zhongguo" (China) or *shijie* (world).[12] Disparaged as a mere rhetorical phrase, yet precisely because of this, it did not directly experience a reinscription or "defilement." Or perhaps one could say that as the dynastic empire disintegrated, tianxia was repeatedly revived as a political, ideological, and cultural keyword at the same time that, precisely because of the fragmentation of this very tianxia system, the term entered into hibernation. After many decades of continuous global reflection on and critique of modernity, and global efforts to portray the many facets and polysemous interpretations and practices of modernity, perhaps it was this very hibernation that enabled tianxia once again to become a keyword, used to excavate and activate different political, ideological, and cultural resources from the history and development of China and East Asia.

Yet precisely because the term "tianxia" had never been eroded by the May Fourth Movement, it can be used directly by today's culture industries as a vacuous signifier of China; its aporetic quality can be used to carry and express both old and new modernist mainstream logic and value.[13] There is no need to quote Žižek directly to confirm what we already know, that the repressed past will return from the future and a cataclysmic moment often arises out of a congealed, momentary flash. Whether or not we can successfully begin anew from the concept of tianxia to recover and activate premodern and modern Chinese and East Asian alternative ideological resources, we are already immersed in, or at least trying to participate in, the construction of the future of China, East Asia, and even the world. Moreover, in the long and checkered history of premodern China, tianxia was already what Deleuze has called a "fold," even if in modern Chinese, tianxia also carries unique memories, traces, pride, and pain, which prompt specific structures of feeling among different generations.[14]

Returning once again to the symptomaticity of *Hero*, we can identify certain repeated traces of tianxia as the fold of Chinese culture. Despite its MacGuffinication of history and despite turning tianxia into an empty sign of China in an international discursive context, the crux of *Hero* nonetheless revolves around the question of what is meant by tianxia. The question is central, whether or not the film refers to tianxia as meaning "all the common people under tianxia" or "the ideals of tianxia" as represented by Broken Sword, or "the business of hegemony," that is, "the unification of tianxia," as represented by the Qin king. Does tianxia refer to a universal realm? Or only to the domain of China? Is it the difference and boundary between Chinese and barbarian? Or the center/margin structure with a dominating and benevolent Middle Kingdom presiding over the world?[15] Is it the hierarchical power order descending from (the son of) heaven? Or the inner logic that makes Chinese civilization self-renewable and self-reliant?

The most direct and self-evident question is whether this so-called tianxia refers to a historical or contemporary China or to a world distinguished from the capitalist world system. Within the internal discursive context of Chinese culture, what barely validates the narrative logic of *Hero* is that its tianxia signifies the modern nation-state of China. For only when looking back from the vantage point of China as a modern nation-state does it become necessary to trace its history for a narrative of legitimacy. While it is possible to push this China narrative back to the legendary Xia (ca. 2100–1600 BCE), Shang (ca. 1600–1050 BCE), and Zhou (ca. 1046–256 BCE) dynasties, regarding modern China, the event of groundbreaking significance as a beginning and foundation was the Qin conquest of six rival kingdoms, leading to the establishment of a unified empire (in 221 BCE).

As Hobsbawm said, with respect to the mythology of modern nationalism, China is one of the few exceptions.[16] The nation-state narrative of China accords with many of the basic elements provided by this myth: China is fairly homogeneous; compared to that of Egypt or Greece, the territory of modern China is situated within the boundaries of its ancient empires; China has a substantially continuous history, thus a relatively continuous civilization and cultural heritage. Hence, the historical significance of Qin Shihuang (the Qin king who claimed to be the first emperor) lies primarily in his unification of tianxia, his preliminary demarcations of the ancient empire, and his laying the foundation for the imperial political model thereafter.[17] Moreover, among his achievements—establishing a unified writing system, a coherent road network, and unified measurements, as well as building the Great Wall as a barrier to the invasion of the nomads from the steppes—the writing system is the one with extraordinary significance. Unified characters have served as the common ground for the culture of China, a country of vast territory and great diversity. Therefore, China's cultural roots are different from those of Europe, which are logocentric—the cultural foundation of its phonocentrism. This parameter underwrites Broken Sword's otherwise inexplicable epiphany in *Hero*. This parameter provides the prop for and supplement not only to the distinctive historical knowledge typical of so-called historical costume dramas, which is unspoken yet self-evident, but also to current concerns.

As I have pointed out elsewhere, in the industrial production of Chinese popular culture, the object of historical narrative has shifted from the precarious and long-suffering empire during the late Ming (1368–1644) and late Qing (1644–1911) dynasties—a period that is closer in time to our modern period and resonant with colonialism—to the much earlier Qin (221–206 BCE), Han (206 BCE–280 CE), and flourishing Tang (618–907 CE) dynasties.[18] The cultural meaning of this change is that the focus of concern has shifted from cultural self-criticism to cultural self-affirmation. The frequent appearance of the Qin Shihuang image in Chinese cinema at the turn of the millennium has multiply entangled symptomatic meanings. Continuing our discussion from above, we can see that the beginning of Qin Shihuang's reign is the beginning of imperial rule; it is also the beginning of (at least one sense of) "China." Being folded within and explained by *Hero*, the word "tianxia" seems to imply the self-recognition and self-representation of China as an (apolitical) modern nation-state.

However, to explain *Hero*'s tianxia this way would make the narrative fall into multiple self-contradictions. If one argues that the idealism about and identification with tianxia/China as one's larger self and as public virtue led Broken Sword to discard his smaller self and private virtue, and that the projection of nationalist mythology is the unspoken yet self-evident premise of his action, then the same logic also supports the decision and behavior of Long Sky, Broken Sword, Flying Snow, and Nameless, who decided to assassinate the Qin king out of their love for the kingdom of Zhao and their desire to rescue their homeland. Thus, in the film, Flying Snow and Nameless ask Broken Sword, "Aren't you from Zhao?," while the Qin king also queries him, "The people of Qin would not assassinate me, so where are you from?"

If the film's narrative logic is to be validated despite the contradictions, tianxia must stand for a larger and more inclusive imaginary than China, as symbolized by the Qin empire. Indeed, with its evacuation of history,

Hero's "historical" framing of the Qin king is clearly not just the one who destroyed six rival kingdoms and established the Qin empire. The king apparently has a much larger vision, aspiration, and ambition. "The six kingdoms are nothing!" the king proclaims. "After conquering them, I will command my cavalries westward to the deserts and eastward across the oceans, establishing a huge territory!" (Interestingly, this last line was quietly erased in the internationally released version.)

The film ends abruptly after the king, with tears in his eyes, orders the execution of Nameless (his actual order is "a thousand arrows through his body"), followed by the caption, "After conquering the six rival states, the Qin king built the Great Wall and protected the country and its people." Thus, we might surmise that Broken Sword's tianxia idealism—as relayed by Nameless—made the king abandon his insatiable ambition to conquer and stopped the Qin army after they destroyed the six kingdoms and unified the empire. However, since the original target market was international (centering on North America/the United States), the "historical knowledge" corresponding to the inner structure of the text—the unspoken yet self-evident premise, whether that is Qin Shihuang or tianxia—is lacking. Quite amusingly, the word *tianxia*, absent from the visual frame, is translated into "our land." Therefore, the only referent that can support the internal logic of the narrative is China, a suspended, empty, and complicated sign. How should we understand the tianxia in *Hero*—the crux of its narrative logic? Is it China's world imagination or the world's imagination of China? Linking it with the year 2003, an extraordinary juncture in China's recent social transitions, or with Zhang Yimou's dazzling role as the main director of the Olympic Games' opening ceremony five years later, we might think it adequate to interpret tianxia as "China's peaceful rise."[19] But to suggest that this is the intrinsic reason for *Hero*'s success at the global box office would be implausible. For whether there is peace in the world or not, "the rise of China" is always accompanied by "the threat of China," by a vaguely remembered, yet, owing to the victor's position, exceptionally powerful logic of the Cold War and by the tensions of a new round of global competition for hegemony.[20] However, it is also unconvincing to suggest that the only basis for the movie's commercial success lies in its gorgeous colors, the ritual aesthetics of the fifth generation as demonstrated by the choreographic arrangements of kung fu, and the Chinese elements or symbols, such as the Chinese zither, chess, calligraphy, and swords. Although new millennium cinema (which follows the Hollywood template) has continued to upgrade its spectacles and dazzling technologies while structuring cultural consumerist fashion, global box-office winners have to be in tune with mainstream logic.

Thus, China becomes an ornate signifier overflowing with meaning, while tianxia turns into a sparsely elaborated sublime object. In their superimposition, they slide off one another, alternating in their aporia. As soon as tianxia serves as the signified of China, the concepts it carries are quietly drained away. Moreover, once "China" is strewn around or positioned within tianxia, the bigger picture, which for the time being can only be called the world, must be refigured, located, and identified. Undoubtedly, *Hero* was unable and unwilling to take on this task. However, from *Hero*, we may discover some core issues in redefining or theorizing tianxia as a new Chinese keyword. If we hope to view tianxia as a possible cultural imaginary and political practice and define it as the world (or the global) or directly call it an alternative to the modern capitalist global system, then this keyword is not only faced with the problem of sorting out the relationship between tianxia and China, but is also still waiting for reinterpretation and reactivation in the present context.

Perhaps even more interesting is that in the actual context of China and, in fact, as part of the global memory of the 1960s, tianxia in *Hero* is linked with, yet marginalizes and conceals, a more proximate and complicated history, memory, and political practice: Chinese revolution, Mao Zedong, and the Great Cultural Revolution. As I have discussed elsewhere, the theme of assassinating the Qin king in a series of films in Chinese cinema, to which *Hero* belongs, has multiple social meanings.[21] These contemporary accounts of the Qin emperor, Qin Shihuang, which we may call historical reassessments or revisionist narratives, contain particular and concrete historical facts related to the political practices from the 1950s to the 1970s. Born and raised in that era, the fifth-generation directors coincidentally selected this assassination story as the main subject of their big-production historical films. However, rather than a direct reflection of their common memory, to the contrary, it appears to be more like a cultural unconscious interrelated with memory/oblivion, revelation/concealment, the political/apolitical, and history/reality. Of course, this is because writing a revisionist account of Qin Shihuang and comparing himself to Qin Shihuang is precisely what Mao did when responding to attacks at home and abroad. However, as the three assassination films chose the assassination aspect rather than Qin Shihuang's great exploits in establishing the empire as their narrative entry point, they seem to have overturned Mao's revisionist account or redressed a historical narrative that had been subverted.

According to the historical materialist view of history of the 1950s–70s, assassins—at least those depicted in "Biographies of Assassins" in *Records of the Grand Historian*—had nothing to do with the inexorable logics of history.[22] Nor were they relevant to the "heroes" generated at the crossroads of deterministic historical trajectories. To the contrary, they were seen as buffoons who, with overconfidence, had attempted to fight against the tide of history. Thus, the three assassination films (in going against this historical materialist view) continue the cultural practice of the 1980s—a seeming reflection on history and culture that is in fact a criticism of current political reality.

However, drawn toward the assassination aspect as the entry point into and identification with this new version of the Qin king's story, this series of films nonetheless reveals some imprints of the Mao era or, more precisely, the era of the Cultural Revolution: namely, a preconceived recognition of the moral justice of rebels and revolutionaries, as well as an emotional structure infused with justice, passion, and an impulse toward martyrdom. It is particularly interesting to note that without exception, all three films ultimately turn from a story of the assassin to that of the king. The admiration for the assassin also transforms into approval of the king. Thus, the Chinese title of the first of these films was changed from *Built by Blood* to *Ode to the Qin Emperor*. Although full of contradiction and hesitation, *The Emperor and the Assassin*, the second of these films, eventually portrays the king, rather than the assassin, as the lone hero who will shoulder the mandate of heaven. *Hero* marks this identificational transition even before the film begins. Moreover, aside from recognizing the assassins' fate in history (because at least they "understood" history, i.e., recognized the king as carrying the mandate of heaven), the film almost completely wipes out from the historical picture of the victors those who resisted that view. The entanglement in Chen Kaige's *The Emperor and the Assassin* lies in the fact that as he consciously or unconsciously rewrites the story of the assassin into the story of the king, Chen cannot help bestowing some cinematic attention on the defeated and the weak.

In contrast, *Hero* is unambiguous: aside from the scene in which Nameless and the king sit in the palace exchanging stories, the film is simply various color-coded versions of a single account. Furthermore, the grand spectacles, without exception, are of the Qin cavalry, the Qin marksmen, and the Qin garrisons. Aside from the four (or five) exceptional assassins, there are no visual images of the collective resistance or collective experience of defeat on the part of the vanquished. The only exception is in the red section. In the story about Nameless, the schoolteacher in the Zhao academy continues to lead the students in practicing calligraphy despite the fact that the Qin army's arrows fall on the school like pelting rain from the sky. But once this section ends, it is instantly identified by the king as a lie. Thus, a collective portrait of those who did not surrender and were unafraid suddenly becomes a cinematic image of fabrication, and disappears in the revised versions: the blue and white sections.

The breathtaking array of the Qin army within the visible frame corresponds with the enormous, visible scarlet character "sword," while the absent presence of the resisters and the disappearance of the image of the collective losers corresponds with the invisible tianxia. These are significant traces in the film. This interpretation may be just an inference from the overall film text. But the complex emotional memory of the Mao era, which has been shaped by the various portrayals of Qin Shihuang, is the crux to explain the seemingly unexpected appearance of tianxia in *Hero*.

With the opening of modern Chinese history, tianxia lost its key position in Chinese political and intellectual history. Occasionally it appeared as a rhetorical enunciation in texts or daily life. But tianxia emerged prominently in the early years of the Cultural Revolution and thus became one of the unusual inscriptions of that specific historical period. Apart from Mao Zedong's famous line "achieve peace and order in tianxia through chaos in tianxia," tianxia, in a way, became one of the iconic terms used by the Red Guards.[23] For example, there was the saying, "Tianxia is our tianxia; the country is our country. If we don't speak out, who will speak? If we don't act, who will act?" "Look at today's state, whose tianxia is it?"—the resounding line in *Tao Wu Zhao Xi* (Denunciation of Wu Zhao) written by the Tang dynasty poet Luo Binwang (640–684)—became part of the manifesto of power seizures and rebellions during the Cultural Revolution.[24] "Take the fate of tianxia as one's own responsibility"—a line from "The Biography of Kong Xiuyuan" in *The History of Southern Dynasties*—became an expression of social and self-expectation for the Red Guards or, more precisely, the younger generation.[25] While this tianxia was variously entangled with the space of power, the political order (as well as its interrogation and subversion), and the connotations of "China" in history and that contemporary moment, at the same time it surely also contained the imagined contours of an alternative world.

When "tianxia" occasionally replaced "the world" in the phrase "care for your country, explore the world"—a standard guideline for youth during the Cultural Revolution—the implication was clear. Perhaps it is this aspect that reveals the key to the issue of tianxia: the reason tianxia could be used (at least in the language used in mainland China) as an alternative global imaginary for the world is that at the time there were socialist revolutions worldwide, there was proletarian internationalism, and, with a reliance on world revolution and a communist vision of the future, there was an alternative to global capitalism. Therefore, "take tianxia as one's own responsibility," the Red Guard saying based in a classical text, could also be a synonymous expression for "take the liberation of all humankind and world revolution as one's own responsibility." "To the Soldiers of the Coming Third World War," a Red Guard poem published in the early stage of the Cultural Revolution, could be an appropriate footnote here.[26]

However, later in the Cultural Revolution when the Red Guard movement had subsided, and tianxia was made over into political and diplomatic rhetoric, it delineated another picture of the world and a different set of international connections. The most famous Chinese diplomatic self-description of that time was, "We have friends all over tianxia." Faced with the Cold War dividing line that blocked the Chinese coast and millions of troops guarding the simmering Sino-Soviet border, Mao Zedong used his third-world doctrine to call for support from the many countries and regions of Asia, Africa, and Latin America. If the fact that in 1971 China was "carried into the United Nations" (in Zhou Enlai's words) by a large number of third-world countries offered corroboration that our friends are all over tianxia, tianxia here meant the vast expanse of third-world countries, which is not equivalent to today's so-called developing nations. Instead, it represented a political force that provided a space between or resistance against the United States and the Soviet Union. It was an international organizational structure known as the nonaligned movement whose foundation was laid at the 1955 Bandung Conference. Of course, to search for contemporary memories of that tianxia, one need only refer to *Hero* to see its complete and utter absence. If *Hero*'s combination of the assassination story and tianxia in the film's third retelling occasionally stirred up dusty memories, from the reassessment of Qin Shihuang to the return of the assassin and then back to the spotlight on the king, this king is no longer the same king, and this tianxia is no longer the same tianxia. That's why the assassin must be nameless, the vanquished who had been slaughtered or conquered invisible, and all trace of tianxia's prominence lost. In the Chinese and world cultural contexts, this absence points obliquely to the cultural trajectory from revolution to farewell to revolution to postrevolution. While *Hero*, through its reference to tianxia, is a small example of China's increasing involvement in the globalization process, the heavily layered meaning of tianxia is not another name for globalization.

Perhaps the key point still lies in the fact that with the arrival of the post–Cold War era, the current world system or, more precisely, capitalist globalization has become the winner with no alternative. The alternatives, or even the relevant utopian imaginations, have all been discarded in a forgotten hole. If the motivation to redefine or reintroduce tianxia is to search for a different world vision or structure, then this search is where the tension or predicament lies. When we try to make use of Chinese traditional cultural resources, we are faced not only with the difficult process of reactivation of those resources, but also with the need to clarify once again the traces and scars left on them by the history of China's long twentieth century. Let us put aside the old propositions of the traditional versus the modern or traditional modernization. It is time to ask: in what sense, from which angles, and to what extent can China serve as a method to sketch an alternative world imaginary?

PART II

Class, Still Lives, and Masculinity

CHAPTER 3

Temporality, *Nature Morte*, and the Filmmaker

A Reconsideration of Still Life

TRANSLATED BY LENNET DAIGLE

In the world of contemporary Chinese cinema, Jia Zhangke is, in many respects, an exception to the rule: he is a director whose films almost without fail depict the lower classes or the majority of society; a director who has continually, from the start, been dedicated to making art films; a director who has fulfilled his social responsibilities as an artist while developing an original mode of artistic expression; a director who has made the transition from independent underground films to commercial mainstream films without losing his vitality and without suffering exclusion from Western film festivals; a director famous for his autobiographical narratives who has finally "grown up" and who has successfully drawn on his experiences to explore broader social issues. As long as China's fifth-generation filmmakers continue to make commercial compromises, and the sixth generation remains stuck—having grown but not matured in terms of style and modes of expression—Jia Zhangke will remain an exception, or even one of a kind.

Actually, after the period in which Chen Kaige's *Yellow Earth* and Zhang Yimou's films had become synonymous with the moniker Chinese cinema and after Zhang Yuan's nomination of "underground cinema" to refer to what Europeans think of as Chinese cinema—both post–Cold War but still Cold War–style designations—the release of *Platform* unexpectedly heralded the arrival of the "Jia Zhangke era" of Chinese cinema in the new millennium's international film world, as represented primarily by European film festivals and American film studies classes.

In some sense, Jia Zhangke, with twenty-first-century eyes of the world upon him, has become one of many paradoxical traces littering world film history, or rather of that branch originating in the European art film. It is similar to the beginning of the twentieth century, when modernism and the avant-garde movements began to turn against, question, and shatter the cultural renaissance and its ideological fabric. The invention of the motion picture camera gave rise to the twentieth century's most important form of art and popular culture (at least in the first half of the century). It nevertheless also revived and reinforced the renaissance space: the fantasy world created by the camera's centralizing perspective and the classical stage spectacle replicated by the silver screen.

In the second half of the twentieth century, during the 1960s, the author, God, and humanity were all declared dead; yet the *politique des auteurs* went against the times and came into being, giving both impetus and a name to wave after wave of "New Wave" cinema around the world, initiating an era of personalized cinema in which auteurs wrote with light. This in turn led to a cultural paradox, since the auteur theory that arose in order to classify and interpret Hollywood filmmakers came to sustain European films made in opposition to Hollywood, and came to be an extension of the critical practice broadly associated with the New Left in the Cold War era. In France and Germany, at least, the auteurs and the affiliated New Wave movements became active participants in—or even the driving force behind—the European and American countercultures during the 1960s and '70s.

As neoliberalism rose to utter dominance in the 1980s and auteur films or European art films gradually exhausted their originality and critical edge, international film festivals—one of the central sites of postwar film creativity—implemented or expanded mechanisms for the identification, nurturing, and classification of non-Western filmmakers and writers. It almost goes without saying that in their role as identifiers of new talent, these European film festivals are in many respects a double-edged sword. They broke the European singular prerogative on art film and opened European and American eyes to the world of non-Western film. But they also, consciously or unconsciously, successfully dictated and regulated the ways non-Western artists understand and conceptualize film, art, and aesthetics.

At the same time, for third-world or non-Western film artists, Europe's film festivals have undoubtedly provided a means of escaping the constraints of crass commercialization as well as severe governmental or cultural realities and have allowed them to continue pursuing their artistic dreams and social critique. But international film festivals also take films with clear, specific cultural concerns and political criticisms and remove them from their local contexts, giving rise to a particular cultural or psychological type of non-Western filmmaker: the combination artist–political dissident, who creates idiosyncratic films nurtured by the strangely—even perversely—insular world of the film festival–art house circuit.

In another sense, postwar–Cold War European art cinema in its very nature perpetuated an unspoken assumption of twentieth-century modernism: namely the counter- or anticommercial nature of art—even if this is undoubtedly an extension of and variation on the antiutilitarian assumptions of classical art and aesthetics, and even though modernist art itself undoubtedly had difficulty escaping market commodification. Clearly, however, since the global market and its cultural and artistic products long ago took over the mainstream, the anti- or noncommercial positioning of art films has taken on an inherently critical cast, in ways that are not necessarily consciously acknowledged. Perhaps it is precisely because of this that the social and cultural reconstruction of postwar art films frequently overlapped with the social and political articulations of the New Left, and that it played an important and even leading role in the global 1960s.

However, even though certain Euro-American art films (including avant-garde, experimental cinema) actualized some form of cultural resistance, or at least a critique of modernity (namely capitalism), the evaluative standards used by international film festivals, whether consciously or unconsciously, embedded mainstream Western values in their classifications for non-Western filmmakers. This situation has led to a somewhat bizarre double standard: the self-referential European insistence on "other" means of expression treats many forms of otherness as either worrisome or praiseworthy signs of lagging on the path toward global capitalism. It has inevitably standardized the methods of representing society used by non-Western filmmakers wanting to pass through the narrow doors of international film festivals. They consequently have reproduced what may tentatively be called Eurocentric ways of imagining the self and others, and have had no choice but to become a referent for the standard Euro-American "non-Western" script. These filmmakers then have had difficulty achieving non-non-Western forms of self-expression characterized by full subjective and cultural self-awareness. Actually, during the last two decades of the twentieth century, European international film festivals' methods of nominating non-Western films centered on Asia (including a surprising but unsustainable interest in Turkish and Iranian New Wave cinema), particularly greater China (Chinese language) films, for which Hong Kong's New Wave was the forerunner, followed by Taiwanese and mainland Chinese new cinema (i.e., the successive appearance of the fourth, fifth, and sixth generations).

Following *The World*, *Still Life* marks Jia Zhangke's second film since his transition from underground to commercial cinema, and from autobiographical to imaginative plot. The film's narrative space—the Three Gorges reservoir, the largest hydro-engineering project in Chinese history and largest water conservation project in the world—is heavy with social symbolism. The massive dam interrupts China's longest river, the Yangtze, at its most dramatic stretch: the Three Gorges region is home to China's most beautiful natural scenery. One finds here countless vestiges of history from over the past two thousand years, and countless poems, songs, and writings praising its landscape. But the area is also rich in water resources, and damming the river to generate electricity has been the dream of three generations of Chinese leaders and hydro engineers seeking to conquer and remold nature, and harness energy.

Actually, the movie includes a seemingly realist episode. As Shen Hong calmly takes leave of her husband and steps on the riverboat bound for Shanghai, the camera zooms in on a television monitor aboard the boat, nearly filling the whole frame, where images of Sun Yat-sen, Mao Zedong, and Deng Xiaoping are successively shown, accompanied by the pleasing, proper voice of a female narrator describing their plans to dam the gorges, followed by a scene of Jiang Zemin at the ribbon-cutting ceremony.[1] Around the edges of the frame, however, the passengers on deck are obscured or indistinct. Perhaps it is precisely this careless glimpse of a shot that casually reveals the film's true intention: to move aside the grand images that lie at the heart of mainstream depictions, and allow us to see with the same kind of casual glance the people behind this canvas—the insignificant little people scurrying to keep up with the giant strides of modernization.

The Three Gorges project was launched in 1994 and completed in 2009, a total of fifteen years. The project was accompanied by a massive migration of people from the reservoir area on a scale rarely seen in human history: the migration of an entire region. Depending on one's point of view, the Three Gorges project is either a marvel of the human control of nature and a milestone in China's century-long modernization, or an environmental and ecological disaster, the moment of inexorable doom toward which history and the present are moving.

Interestingly, within the filmic space we hardly ever see any large-scale hydro-engineering works, and, aside from the male protagonist Han Sanming's job sites, the film hardly shows us the ubiquitous ruins. On the contrary, the film is filled with scenes of very ordinary bustling streets and densely packed dwellings typical of a small city in southwestern China. But it is a way of life that can be absolutely and permanently cut short at any time by the word "demolish" (*chai* 拆) written and circled in whitewash on walls of buildings slated for removal—a sight so ubiquitous that it came to symbolize Chinese urban life in the 1990s.

In one of the film's few lighthearted moments we see Han Sanming and a coworker splashing water on each other after a day's work in the hot sun, when suddenly something outside the frame attracts Han Sanming's attention and he worriedly calls out to the owner of the inn. Not until the camera pans to the innkeeper do we see a group of workers writing "chai" in giant white strokes enclosed in the customary circle, on the side of the inn where it says Chinese People's Pavilion and Guest House. Even though this means the end is near, that the innkeeper will lose his home and livelihood and that Han Sanming will lose his humble but inexpensive lodgings, the innkeeper can only muster a few feeble curses, to which the workers give the routine response that they are just doing their job. In the next sequence, a wide-angle shot shows a small building on a hillside and a mother and daughter looking out the window. But in the lower right we see another huge, white, encircled chai, adding a sense of alarm to this everyday scene. As the camera pans to the right, past the chai, a high-angle shot reveals the innkeeper hobbling down the street.

Still Life depicts a time close to the project's completion. The narrative ambience is permeated with a sense that the countdown has begun. Signs indicating how high the water will rise during the project's third phase appear everywhere, as if the filmic space itself tells a story of flooding. In fact, the filmic space, and the time period and background that unfold through the narrative, make *Still Life* into something of a contemporary Chinese parable: rebuild or drown, create or destroy, remember or repress, an era's dream come true or a complete rupture with history. The film is built on an extremely old narrative trope: the search. A man and woman with nothing in common, he from the lower class [Han Sanming], she from a higher class [Shen Hong], come to the Three Gorges separately looking for their spouses.[2] Thus, it is personal stories that motivate and dominate this parabolic, collective social site. The primary plot takes the form of a free-flowing melodrama, full of fortuitous encounters and missed opportunities. But Jia Zhangke refuses to construct fantasies and instead uses a seemingly unpremeditated, informal, documentary style of exposition.

Still Life exhibits just those characteristics that could allow us to make the broadest or most crude distinctions between art and commercial film: large numbers of long takes, and a slow, drawn-out editing rhythm. Perhaps it goes without saying, but the ideas and qualities embedded in the long takes and slow editing characteristics of art film—as opposed to the "short" and "fast" of commercial film—are among the ways that films produce their cultural politics. Long and slow are contrasted or counterposed with short and fast, indicating a nonconformist stance toward the speed and efficiency prized by modern, capitalist logic. The opening sequence is an extremely long, seemingly endless and boundless take, panning across the passengers on the deck of a Yangtze River freighter, like a long painting scroll depicting the lower rungs of Chinese society—the enormous lower class, the majority of society, or one could say the huge base of the pyramid supporting the Chinese miracle—before finally revealing and alighting on the male protagonist, Han Sanming. This sequence is followed by more long takes capturing Han Sanming traveling and searching.

It is precisely these shots following Han Sanming through bricks and rubble, through slum-like temporary housing for the poor and past reinforced concrete structures seemingly under construction but actually being demolished, that delineate the contours of this massive and perverse space: an unprecedented and unrepeatable engineering project, whose completion heralds the complete destruction and submersion of the space itself. In light of the impending flood, this discarded space and community have come under the rule of casual violence and organized crime.

Three long takes are worth mentioning: the first shows Han Sanming calling Xiao Ma's mobile phone during a rain shower that has brought work to a halt.[3] The camera pans toward the source of the faint ringtone, ultimately revealing not far away beneath the rubble the dead body of the childlike young man. The second depicts Shen Hong and her husband, Guo Bin, meeting and deciding to break up, with a stationary shot filming this long-separated couple who may still have feelings for each other, but who have long since ceased to be a couple in anything but name. The third comes at the end of the film as Han Sanming's fellow workers on the demolition site decide nearly on the spur of the moment to leave and accompany him to the Shanxi coal mines to find work. The camera films these migratory, drifting men against the backdrop of China's vast territory, walking out of the depths of the frame and turning toward the right, then shifts to a medium shot of Han Sanming's back, while in the background is one of *Still Life*'s most important, absurd, and symbolic of images: a figure holding a long bamboo pole walking on a steel cable across the Yangtze, a river once considered an insurmountable natural barrier.

The background image of the final shot may work at an allegorical level to comment on the lives of the Three Gorges dam, or perhaps all of China's internal migratory lower classes, full of imminent danger, lives hanging by a thread. Or it could be read as a tragic footnote to the choices and aspirations of the people in the film: In 2005, the year *Still Life* was filmed, news reports of accidents in the Shanxi mines repeatedly shocked Chinese society. The frequency of the accidents and dramatic increase in casualties revealed what was only the tip of the iceberg of problems facing China's poor. A protest video about the mining disasters popular on the Internet at the time was titled "There Is an Occupation Called Making It Back Alive."

There is one particular long-take sequence that reveals or explains the social significance of this space: it opens with a panoramic shot of the demolition site and the workers swinging their sledgehammers, using the most primitive of methods to tear down modern reinforced concrete buildings. In the foreground, Han Sanming stands for a brief moment before taking off his shirt and swinging his hammer. The camera pans and gradually moves in on a silent and seemingly abandoned heap of rubble, when suddenly a group of workers covered head to toe in white protective clothing and carrying sprayers rises from the rubble in a manner reminiscent of science fiction films, creating a powerfully surreal atmosphere. The camera follows the workers as they spray disinfectant over the rubble heap, allowing the audience to see formerly enclosed homes, their walls crumbled, now lying exposed and part of the external environment. The decorations and awards that remain on the walls reveal the dreams, passions, and memories of the inhabitants. It's a type of scene normally found in war films, the feel that Picasso's *Guernica* tries to transmit. Yet this film is dealing instead with a construction site that is the focus of worldwide attention.

In *Still Life*, Jia Zhangke paints a fairly dark picture: during the final phase of the Three Gorges project, migrants are forced to leave their homes for the northeast or Guangdong—China's northernmost and southernmost areas. The "closest" destination is Shanghai's Chongming Island. These people closely connected to the land are uprooted and moved to places where the terrain and culture are very different, while those who refuse relocation are forced into slums or, like Old Ma and family, to live on boats adrift in the Yangtze. All of them represent the most prominent social landscape of globalization: a metaphor of flux.

After the Three Gorges project and the ensuing mass migration had thoroughly destroyed the communities in the dam area, the people who remained were without the most basic social protections or means of self-preservation. In *Still Life*, the area has already been reduced to a primitive criminal state in which violence is the only solution. We see unemployed men, forced to migrate to find work and subsequently injured on the job, helplessly, unreasonably, and pointlessly asking the bankrupt factory's manager to compensate them for their losses, and forced to rely on the money their wives earn from prostitution; while Old Ma clearly relies on the fists of his deckhands to maintain order in his shipping business. In the background, never appearing except as a photograph in a flier, the "Lady from Xiamen" is apparently in charge of "office building demolition," while her lover (bodyguard? henchman?), Shen Hong's husband, Guo Bin, is clearly a powerful criminal figure.

Aside from the demolition crews (with whom Jia Zhangke sympathizes and identifies to some extent), every scene with crowds of people includes some bandaged heads or bloody faces. Guo Bin's place of work exists in an especially great swirl of noisy activity, in which violence is met with violence. Jia Zhangke has never avoided these themes in the past, but neither has he fixated on or amplified their cruelty as he does here. In a blurred, distracted mode, Jia Zhangke's long takes create a visual caress that touches everything in this soon-to-be-submerged landscape—people, things, scenery—as if seen through the eyes of Han Sanming and Shen Hong, who are drawn to the area by their love. Perhaps this is the origin of the film's English title, *Still Life*. Actually, following the example of European art film, it is space—and not people—that plays the leading role in the film. Here it is the Three Gorges, the reservoir, and the area soon to be flooded. What traces, reveals, or speaks for this leading role is the movement of the long take. That is to say, in the dialogue between Jia Zhangke and the Three Gorges, or Jia Zhangke and the reservoir area, everything in the film is a kind of "still life." The translator of the film's title into English bestowed a sense of desolation and longing absent in the Chinese title (which translates literally as "The Good People of the Three Gorges").

Here, however the film exhibits an interesting cultural symptomaticity. One could say that the film basically follows the conventions of art films and makes space a primary character, albeit a palimpsestic space condemned to disappear, or already gone: the majestic scenery of the Three Gorges, the riverbank towns, the future reservoir, or the soon-to-be-depopulated countryside. But it would be more accurate to say that spaces such as the future reservoir area or the Three Gorges District—already gone or inevitably fated to disappear—float suspended in the distance, above or beyond the narrative and the text.

Thus, the visual space of *Still Life* has become a "site" in the narrow sense, a temporal appearance of a spatial form. Clearly, within the range of Chinese art cinema, or rather in the tradition of post-Mao film, *Still Life* is the first to accomplish the inversion of cultural and visual themes of fifth-generation Chinese cinema (or rather fifth-generation-style film). No longer is space given priority over time, and no longer is the time of progress, reform, and life swallowed by Chinese historical and geographical space. Rather, it is temporality, that is to say development or progress, that sweeps away historical and natural spaces like a hurricane and rewrites them, as if once again corroborating a compressed experience of time: contemporary China experienced four hundred years of European capitalist history, from the Enlightenment to the critique of modernity in the thirty years leading up to the turn of this century.

Yet perhaps we need to consider the prehistory of this late modern period of China's history of modernization. Without even going back as far as the Ming (1368–1644) and Qing dynasties (1644–1911), we can already find the outstanding recurring themes about modern China's historical narratives and space-time imaginaries: the movements to reassess Chinese culture and history in the 1980s, in which fifth-generation filmmakers played such an active role, actually (and also as a form of imaginary) were a repetition in a transformed sense of May Fourth cultural movement themes.[4] The prominent spatial aspect of May Fourth preoccupations became a direct vector in these later movements for the notion of the extraordinary structural stability of Chinese history, in which the hope for redemption lay in a reactivation of time, or more precisely in allowing the time of "world history (i.e., capitalism)" to replace or substitute for "Chinese time."

Even more interesting, the legitimation of the Three Gorges project and its enactment as a heroic feat are in effect the reappearance and fulfillment of the temporal-historical narrative of the late 1950s and the Mao era. Not only is it the realization of Mao's own personal dream ("Walls of stone will stand upstream to the west / To hold back Wushan's clouds and rain / Till a smooth lake rises in the narrow gorges") and noble sentiments ("Ten thousand years are too long, seize the day, seize the hour!").[5] It is moreover the enactment of a demonstrative logic of that era that seems fantastical in light of today's mainstream thinking: "There is no Jade Emperor in heaven, no Dragon King on earth. I am the Jade Emperor, I am the Dragon King. Tell the mountains and hills to open the way, I'm coming!"[6] "The earth is a bauble. . . . I will carve it as I please." Perhaps it goes without saying that in these two quotes, "I" must definitely be capitalized, because even if this "I" cannot be directly identified as the proletariat—the once and future subject of history in Marxism or the international communist movement—the "it" is undoubtedly a reference to the people ("the people, and only the people, are the motive force of history") and not the individual.[7]

In the current moment, we probably do not need to offer a meticulous explanation that in the post-Mao era, the capitalist transformation that is referred to in China as "reform and opening"—in the sense of modernization and industrialization supposedly taking the nation-state as their unit, and in the logic of catching up and overtaking by which underdeveloped countries compare themselves to developed Euro-American countries— far from being a rupture with the Mao era, is deeply, intimately, and directly intertwined with it. Consequently, the communism and socialism of underdeveloped countries in the twentieth century can be seen instead as a form of state capitalism actualized under specific historical conditions, though such a narrative is incapable of revealing, and may even conceal, political and cultural tendencies of the twentieth century's international communist movement, particularly the realities of Cold War socialism. But what makes *Still Life* such a valuable filmic moment is its ability to stop and look back and try to capture in a series of "still lives" spatial images that will be destroyed, submerged in the ceaselessly accelerating flow of time.

Yet another cluster of social and cultural symptoms is reflected in the changes that have occurred between fifth-generation films (particularly the earlier ones) and Jia Zhangke's (and perhaps the sixth generation's) respective means of representing history, the present, and space-time: namely, China's "progress," or more accurately the march toward capitalism and China's economic "rise." Rather than making it easier for films to explore cultural themes, these changes have made it dramatically more difficult. In the past, in the Mao era (1950s–70s), the people (those classified as workers, peasants, or soldiers, those clearly included in the capital "I") briefly eclipsed the new person of modern Chinese culture and literature (the delicate, sensitive, pale individual) and firmly occupied the place of the social and historical subject, occasionally using what would by Euro-American standards be considered "noncinematic" or even "anticinematic" methods to change or settle once and for all the "subjectless sentence" that characterizes Chinese cinema.[8]

However, in the new era, the fifth generation's resurrection of the May Fourth Movement's Enlightenment critique also reinstates, in a seemingly logical fashion, the subjectless film. Not only are people no longer in control of history and narrative, they once again become prisoners of or sacrifices to society or their environments, and almost no people or roles exist who can occupy the visual position of the camera and become the agent of the narrative. Consequently, the cinematic gaze on its human objects must forego the fiction of the hypothetical character on which it had depended, and must unexpectedly reveal itself for what it is, and it is precisely this internal fracturing or disappearance of the position of the subject that renders difficult or impossible the suturing demanded by mainstream cinema. Consequently, examination of fifth-generation films, particularly the earlier ones, is likely to reveal that, despite recurrent difficulties in filmic expression, as well as that of an agentive subject, each reconstruction is highly unique and rich.

In *Yellow Earth*, for example, leaving aside cultural politics and aesthetic concerns, it is still not difficult to read it as a drama about different subject positions and intersubjectivity. The random placement and clashing of the film's revolutionary songs and folk songs not only reflect official practice and rural practice respectively, but also link four subject positions that cannot be subsumed under the binary oppositions modern/traditional, revolutionary (reformist)/conservative. First, Gu Qing, an Eighth Army soldier sent to the countryside to study and record folk culture, an outsider representing both revolution/radical change and enlightenment/modernity. Second, Cuiqiao's father, the expression of Yellow Earth or Old China, which becomes simultaneously the logic of the land and of nature—"This old yellow earth . . . how can you not respect it?"—and the spokesman for traditional, conservative values. This position also occasionally provides glimpses of "the people": still not remote, and still looked up to in reverence. Third, Cuiqiao: the female position, an oppressed position, also implying the sons/daughters of May Fourth: oppressed, repressed, and exploited to the point of unreservedly welcoming and embracing the possibility of any kind of change, even if it does not promise a vision of liberation. Finally, Han Han: shared with Cuiqiao, a position culturally signifying the children's generation, and of course the only position of youth in the May Fourth sense, a position of revolt and reform in terms of expectations and intentions.

Interestingly, because of this position, Han Han occupies the role of a modern, revolutionary new person or individual. He stands out within the film's narrative due to his playing a more important role within the father-son order than Cuiqiao and due to his speechless or rather mute condition. Thus, in the last scene, he is the one running against the feverish flow of the crowd toward Gu Qing, but ultimately, he faces a blank and open horizon. For me, the positing of different types of subjectivity and the filmmaker's identification with different subjects is not only an expression of the still-vibrant socialism of the time or a historical memory of the Mao era. It is also an expression of the ritual cleansing undergone by the sent-down youth and the emergence of a special emotional connection they felt toward the rural land, the village, and the peasants or people.[9] It is a form of moral discipline and honesty shown by those who lived through the twentieth century, especially the socialist era, and who therefore have faced the reality or predicament of China's past and present.

Perhaps compared to Gu Qing, the father of Cuiqiao and Cuiqiao herself, the director has invested Han Han with more autonomous imagination or subjective self-consciousness. Thus, Han Han's speechlessness or muteness signifies or reflects "China" and its realities and cultural constraints in the early 1980s. As in the scripts of fourth- and fifth-generation directors in the late 1970s and early '80s, a wandering, speechless, or mute or delirious madman or fool becomes a necessary ornamental signifier in the filmic space. Such a character serves as a noticeable, if obscure, vehicle for a latent historical consciousness, as well as a semiconscious self-referentiality about the situation of intellectuals and artists in the new China.

But as I have already discussed, in early fifth-generation films, when variously signifying characters are unable to take up the subject position of the director's narrative or viewpoint, or are refused this task, or when characters serve only as objects of the gaze, an extremely important discursive manifestation of subjectivity and the most powerful means of depicting the subject is actually the undisguised film camera. It is precisely this inability to achieve, or refusal of, the camera's suture, as well as the painstakingly unconventional compositions—particularly the abundance of long takes—that reveal the existence of the camera. The camera stands in for the plot and the human psychodrama for time—suppressed and swallowed by space, but trying to burst out of and tear open its closed, suffocating power. Perhaps it goes without saying, but in this instance the autonomous camera undoubtedly becomes or is acknowledged as the very self-same operator of the camera connected with the discursive context and occupying the place of the subject, what French auteur theory described as the auteur-director.

Jia Zhangke not only rejects the possibility of a love story, he also rejects the Three Gorges area's rich dramatic potential. He chooses to focus instead on the reservoir and the everyday life of China's poor. The film's truly moving reality fills this story of lost love with a permeating sense of despair, as if the two leads will never find whom they are looking for, and this world, soon to be submerged, will erase their only remaining hopes. Faced with this unavoidable ending, the two characters, or at least Han Sanming, have arrived too late. Early on, the address he has carefully preserved on a cigarette box has long since become nothing but a vaguely distinguishable smudge in the wide expanse of the reservoir, a blotch soon to be lost in the depths. Melancholic, nostalgic—perhaps it is Jia Zhangke himself who wishes to salvage something from this unprecedented flood, to save some images, to preserve the tenuous connections between individual and society, the past and present, culture and the material world.

Perhaps as a result, the movie has novelistic chapters: "Tobacco," "Alcohol," "Tea," "Candy." These chapter headings represent small luxuries of Chinese life, or traditional gifts that have smoothed the way for social relations and served to bind Chinese society. Yet in every section of *Still Life* these small catalysts nearly always fail to achieve communication, exchange, transmission, or emotional bonding. Admittedly, in the first section the old man at the inn accepts the cigarettes that Han Sanming gives him as a gift. But soon his inn will to be reduced to rubble, and the owner will spend his remaining years alone and lonely at some transfer station or migrant camp holding the placard of his little inn. Xiao Ma, who asks Han Sanming for a cigarette and drinks with him, is a likeable and humorous youth who is thoroughly immersed in the fantasy world of Hong Kong films (such as *A Better Tomorrow* or *The Bund* or one of Chow Yun-fat's "stylish gangster movies"). His plea to Han Sanming, "Be my brother, I'll cover you," is of course completely without value or meaning, something that is clear from the start. As the innkeeper says, "This kid has no future." Han Sanming later uses cigarettes as a burnt offering, lighting them one by one before the body of this child who has died a violent death.

The second section, "Alcohol," starts just after a gift of liquor has been rejected. At the end of the first section, Han Sanming takes out two bottles of liquor from his hometown and offers them to Ma Laoda, the older brother of his ex-wife, addressing him as *ge* (brother). Ma's response is, "I'm not your brother, and I don't want your liquor." The camera remains fixed on this awkward moment between Han Sanming and Ma Laoda, the former holding up the two bottles, until the scene gradually fades. Without question, alcohol binds Sanming with Xiao Ma and with the demolition crew, helping set the latter on the long journey they are fated to travel. Most profoundly, when Sanming brings up the dangers of coal mining, saying, "When you go down in the morning, you never know if you'll be coming back up at night," the men can only keep drinking in silence. Is this a male expression of sadness? Camaraderie? Or just a helpless resignation to fate? What tobacco and alcohol together articulate are no longer social bonds, but rather perhaps a new, if vague, expression of class identity. Or at least a pledge between people facing their final destiny that some help will be offered in time of need, even if no pledge to share the burden is implied.

In the third chapter, with its multiple plotlines, tea provides the link to the female lead Shen Hong, who has come to the Three Gorges in search of her husband. Unlike Han Sanming, the sequence with Shen Hong starts with a close-up of an abandoned factory space, highlighting the (class) identity of the female lead and the different types of people they are looking for—one rural, one urban. At the same time, we are given a glimpse of a different pace of life. Han Sanming lives in step with a slower rhythm shaped by village life, its traditions, kin ties, and beliefs. He has come searching only after a sixteen-year absence. Shen Hong's is an urban rhythm, fluid, drifting, unmoored. Two years of absence is cause for concern, and two years of waiting is already a very long time. An interesting detail: when an employee of the bankrupt factory is unable to open the rusted lock [of her husband's locker], Shen Hong picks up a hammer that happens to be lying around and quickly knocks off the lock. Tea, the common Chinese beverage, is the most ordinary thing one can offer guests. But Shen Hong's tea is some she found in the abandoned locker of her husband, Guo Bin. In the next scene, Shen Hong, alone and lonely, opens the bag and pours an excessive amount of leaves into a cup just before the scene cuts. We don't see her pouring her own water and don't know if she drinks this cup of bitter tea. But as the plot unfolds, we realize that at this point she resolved to leave her husband.

Related to the theme of tea, in the plotline devoted to Shen Hong, is her continual and symbolic action of drinking bottled water. We see that every time she has an empty bottle she makes sure to fill it up. This action and this little prop are meant perhaps to intentionally signify thirst: emotional, physical, sexual. She is careful to keep a water bottle with her, even though it is not necessarily one worth keeping, but instead a consumer good meant to be used and discarded. This seems to be an allusion to Shen Hong's marriage or love life, a portrait of the shifting, unstable modern world and present-day China. Everything is being mercilessly cast aside. The things you are trying to preserve may be things that were never meant to last in the first place.

It's also in this section on tea, in a medium shot of Shen Hong, that a bizarre, even ugly building suddenly ascends into the air. (Actually, when we first see Shen Hong, she steps off the boat midframe in Fengjie; in the background a UFO shoots past above the horizon. In a parallel scene, Han Sanming also sees a UFO go by.) Everyone else in the scene is silent and indifferent. When everything in the ancient land of the reservoir district has become disposable, no one takes notice of whether a building is still standing or has disappeared. Such things have become commonplace.

An interesting, if "unconscious," gender discrepancy comes out here. The film's two major images of fantasy, the UFO and the crossing of the Yangtze on a single steel cable, correspond to Shen Hong and Han Sanming, respectively. But the image of the UFO shooting past occurs behind Shen Hong's back. She remains completely unaware of it, signifying perhaps that she is completely immersed in her marital problems, not realizing, even though she is well educated and from the petit bourgeoisie, that her marriage is only a tiny part of a huge, crumbling canvas. The crossing of the Yangtze on the cable, however, occurs in front of Han Sanming, in his field of vision, even though he is in the foreground, indicating perhaps that Han Sanming is fully aware of his social status and social fate. Though he has never joined the criminal underworld like Xiao Ma, the life of a manual laborer in today's China and in the world is filled with violence and is expendable. Yet the tone is not one of sorrow, but rather of generosity. Here the "correct" representation of class and gender is once again shown to be paradoxical.

Then there is the film's final section, "Candy": a luxury product during times of scarcity, and a superfluity in times of wealth. "Candy" can also be used in a somewhat old-fashioned way to refer to a sweet, intimate relationship. Yet at the beginning of this section, as Xiao Ma and his "boys" set out to stamp out some trouble, probably some kind of gang dispute, he gives Han Sanming a Big White Rabbit—a famous, bygone brand of candy from Shanghai—and arranges to drink with him when he returns. Xiao Ma also shares the candy with his mates, asserting, in the style of a Hong Kong gangster film, "Brother Guo will make sure we're taken care of"— reflected in the "generous" treatment he ultimately receives when his body is discarded on a rubbish heap.

When Han Sanming orders food and liquor and awaits Xiao Ma, long past the time he is supposed to show up, the camera pans to reveal the diners at the next table and thus another absurd image: four actors in full Peking opera dress and makeup, who do not drink, eat, or talk, but stay focused on their own handheld video games. Another postmodern intervention, both absurd and realistic: in this space the premodern and postmodern meet, like Xiao Ma's immersion in the suave images of Wu Yusen's action films.[10] But located in the everyday ranks of the proletariat as he is,

Xiao Ma's relationship with Han Sanming is not and could not be characterized by the type of heroic self-sacrifice one finds in the legends of Wu Yusen's films. Rather, they display the kind of modest mutual aid one finds among the bit players, such as the modest offerings and burial that Han Sanming gives to this young man who doesn't even have a real name.[11]

Ultimately, the original implications of candy, the care and intimacy, are expressed in the relationship between Han Sanming and his ex-wife. In a half-collapsed building somewhere, Ma Yaomei gives a Big White Rabbit to Han Sanming, who unwraps it and takes a bite and gives the rest to her. A bit of love and warmth, a couple kept apart for sixteen years and wanting to reunite, but still separated by thirty thousand RMB.[12] So Han Sanming decides to go down into the mines once again despite the dangers. This slight sweetness is thus mixed with too much bitterness. Jia Zhangke portrays a child on the river steamer who sings popular love songs, appearing individually with Han Sanming and then Shen Hong. Perhaps the feelings these couples had for each other once resembled these love songs but ultimately, they bear little relationship to their personal lives. In this overwhelming and cruel reality, love is considered a luxury, even a myth.

After tobacco, alcohol, tea, and candy lose their social, catalytic, and communicative significance among the lower and marginalized classes, Jia Zhangke continues to use another catalyst, the only one with no connection to human emotions or people at all: money. Here, money is not just a number with financial meaning. It has a kind of material aspect: paper currency. For as far as the Chinese lower classes are concerned, they have fallen off the imperialist map of finance capital. Money runs through the entire movie. When Han Sanming lands in Fengqie, he is dragged into what was formerly something like a circus tent, where a magician holding a stack of white paper strips recites a mantra that the "Information Age" is full of: "If you want to float on water, you need U.S. dollars." He proceeds to turn them into Euros and RMB. Then claiming to own some sort of intellectual property rights to his trick, he requests or, better to say, extorts "tuition fees."

Later, the local demolition crew asks Han Sanming if, in the boat on the way over, he saw Kuimen, a famous site in the Three Gorges. When they are met with his blank look, they produce an RMB note decorated with Kuimen scenery. In response, Han Sanming produces a different note with a famous scene from his hometown, Hukou Falls on the Yellow River.

Later we see Han Sanming holding one of the notes up to compare it with the wide, mist-covered Kuimen in front of him. Profoundly and ironically, as tourists flock to see these places for the last time, places that have been cherished and elegized for millennia, Han Sanming, who has come drawn by love lost, has taken absolutely no notice of them. This small detail reveals the divergent interests of different classes. It is also in this detail that money comes to convey memory and homesickness. As Han Sanming prepares to take leave of his demolition team coworkers, his parting words are a promise that the image of Kuimen on the money will remind him of them. Yet in the end they don't part company. They all go with him to the Shanxi coal mines, motivated by the higher wages for which they may end up giving their lives.

This is the force motivating China's 240 million migrant laborers to leave their homes: job opportunities, ideally with higher salaries, even if the price to be paid is excessively dear (actually, Jia Zhangke already explored the cost of life in his previous film *The World*). While the mysterious woman from Xiamen who seems to possess supernatural powers in the reservoir area undoubtedly derives her powers from money, or rather from the submerged connections between power and money, Jia Zhangke dispassionately explores the interaction of money and emotion. In the face of money, the marriage of Shen Hong and Guo Bin proves to be as flimsy as paper, while Han Sanming's simple desire to be with family must be bought with money he doesn't have. The tragic backstory, whose gender formulation one could interrogate, is that Han Sanming originally bought Ma Yaomei as a wife from a human trafficker. Ma clearly could not abide such a commercial marriage, and so accepted her liberation by the police based on criminal kidnapping and human trafficking. But as a consequence of this liberation and her choice, she may end up being resold by her brother, for her own and perhaps her daughter's survival. Actually, the person he was originally looking for was his daughter, who, out of the same motivations as her mother, has long since left for work in Shenzhen. Thus, in *Still Life*, this story of an epic journey in search of love is not a momentary eruption full of dramatic tension but a dramatic exhaustion of emotion in the face of reality, particularly financial reality.

Ultimately, what makes *Still Life* so appealing is something I keep coming back to, namely Jia Zhangke's postmodern interpolations: the sudden ascension of a UFO, the shadow of a man, in Han Sanming's field of vision, crossing the Yangtze on a cable. When the smooth, unhurried documentary style is already characterized by highly realistic absurdities, these radically absurd images become organizing elements that harmonize the picture of reality. In some sense, the camera appropriates the scenes documented from Han Sanming's point of view, often creating an even more absurd feel than typical postmodern embedding techniques: a group of middle-aged sex workers who appear, when called, on a half-collapsed balcony offering their seductive poses, almost as if in parody of brothel demeanor; a red-and-white bag made of woven plastic, abandoned on a pile of broken rock, from one end of which protrudes the head of Xiao Ma, who has apparently been beaten and cruelly stuffed into the bag; the flustered and exhausted former union head meeting with angry workers in the decommissioned factory, while the remnants of pictures of Marx, Engels, Lenin, Stalin, and Mao hang above his head, serving as a historical reminder or as caustic irony; the painted opera troupe in the restaurant, immersed in their video games. Yet if we expand our view to include independent (underground) documentaries about the Three Gorges region (particularly those that have garnered international acclaim, such as *Before the Flood* and *Bing Ai* (Bing's love), we can see an interesting, recurring observation: that reality in contemporary China and the third world in general is foremost the reality of the spread of capitalism or primitive capitalism, in which money replaces tobacco, alcohol, tea, and candy as social cement and lubricant. But in the era of globalization, a third-world artist can no longer, as Zhan Mingxin asserted many years ago, write like Sherwood Anderson, or write in a realistic, transparent style. Even though China and poorer third-world countries are still experiencing a Sherwood Anderson or Charles Dickens–style reality, this reality cannot be borne by a highly formalized, commercialized, conventionalized realism. That kind of Sherwood Anderson realism has already been declared illegitimate in the European present, and postmodernism the only available option. To loosely appropriate a construction used by Hardt and Negri in *Empire*, one of the fundamental characteristics of globalization is the disappearance or at least withering of the second world, and the ubiquity of both the first and third worlds. Interestingly, or tragically, faced with the globalized present, we are only able to use first- or perhaps second-world writing techniques and standards.

Another example: the experiences of independent documentary director Feng Yan making a film about the Three Gorges reveal other aspects of these difficulties. In 1988 Feng Yan went to Japan to study environmental economics. At the 1992 Yamagata film festival, she happened upon the work of acclaimed documentary filmmaker Shinsuke Ogawa. Feng Yan's transformation into a documentary director has already become something of a legend in Chinese film circles. The majestic series of documentaries created by her mentor and idol Ogawa record, on a vast spatial and temporal scope, the struggles of Sanrizuka farmers against the construction of Narita International Airport. The production team's eleven years of participant documentation became an integral and prominent part of the movement itself. So in 1994 when the Three Gorges project started, Feng Yan took her camera and went to the reservoir site in the hope of recording this historic event (and perhaps, like Ogawa, becoming involved).

What she was unprepared for was that the inhabitants of the area were actually looking forward to the building of the dam. The news that construction was about to begin sent the whole area into a joyful frenzy. As Feng Yan tells it, the primary reason for this was that the dream of taking advantage of the huge elevation drop—the waters of the Yangtze "falling from the skies" to create energy—had been at the core of China's century-long modern dream. Therefore, over nearly the past one hundred years of projecting and imagining, hardly anything has been built and hardly any investment made in the reservoir region. Thus, the local residents were trapped in difficult and remediless natural and material living conditions, on the one hand, and were placing all their hopes in the project, on the other, trusting that once the dam went up they would finally have a share in the huge promise of modernization. I believe this situation to be one of the absurdities faced by countries late to undergo modernization: huge national construction plans can cause certain pieces of land to be discarded or set aside, to the extent that they become nothing more than temporary resting places in the minds of local residents. When this enormously expensive and shockingly expansive project kept getting delayed for various reasons but never canceled, the people in this area lived for generations in a state not unlike something out of *Waiting for Godot*. So as far as they were concerned, the Three Gorges project was, if not a gift from heaven, then at least the end of several generations of waiting. It is also a formative part of the reconstruction or self-remaking of modern Chinese culture in the wake of the tragic clash with Western imperialism in the late nineteenth century, representing infinite hopes for modernization, faith in historical progress, and yearnings for reform and change. According to the blueprints for Westernization and modernization, villages, farms, and rural life and culture are designated for the most part as historical traces destined to disappear (or be destroyed). Not only are they viewed as completely without positive value or meaning, they are given no structural position within the culture.

In Feng Yan's case, even though the situation was the opposite of what she expected, she stayed anyway and began following the lives of several local women as a way of charting this project and the dramatic changes it caused. One of the women turned out to be an exception of sorts, a female villager named Zhang Bing'ai. Only she obstinately fought back. She refused to move and opposed the dam, out of love for her home and the soil. Feng Yan filmed longer than Ogawa did, so one can imagine how much material she had to work with. But strangely enough, at the turn of the millennium, when she finally started editing the material, the only film she completed, and the one that ended up winning her international acclaim, was the story of this exception: *Bing Ai.*

What is thought provoking for me is that, on the one hand, the vast logic of global capitalism destroys everything in its path; yet on the other, oppositional cultures are not only weak and marginalized, they can only react to and position themselves in predictable opposition to their enemies, and are unable to create their own, constructivist, alternative logics. Thus, they are unable to create their own structures within which to mobilize, share, and organize. Ogawa's landmark films were made in the exceedingly complex cultural environment of postwar Japan. They reflect the mutual interdependence of revolution and resistance in the global 1960s. Yet with the 1960s long gone and the post-post–Cold War period upon us, when those who suffer have been stripped of their moral value and hopes for the future, it would seem that there is no other choice but to rely on the models created by Ogawa and others in the 1960s in order to understand the narrative logic and narrative significance of the current plight of society and the rapacious course of modernization.

If we move from *Bing Ai* to the work of director Li Yifan, including his documentary about the Three Gorges, *Before the Flood,* we come upon an even richer exploration of China's social and cultural ills. Li Yifan, who started his career with *Before the Flood,* was also responsible for the documentary *Village Archive*, in which he turned from the displacement caused by the Three Gorges dam to the subtle symbiosis between Christianity and local elections. In August 2008, as part of the joint exhibition *Microscopic Narration: Social Images by Zhang Xiaotao and Li Yifan* at Beijing's 798 Iberia Center for Contemporary Art, Li presented his first piece of installation art, titled *Law Archive*. A steel-ribbed tunnel leads visitors toward the exhibition hall, which is largely enclosed in a steel mesh, turning it into a giant cage. Around the cage are densely arranged old personnel files: the files that renowned labor lawyer Zhou Litai accumulated working on behalf of injured workers in Shenzhen and Chongqing. Televisions suspended at different heights inside the cage broadcast interviews with Zhou's clients who have been denied compensation.

On the opening day of the exhibit, several dozen bare-chested workers wearing black shorts and black masks (black fabric bags with three holes cut in them) squatted in rows on one side of the hall. Photographs of this piece exhibited later were pointedly named *The Abusers and the Abused*. When they left, all that remained were their shoes, perversely and somewhat savagely arranged in rows. Their "fashion sense" clearly marked them as what would be called in China bandits or petty criminals. But spectators, reporters, and art critics all instantly identified them as "terrorists." In one corner of the hall, outside the fence, two people dressed as workers continually fed the contents of the document folders into a paper shredder. The shreds were then once again formed into sheets of paper, which appeared on a desk next to the shredder, where amputees (due to work-related injuries) copied with traditional writing brushes the text of Rousseau's *Social Contract*. The finished copies were framed and hung alongside the entrance tunnel. In the words of the exhibition catalog, this was a kind of "micro narrative," Li Yifan's research in social "pathology."

Even setting aside for a moment the interactive relationship between Li Yifan's *Law Archive* and the other work on display in the main hall, contemporary artist Zhang Xiaotao's *Dense Fog*, Li's installation pieces stand on their own as both shocking and thought provoking. The visual statement created by the densely packed personnel files that refuse to disappear, and the hooded workers, along with Li Yifan's photographs of them and the name he has given them, all indicate a clear conceptual framework: exploitation, violence, hardship, and how they inevitably lead to the brewing violence and risks taken by people who feel they have no other choice.

Here *The Abusers and the Abused* is obviously not invoking the concept of harmony as used in psychology and psychoanalysis.[13] Rather it subtly evokes oppression and resistance (or is it resistance and oppression?). The unhesitating identification of "terrorists" unexpectedly drags a Chinese matter into the American-made post 9/11 world of antiterrorist ideology, raising new questions: What precisely are the causes and processes that lead to terrorist attacks or movements? Could it be that behind appalling acts of terrorism lies a history of violence and oppression? Aside from retribution through terrorism, do the oppressed and exploited have any other option? As for the exhibition as a whole: How do the elements outside the fence and to the side—the paper shredder, recycled paper, and the workers copying *The Social Contract*—relate to and enter into dialogue with the "scenery" inside the cage? Li Yifan explains, "I'm not trying to shock or frighten people, and I'm not trying to simply deconstruct society; I'm trying to create a new awareness of lower class society and new methods for examining contemporary social issues."[14] But is Rousseau's social contract to be considered a symptom or a solution? If it's not a new method for creating awareness of or discussing the lower classes or modern society, then exactly where in these installations and texts are these methods (potentially) to be found?

Returning to Jia Zhangke as the director of the "art film" *Still Life*, I would suggest that the postmodern *Still Life* can be regarded as or read as a national fable, while the live performance of *The Abusers and the Abused* and the modeling and naming of terrorists combined with Rousseau's *Social Contract* grant this micronarrative a strikingly macroscopic or broad significance. Thus, when Jia Zhangke calls his piece *Still Life*, he captures and records a series of images in time. He touches time and freezes time, the most prominent image being the various watches that Wang Dongming/ Wang Hongwei has hanging beside his end table—a spatial image of time. This, despite that in the film this frozen scenery, longingly gazed at, is about to be destroyed in the hurricane of modernity. The implications of the term *Still Life* allow Jia Zhangke to avoid having to depict progress, the past and the future.

But perhaps due to the restrictions of the medium in installation art, or perhaps due to Li Yifan's own personal artistic choice, *Law Archive* opens a window on the future. And the role of the elements outside the cage is surely to suggest a solution. But is the solution to destroy and rebuild? Or establish the social contract? If the former, does this point to revolution? If the latter, then hopes are pinned to reform and rule of law. The latter, which is the dominant consensus within the Chinese intellectual community, the basis of its knowledge and discourse, is the logic of the post–Cold War victors: that capitalism is superior to and higher than socialism. In China, a (post) socialist country, comprehensive capitalist development—particularly democratic governance and implementation of the rule of law—is seen as an effective solution, or even the only solution. What this fails to acknowledge is that the problems China faced at the turn of the century, particularly the problems with rural workers, are linked to the historical debts of socialism (the urban-rural dichotomy created by the household registration system). Clearly this is a problem related to the global spread of capitalism. Thus, spreading or strengthening capitalism is not only trying to cure the wound using the weapon that made it. It is an old capitalist cure for a new global malady. Moreover, this old cure is one of the causes of the new disease.

Linking these things once again to the Three Gorges project—a strange case of advance and retreat, construction and demolition—and to *Still Life* and *Before the Flood*, what comes out is not just a matter of art or the difficulties of artistic expression, but the difficulties faced by China and by the world in the era of globalization. *Still Life* won Jia Zhangke the Golden Lion at the Venice Film Festival, once again confirming his international status as an auteur. But this does not change the marginalized status of critical or oppositional culture in the era of globalization. And it cannot respond to, not to mention solve, the urgent question of whether or not culture can provide an alternate path.

CHAPTER 4

The Piano in a Factory

Class, in the Name of the Father

TRANSLATED BY JIE LI

The Piano in a Factory was an exhilarating highlight and a morale booster when it was released in 2011. Costing a mere five million RMB—a shoestring budget by the current standards of the Chinese film industry—it lacks the luxurious style of a Hollywood film, but it is also not an overly sentimental American B movie or sitcom. It is even free of the affectations of art films often seen at European international film festivals. Low budget, but by no means shoddy. On the contrary, the film is full of fun and feeling, style and tact, laughter and tears. In this unique, original, and enchanting film, we reencounter a few long-lost friends: sincerity and down-to-earth reality, workers and factories, dignified labor and creativity. Not only a bittersweet comedy about a father who used to be a worker, it is also a group portrait of a class. It is a heartfelt visual tribute to a bygone era as well as a passionate alternative imagination of the future.

A rare treasure of contemporary cinema, *The Piano in a Factory* is a simple story filled with joy and pathos. Its protagonist, Chen Guilin, is a worker laid off from a state-owned steel mill and a single father who raises his young daughter and supports his elderly father. He makes a living by managing a small band that does gigs for weddings, funerals, and product promotion. His ex-wife, Xiao Ju, who has hooked up with a sugar daddy, suddenly returns to fight over the custody of their daughter, who says, "I will follow whichever parent can buy me a piano." Chen Guilin tries to borrow money, scaring off all his friends. Emboldened after a drunken feast, he and a few pals try stealing a piano from a school and are collectively detained. Desperation gives rise to a maverick solution: Chen gathers a few old craftsmen from the steel mill, now scattered as peddlers and gangsters, to build their own piano, literally a "musical instrument of steel."[1] While making the piano, side issues keep arising to discourage Chen Guilin from the custody battle. Finally, they complete the piano, a steel piano: "For our brother, let's do something awesome, let's fight for our dignity!"[2]

Such a plot is not far from melodrama. Yet unlike ahistorical portrayals of the pleasures and sorrows of the middle class, this simple story is saturated with the imprint of two major historical eras. Already distant are the "years red as fire" from the 1950s to the 1970s, when industrial workers—the country's leading class—laid the foundations of the nation's industrialization process. Not so distant, yet already dull and muted, is the last decade of the twentieth century, years of traumatic change, when "the brave warrior amputated his snake-bitten limb": during market reforms, large state-owned enterprises went bankrupt and factories "spat out" workers. "Previously, everyone was part of a collective, but all of a sudden, everyone had to become an atom. Shenyang (or all old industrial areas) became a sheet of loose sand, and everyone became 'independent.'. . . This was a long process: some workers lost their jobs as early as 1985, while others persisted until 1999. Over this long stretch of time, everyone struggled for their livelihoods. Some families split apart; some left for elsewhere." Rather than any overinterpretation of the text, director Zhang Meng consciously wanted "to tell the story of a lost class through the case study of a family."[3]

Remarkably, the film does not simply show a panorama of misery or mark out submerged memories of bitterness. To the contrary, this is an extremely sunny story, an unrestrained and bountiful film. When the fifth generation first emerged in the 1980s, when Chen Kaige and Zhang Yimou were still young, they ruefully observed, "With a full stomach we portray worry and grief, yet they (Northern country folks) sing of joy on an empty stomach. . . . But in the end, the stories we wrote with light were heavy, thick, and solemn. Their categorical despair had everything to do with our having embraced an open but empty future vision."[4] Today, the future has arrived, but in this brave new world, "you make money, spend money, make more money—you hold onto money to live and to die. We have all become so good at using money to calculate and compensate for spiritual withering and loss. Hardly anybody remembers how we got to where we are. Everyone walks in the cloud of money and looks to a higher point in the clouds."[5]

Therefore, the director Zhang Meng set the tone for the film as "sad without lamentation, just a tearful smile."[6] The first scene after the opening sequence—a funeral full of black humor—is an ironic self-reflection on the film's comedic form. The image slowly fades in with the gloomy prelude of the Soviet song "Troika" on the soundtrack. Dressed in black ponchos, Chen Guilin's little band plays in the rain. As an offscreen mezzo-soprano voice begins to sing, the camera tracks horizontally to reveal the singer, Shu Xian, in a blue concert dress with a coat draped over her shoulders and holding a black umbrella. Suddenly, an offscreen voice shouts, "Stop, stop, stop!," which in Chinese is the same as "cut, cut, cut"—the special command of the film director. Telling his band to stop playing, Chen Guilin faces left and deferentially addresses someone offscreen: "What is it? What is it brother?" "This melody is too painful. . . . The old folks will be dragging their feet to that tune."

After Shu Xian stops him from defending the Russian song, Chen Guilin decides to change the tune: "Let's play 'Rising Higher Step by Step' B flat." The cheerful, perky melody and the band's altered body language change the atmosphere. The camera tracks leftward to reveal a mourning canopy. A mélange of old and new customs, the children, dressed in traditional white mourning clothes, kneel before a photograph of the deceased, draped in black crepe, with a hanging scroll that reads, "With profound sorrow we grieve our mother." This sequence concludes with a panoramic establishing shot: a corner of the old factory district, an empty mourning canopy attended only by paper servants, and huge smokestacks in the backdrop puffing out white smoke.[7] Tragedy is to be staged as comedy, and the command for the dead to leave swiftly with lighthearted steps comes from a disembodied and authoritative voice. Beyond accounting for how Chen Guilin and his friends make a living after losing their factory jobs, this first scene is also sharp, witty, and self-referential. Tragic reality can only be staged as comedy: though ignorant of their destination, people should still walk briskly and merrily forward. The film's double self-consciousness, not only of reality but also of cinematic narrative, sets the tone for the seemingly light treatment of a heavy subject.

In fact, Zhang Meng's exuberant film consistently and ostentatiously flaunts its cinematographic style: frontal camera positions with many horizontal tracking shots; characters moving horizontally within the frame and the set (entering left and exiting right or vice versa). In a few scenes, the camera also tracks forward or backward, emphasizing the depth of field and creating a vertical axis that crosses the horizontal axis at a right angle. The camera position in the opening shot is a full shot from a fixed position. Against the backdrop of an industrial wasteland, the protagonist, Chen Guilin, and his ex-wife, Xiao Ju, standing side by side facing the camera, discuss their divorce and the custody of their child. Such camera work seems to violate a commonplace taboo of film narrative: the frontal camera position highlights the two-dimensionality of the cinematic image, whereas film textbooks tell us that the basic enchantment of cinema is to create an illusion of a third dimension.

The horizontal tracking movement is an even greater taboo: the golden rule of narrative feature films is to conceal the cinematic apparatus and to displace the look of the camera into the perspectives and psychologies of the characters. Camera movements (zooming in and out, panning, tilting, and especially tracking shots) all betray cinema's mechanical nature and cannot be easily disguised, so they are rarely used in such a flamboyant manner (except for special effects). Yet Zhang Meng dares to take such formal risks and develops this "uncinematic" or even "anticinematic" idiom into a highly original cinematic expression. Moreover, he does this without the exhibitionist self-exposure that plagues so-called art films when directors "bare all." To the contrary, this stylized language fits perfectly with the story, not only enhancing its quirky comedy but also conveying the film's heavy themes with poise.

Vividly yet in an unassuming manner, the variation of the film's stylized language already lays out the filmmaker's social consciousness. Right after the opening credits, the ex-wife Xiao Ju's carefully worded yet callous self-justification is spoken over a dissolve: "Divorce is a two-way street." As the image starts fading in, she continues, "You cut me some slack and I'll do the same for you." Through a frontal low-angle shot, this (former) couple stands shoulder to shoulder, staring ahead without eye contact. In the backdrop is an empty, dilapidated, yet still monumental industrial structure. The next few shots alternate frontal medium shots of either the husband or the wife. The fragmented framing of each shot emphasizes the relationship of strangers between this divorced couple. Chen Guilin replies impassively and crisply, "Divorce is divorce. Don't talk rubbish. I agree." This scene opens the curtain on this absurdist comedy about marriage and family. Later, in a low-angle tracking shot, Chen Guilin explains to his father, who is sitting on the back of his motorbike: "Xiao Ju's come back. She wants a divorce. I agreed. She's now with a guy who sells fake medicine. She's happy. She's finally fulfilled her dream of an easy life." This is not only a family black comedy or a father's tragedy. In telling the story about a class, it also captures the receding view of a turbulent epoch, conjures up a forgotten era, and perhaps even reenvisions a utopian future.

In the first half of the film, the mise-en-scène of walls, doors, and windows often establishes narrow but not altogether closed perspectives and spaces—apt metaphors for the social status and survival space of Chen Guilin and company. As the camera's tracking movements reframe, decenter, and displace immobile characters, as their voices and dialogue continue offscreen, we can readily visualize the working class's experience of marginalization as they plunge into their doomed historical "destiny." Various objects in the foreground often block out or obscure the characters. This may have to do with location shooting for a low-budget film, but in *The Piano in a Factory*, such mise-en-scène provides apt commentary on the social reality of its characters. Two exceptions to this eclipsing of characters illuminate the originality and significance of this visual expression. First, in the process of making the piano, Shuzhen lays bare the brutal truth in a moment of exasperation: "Even if you make a piano, Xiao Yuan won't stay with you."[8] After this, the camera tracks slightly back and leaves us with a gloomy and empty factory workshop. Then, in the dim evening light, accompanied by almost jovial accordion music, Xiao Ju and Xiao Yuan, mother and daughter, hold hands affectionately and stroll toward the camera from a distance. In fact, Xiao Yuan is the only figure who always occupies the film's deep space. Does this mean that Chen Guilin conceives of a better future for his daughter? Or does it just mean that the child will change her class status and destiny in her choice between father and mother, just like the daughter of Chen's former worker friend, Fat Head? In the foreground yet out of focus, a blurred figure crosses the frame from right to left—this is Chen Guilin on a motorcycle. Cut to a frontal shot of the factory dormitory where Xiao Ju watches her daughter ascend the stairs and then exits screen right. At that moment, Chen Guilin on his motorcycle enters screen left and watches his ex-wife depart with mixed feelings. Cut to Chen Guilin clumsily yet dedicatedly knitting a pair of woolen pants for his daughter. Now without a wife, he must be mother as well as father, yet his love cannot be converted into a father's "capital." The image fades to black.

In another instance, when Chen Guilin cannot afford the cost of being a father and resigns himself to giving up the battle over custody, we see again the mise-en-scène of the prologue. But this time, a level camera position replaces a low-angle frontal fixed shot. The divorced couple no longer towers over the audience, as if protesting against their fate, but instead occupies only the lower third of the screen. Following their realist dialogue ("You can take Xiao Yuan." "Why?" "I don't know how to explain." "You won't blame me, will you?"), the camera travels forward, between, and past the two characters, literally pushing them out of the frame. While the image shows the dilapidated factory and little else, the two continue to speak, as if with some remnant affection: "Time goes by so fast. Xiao Yuan's grown up so quickly." "Just like it was yesterday." "When she was born, she was only six pounds." "Six pounds, four and a half ounces." "No, six pounds, four and a quarter ounces." "How could I be wrong? I was the one who gave birth to her." "How could I be wrong? I was the one who weighed her." This familiar dialogue of a parting couple not only fills the awkward moment, but also marks the film's self-reflexive narrative: a shared life can no longer be remembered; their memories do not even agree on the simplest facts. Perhaps this banter over domestic trivia refers to the formal logic of the film itself: its level camera position and tracking movement bring theatricality and staginess to the mise-en-scène and expose the film's own fictionality. But its referent might be the formal transparency of realism or the realist illusion that often, if not always, obscures reality. Perhaps the representation of reality and the reality of representation are irrelevant here. What matters are rather the intensity of memory and the structure of feelings.

Even more powerful, however, is the development and variation of the film's formal language. When Chen Guilin successfully bamboozles his former coworkers—skillful and talented worker artisans employed by large industries from the 1950s to the 1970s—to gather in the old factory to build a piano, the camera gradually reduces and eventually stops its highly autonomous movement, which often abandons the characters. Characters now move in deep space. Moreover, a level and stable camera (often taking a low angle) chronicles how, when they return to the factory to perform collaborative work, they also unexpectedly regain a sense of dignity, honor, and especially the happiness of labor and creation. The poised montage sequences, with focus, ease, and calm, consist of foregrounded close-ups of individuals doing various types of work. Human beings once again dominate the screen and control the camera's movement and rhythm. Tracking shots are now synchronized with the characters' movements and create panoramic scrolls that lay out the factory's various labor procedures. The cinematic climax comes at the end of the film, after Chen Guilin gives up his fight over his daughter's custody. Accompanied by orchestral music and flamenco dance, former workers gather once again in the factory to build a piano, a "steel musical instrument." This sequence begins with three rapid shots in deep focus, showing how a creative community rallying around more than mere economic interests—the father's "capital"—can now command a three-dimensional social space. Next, we see shots of "steel fireworks" from the casting process, once symbolizing productive vitality in old industrial theme films. This scene is shot mostly from a low angle. If this camera position suggests a stage, then it also recognizes a group portrait, a subject, a historical and real subject position. At the same time, this camera position rallies an admiring gaze from us, the spectators, toward the miracle of labor and creation.

When *The Piano in a Factory* became the "most highly praised film of 2011," it was described in contradictory terms as both "real" and "surreal," "true" and "fantastic." This made me think of the way Latin American authors responded to the term "magical realism," ascribed to them by Western literary critics: no magic, only reality, our own reality, the reality of Latin America. Perhaps in this instance, Zhang Meng could also respond to those who describe his film as "fantastic realism": no fantasy, only reality, the reality of old industrial districts, the reality of laid-off workers.

Apart from its unique formal language, the film is also striking—and difficult to categorize—for its multiple music and dance interludes that interrupt the flow of the narrative. Of course, these include the diegetic street performances of Chen Guilin's band as they try to make a living. But there are also imaginary musical interludes, framed as if under a spotlight on a stage, that are not part of the narrative. For example, after a dinner party full of booze, Chen Guilin and his buddies embark on the "grand enterprise" of stealing a piano. Taking a ride in a refrigerator van with chilled pork hanging in the foreground, they sing and dance in drunken revelry, accompanied by extradiegetic music. Between their failed piano theft attempt and police detention, Chen Giulin gives a superb solo performance, like a concert pianist, amid whirling snow. Moreover, what delighted many

audiences and puzzled some others are the grandiose song-and-dance sequences in the film's denouement. On a cart rolling on tracks toward the
camera, Chen Guilin's band offers a spirited performance of Latin dance
music, as if on a festooned vehicle in a parade, while Shu Xian leads a group
of female dancers in red flamenco dresses with a few guys in white shirts
and black trousers posing as matadors. Parallel editing weaves this grand
musical sequence into a montage of the final assemblage of the finished
piano, creating a hearty and soul-stirring grand finale.

These theatrical musical sequences make the film especially enchanting and meaningful. Its invigorating song and dance performances reject
tragic postures, even though a politics of tragedy has always been an effective strategy of self-representation and practical mobilization for subaltern
or vulnerable social groups. A politics of tragedy enumerates the iniquity
of the opponent and displays the miseries of the self. In order to attract
societal attention and reform initiatives, it plays up the contrast of how
"wine and meat rot behind vermillion gates while on the roadside people
freeze to death."[9] However, the legacies of the twentieth century show that
the enemy's crimes do not naturally translate into one's own righteousness,
which must be pursued in theory as well as in practice.

Moreover, a new global consensus has already successfully wiped out the
moral high ground of misery, the ponderous cultural legacy of the twentieth century. By the turn of the twenty-first century, unemployment—created
and exacerbated through neoliberalism, globalization, and the financial
tsunami—has turned into a global theme. Yet only a handful of movies
have dealt with this subject, setting aside for the moment Hollywood films
that provide imaginary solutions to real-world problems, such as *The Pursuit of Happyness*, *Fun with Dick and Jane*, *Up in the Air*, and so on. The
British film *The Full Monty* and the Spanish film *Mondays in the Sun* have
resorted to tragicomedy rather than tragedy or drama as narrative genres.

But in *The Piano in a Factory*, musical sequences not only formally reject tragic gestures, they also turn into a perhaps unconscious yet meaningful cure. They hark back to the cultural life of factories and work units
of a bygone era, a socialist culture that tried to create new human beings.
In its refusal of tragic gestures, the film also does not deliberately highlight material poverty in its plot or moral signification. Needless to say,
material deprivation—poverty or the shortage of everyday necessities—is
at the core of the modern world's class-based reality, of the helplessness

and sorrow of individual lives. In the late 1990s, poverty became the focus of Chinese literary and artistic productions that thematized the sharing of hardship. *The Piano in a Factory* does not evade material deprivation in the lives of its characters. Yet its plot focuses not on subsistence but rather on affluence—on whether a father can afford to give his child a piano. A piano is by no means a necessity of life and remains a luxury even for the middle class. Hence its significance goes beyond wealth and poverty in terms of food and clothing, shifting instead to a new dimension: "In the Name of the Father."

As a result of economic reforms, the transition of state-owned enterprises, and the shock waves of unemployment that began in the late 1980s and accelerated in the 1990s, tens of millions of people—once state-owned enterprise workers who were the "middle layer" (a de facto middle class) in both social and economic terms—fell into the bottom of society and became the poor. Yet all relevant discussions and representations seem to have ignored or avoided an even more important aspect of this process: the radical upheaval in the social status of workers in state-owned enterprises, especially in cultural and symbolic terms. I am not just talking about the extinguishing of the so-called sacred political halo hovering above the working class. Rather, as Liu Yan has incisively pointed out, "Just as important is the symbolic death of workers as the father. . . . When Chen Guilin tried to keep his daughter with a piano, he wanted to claim his masculinity as a man and a father. On the other hand, this was subservient to a new symbolic order. His fantasy is to use an object to exchange for his father status, but in a world dominated by exchange value, he will never be able to gain the name of the father."[10]

In terms of psychoanalysis and political symbolism, the most meaningful of the film's many subplots concerns the smokestacks of the industrial zone. Zhang Meng narrates this subplot in great detail. First, Chen Guilin visits Wang Gong and suggests giving value to the smokestacks through "creative transformation."[11] Then we see the assembly of bicycles and motorcycles in front of the abandoned workshop, giving off an illusion of a workers' meeting. Wang Gong stands on a promontory and gives an earnest speech to rescue these two smokestacks from being demolished. Full of black humor, his drawings on the blackboard transform the smokestacks into rockets, giraffes, and bungee jumping-off points. In shot–reverse shot, we see solemn medium close-ups of (former) workers listening attentively to him. The conclusion of his speech is intriguing: "If we succeed, this will be a pretty tourist attraction. If we fail, this will be a fond memory." Whereas the professional yet comic drawings on the board are juxtaposed with deep feelings in the scene, these last lines are pungent and ironic. If former industrial or socialist historical spaces (chronotopes) can survive into the present day, then they will become a pretty tourist attraction on the consumer circuit, much like the preserved industrial district of *24 City* or the hang-out scene of 798.[12] Otherwise, they only turn into memories that have not been and cannot be narrated, memories that nevertheless remain beautiful and unforgettable for those who possess them.

Thereafter, when an exhausted Chen Guilin gives up making a piano and the custody battle over his daughter, the crowd gathers on a slope to witness the demolition of the smokestacks. Zhang Meng does not use psychoanalysis as his main scaffolding in *The Piano in a Factory*. For despite Slavoj Žižek's efforts to politicize psychoanalysis, the use of psychoanalysis often turns history and society into personal melodrama rather than vice versa. Yet Zhang Meng is clearly aware of the symbolic meaning of the smokestack episode: "Those two smokestacks are the phallus of the working class. Cut them off! No more nonsense. This has nothing more to do with you. We have pushed out an old industrial age to usher in a new industrial age."[13] Therefore, the blasting of the smokestacks not only extends and reiterates Chen Guilin's feelings of helplessness as he reluctantly gives up his daughter, but also provides a straightforward castration scene for the symbolic death of the worker as father.

To further elaborate, I believe that the old working class truly befit "the name of the father" as masters of the country and the leading class. Such an identity was not merely a political halo, but rather had a real economic basis and support in the form of collective property rights. Throughout China's modernization and industrialization process from the 1950s to the 1970s, the substitution of capital with labor—primitive accumulation with Chinese characteristics—prevented the direct manifestation of property rights in a shareholding system. But it did enable a particular form of social production and social organization: the *danwei* (work unit). The latter was not only a system with a sense of belonging and security—one felt secure about births, old age, sickness, and death. It also gave rise to a society and cultural practices that were alternatives to capitalism and the societies it has produced. This is the origin and correlation of Zhang Meng's memory and the plotline: "These rough steelworkers may be engaged in menial and coarse labor, but each of them is capable of music and is full of tenderness. They even sing in the workshop, and this in itself is a fascinating combination of reality and absurdity."[14] Or was it that he had inadvertently discovered a piano homemade by workers?[15] This is clearly not just the regional color of the Northeast, but rather yesterday's creation and today's remnants of the danwei system's amateur cultural life or "entertainment for the masses." It is for this reason that at least some old workers may well be simultaneously the piano makers and piano players.[16]

Zhang Meng describes the film's dramatis personae as "a lost class."[17] The media often rewrites this label as "a disappearing class." This expression, along with its revision, shows a blind spot in our social field of vision. If "class" here refers to what we normally understand as the working class, then since the 1980s, they have truly been "losers" in the political, economic, and cultural sense. Yet they have not disappeared. True, giant state-run enterprises "spat out" tens of millions of workers. (In the documentary *West of the Tracks*, we see tens of thousands of people driven not only out of their production spaces but also out of their living spaces—dilapidated factory dormitories that were nevertheless their homes.) Meanwhile, all kinds of processing factories sprang up along coastal areas and, with their humongous appetite, swallowed up hundreds of millions of migrant workers from rural areas.

The working class not only did not shrivel, let alone disappear, but instead grew at an unprecedented scale. Few have studied the old and the new working classes together, not only because mainstream discourse and media consciously and effectively cut off the simultaneous discussion of unemployed urban workers and rural migrant workers. Just as importantly, these two sets of workers are worlds apart in their class status even if they both engage in industrial production and factory work. Hence one really cannot conflate these two groups of people and their two distinctive modes of existence.

Even for state enterprises, the one-word change from "state-run" (国营) to "state-owned" (国有) changed their ownership and property rights—the entire basis for the political halo over the old working class as the leading class, the masters of the country and "the Republic's eldest son." Not only ideology but also laborers' property rights created different subject positions and different relations of production. In the film, Chen Guilin parodies, in the style of Wang Shuo, a Maoist slogan: "We will overcome all difficulties. If we don't have enough difficulties we'll create them."[18] The original slogan came from the Daqing oil field's "iron man," Wang Jingxi: "If we have the conditions we'll do it. If we don't have the conditions we'll create them." This is followed by Wang Gong's unassuming reply: "We workers can do anything if we put our mind to it." Even if we consider the latter a platitude from a bygone era, the miracle of making a piano from scratch shows us that an alternative production relation, subject position, and self-image had indeed created different lives and a new social collective.

Significantly, *The Piano in a Factory* is almost the only feature film to represent the tsunami-like transformations that have touched tens of millions of lives and changed Chinese society over the last twenty-some years. As much as this film gives us a glimpse into the decades that have thrown tens of millions of lives off track, it also memorializes a forgotten prehistory—the "red and fiery" era—and that era's human beings, endowed with dignity, passion, imagination, and creativity. When People with a capital P—an effective social rhetoric—fill up screens across China, much more imperceptible and quietly effaced are the real human beings belonging to an alternative value system. The film's most tearjerker and touching sequence is when police come to arrest the "gangster" Brother Ji. Dressed again in his old working clothes and making a sand mold with skill and focus, he calmly says to them, "I've gotta finish something and then I can go with you." With poise, he turns on the conveyer belt and, after carefully examining the sand mold, he walks over to Chen Guilin and speaks plainly and solemnly: "Guilin, there's no problem with the sand mold. I've finished my part." With broad strides, he walks out of the workshop. Shot with deep focus and backlighting, the bright haze from the factory gates in the middle backdrop delineates his silhouette between that of two police officers in a frame within a frame. Brother Ji's dog then jumps out from the lower edge of the screen to follow his master. The mise-en-scène is reminiscent of a Hong Kong gangster film. But what makes this scene soul stirring is not only a sense of righteous brotherhood, but also the dignity of workers, the pride in vocational skills, and the bleak despair of losing the power of one's labor.

In fact, it is around the supporting role of Brother Ji that the film sketches the minidrama of the historical destiny of the former industrial working class. In a previous scene, an invigorating montage, we view the last stage of the production process (yet not assembly-line style): the creation of the sand mold by Brother Ji. Seen through the double doors of the oven that create a frame within a frame or a ministage, Brother Ji fixes the sand mold on a cart on the conveyor belt. He and his coworkers push the mold into the oven. The doors close slowly before the audience like a stage curtain, eclipsing the scene of collective and collaborative labor, gradually obscuring the group shot of workshop members in blue smocks. The curtain falls over an era, over an entire class. The same oven doors opened to show Brother Ji working before his arrest in the aforementioned scene. Momentarily, this image disappeared into the light as his buddies saw him off. Therefore, the film is a belated backward glance from the edge of the abyss, a visual tribute to that unmourned yet bygone era and a reverential salute to its collective heroes.

Besides the main plot of Chen Guilin's attempt to keep his daughter, these digressive episodes seamlessly enrich this fresco of a class full of fraternal solidarity. Plot tangents about Lightning Fingers (retired thief), Fat Head (full-time drifter), and Brother Ji constitute the behind-the-scenes desperate struggles and helpless degradation of laid-off workers. For example, the reconciliation and chase scenes to apprehend the culprit who impregnated Fat Head's unmarried daughter again borrow from a gangster film style, showing the identification and fraternity of those who share the same plight. Except that this time, "proletariats of the world unite" has reverted to "all men are brothers." However, the scuffle in the billiard hall confronts only a few idle youth—not villains, not even juvenile delinquents. A gang of men with murderous looks could end this chase scene only by shouting "Get out!" The story of Fat Head's daughter is but the tip of the iceberg of adolescent life among workers after the layoff "tsunami."[19]

Never pretentious or precious, *The Piano in a Factory* even rejects tragedy. But its fullness of emotions is an important aspect of its enchantment. Needless to say, this is due first and foremost to the director's identification with the restrained passion and trauma of his father's generation of the Chinese working class. But the direct expression of the film's emotions lies clearly with its music. Zhang Meng very consciously chose music from the former Soviet Union and Eastern Europe. For an audience who lived through that history, such music reconnects them with that ardent epoch: "I wanted music with a socialist style of orchestration, so I chose Russian and East German music to preserve certain nuanced feelings."[20] The melodies and rhythms of such music successfully and inherently compose and reproduce the socialized industrialization processes of former socialist countries.[21] Though somewhat incongruous with the popular music in the film, such music is often used in counterpoint to the film's plot. Interestingly, for the film's anticipated audience who belong to a younger generation, this music outside the realm of their own lived experience does not so much elicit submerged memories as it successfully narrates the film: along with the estrangement of former factory spaces and workers, the music further connotes a sense of banishment and oblivion. Much like the film's well-crafted cinematographic position, composition, and movement, such music both defamiliarizes old industrial districts and endows them with wondrous beauty, blending a modern wasteland with human feeling. Through music, but not only music, *The Piano in a Factory* strikes a chord with our most genuine sentiments, especially luxurious in this fickle age. Such genuine sentiments evoke a special space and ambiance, as well as the special body language of the actors: intimate yet relaxed, high-spirited and contented, an era so far away, as if from another world. These genuine sentiments also reopen the rusty gates of memory. Indeed, *The Piano in a Factory* evoked childhood memories among a younger film audience, reminding them of their lives inside the factory compound, of its aura and value. Besides reminding them of their proud status as the sons and daughters of workers, the film also triggered for the first time a public discussion of the "silent other side" of the transition of state-owned enterprises—that unemployment tsunami that affected tens of millions of lives.[22]

Here, the memory triggered by emotions manifested special meanings in the intertextual coordinates set by critics and audiences. When commenting on *The Piano in a Factory*, almost every media report and Internet commentator compared it to the former Yugoslav director Emir Kusturica's *Underground* and the German director Wolfgang Becker's *Good Bye Lenin!* For me, these intertextual associations are in themselves quite intriguing. Apart from their shared absurdity, *The Piano in a Factory* has little in common with *Underground*, and, apart from black comedy, it is hardly comparable to *Good Bye Lenin!* These intertextual nodes instead highlight the cinematic narrative of former socialist countries that bridge the Cold War and post–Cold War eras. Zhang Meng responded this way: "Both *Underground* and *Good Bye Lenin!* depicted the interior feelings of people undergoing momentous transition. I am very satisfied to have captured sentiments comparable to these masterpieces. We have hardly experienced changes as abrupt as the fall of the Berlin Wall, but ordinary people's emotional responses to such historical rupture are quite similar. Such feelings are difficult to capture but most worthy of documentation and expression through cinema."[23] Indeed, in the two decades after the Cold War, few directors so keenly and profoundly responded to social reality while maintaining such a sober view of history. Yet beyond similar themes and historical contexts, *Underground* is a postmodern caricature of a bygone history, whereas *The Piano in a Factory* is more of a minipanorama that takes an alternative narrative tone. Kusturica's film is playful and absurd throughout: even with tears in the characters' eyes, thick smoke rises out of their nostrils. The film's cynical attitude toward history makes that smoke so majestic, we cannot tell if the sparkle in the eye is a tear or a sly smile. Zhang Meng, on the other hand, solemnly identifies with his characters: "Cinema is my only method for revisiting that way of life. I am filled with longing for that era. The memories of growing up in that collective are quite beautiful and cannot be summarized by the term 'iron rice bowl.'"[24] "We should not forget the essence of socialism, that red thing deeply seared into our hearts, that pursuit. If we forget that, our images will have no personality or character."[25] Similarly, when *The Piano in a Factory* opens up sealed memories, historical depth extends from this rather postmodern film (as opposed to the total flatness of *Underground*). Yet the lost class shows not only its back, not just nostalgia or mourning in the style of *The Twilight Samurai*, but rather unexpectedly opens up a future horizon in the midst of deep historical space.[26]

Perhaps this bygone history depicts and summons a future generation.

PART III

The Spy Genre

CHAPTER 5

The Spy-Film Legacy

A Preliminary Cultural Analysis of the Spy Film

TRANSLATED BY CHRISTOPHER CONNERY

Ang Lee's unexpected box-office hit *Lust, Caution* (色·戒, 2007), albeit only a quasi-local film, put the spy film back on the map in China, and the nearly equal success achieved by two genuine home products—2009's *The Message* (风声, dir. Chen Guofu and Gao Qunfu) and *Qiu Xi* (秋喜, dir. Sun Zhou)—signaled China's embrace of the global spy-film craze. Indeed, the vigorous reemergence of the spy film, after languishing in relative obscurity for some years, was one of several unexpected developments in cinema at the turn of the new century. Yet these films, with their qualities of hesitation, self-doubt, introspection, powerful emotions flowing in unexpected directions, and heavy-heartedness, contrasted powerfully with the spy films of the Cold War era, marked by pervasive anxiety, bursts of violent combat, and menace threatening from all sides. The spy film, in a strict sense, is less a film genre than a film with a specific theme. Even so, the spy film between the 1950s and 1970s formed a most distinctive presence on the world screen. Erupting onto the scene fairly rapidly, its achievements included the James Bond films and numerous youthful, action-filled spin-offs. The spy film also made its mark in Hollywood film noir, and exemplars counted among the most acclaimed of the B movies. It became a significant component of mass-entertainment film in the Soviet Union and Eastern Europe, and became a major narrative mode within worker-peasant-soldier art, literature, and film in China. On both sides of the Cold War division of the world, in fact, the espionage theme formed a primary mode of narrative cinema, qualifying as a distinct sub- or quasi-genre.[1] Rather than viewing this development as a product of film-industry demands, or as a response to film consumers' psychological needs, it would perhaps be more useful to view this development as a cinematic narrative hot spot produced within a specific historical context: the Cold War, with its division of humanity into two armed and mutually hostile camps. In my view, the spy film's status as sub- or quasi-genre derives primarily from its status as the classic Cold War genre. Consequently, the sociocultural riddle presented by the historical trajectory of the spy film, which not only did not die a natural death with the end of the Cold War but was reborn in an age even more marked by the secret and the surreptitious, is worthy of some investigative attention. It is also important and useful, and now more than ever, to cut through the fog of historical amnesia created by postmodern cynicism, and to search the margins of cultural production in order to re-interrogate historical experience.

For this essay, by "spy film" I refer to a narrative cinematic mode within the New Chinese cinema from the 1950s through the 1970s, and I recognize that the category is not a rigorous one. In this period, films of this kind were divided into two seemingly unrelated subtypes. One was the story of the "undercover agent who infiltrates the enemy's inner sanctum," which refers to the subject matter of these narratives.[2] The other is the counterespionage film, a generic denomination that is suffused with Cold War ideology. The difference between the two types is encapsulated in a bit of dialogue from one of the best-known spy films, *At Ten O'Clock on the National Day* (国庆十点钟, dir. Wu Tian, 1956) which mentions both the "concealed struggle against a visible enemy" and the "visible struggle against a concealed enemy." The first depicts the Communist Party member's infiltration into the enemy's (usually the Guomindang's) military or intelligence apparatuses and his engagement in a battle of wits and strength, the successful outcome of which allows the party member to obtain and convey intelligence guaranteeing the victorious advancement of the revolutionary undertaking. The other depicts how a member of the CCP intelligence or security services, with uncommon resourcefulness, is able to see through and outfox a dissimulating enemy (usually a spy sent from Taiwan or the U.S., or a Guomindang undercover agent left behind after the retreat to Taiwan), thus foiling the hidden plot. It is a not uncommon plotline, in the latter type, for one of "our" agents to assume the disguise of an agent sent by the Guomindang from overseas in order to infiltrate the enemy organization.

In the 1950s, this type of film, conforming to international standards and also following Soviet generic divisions, was categorized in the adventure genre, but this name never became common and did not persist. Although "adventure" describes the plot type of a given narrative form, it does not depict what is virtually the only object of narration within this plot type: the secret battle line in the struggle with the enemy. Although even up until the present, the undercover agent plotline, in fiction and in film, is a more appropriate and apparent designation of this particular narrative type, I nevertheless prefer not to use it. This is not merely because the term "undercover agent" is so closely and clearly linked to Hong Kong gangster or cops-and-robbers films, in a manner quite distinctive to Hong Kong. These films emerge out of Hong Kong's history of collaborative colonialism and thus express a specific form of subjective anxiety.[3] My most central reservation is that the undercover agent category obscures the rich significance of the spy film as a social symptom for the Cold War and post–Cold War periods.

The Chinese spy film, in the context of worker-peasant-soldier feature films from the 1950s through the 1970s, is distinctive and exceptional in many respects. In contrast to other films from this period, the plot of the spy film takes little from folk-based cultural production, drawing primarily on urban mass culture. Interestingly, after 1949, the spy film is the only Chinese film phenomenon that is in line with international tendencies. It is also the only group of films with a unified and distinctive narrative form, one with at least quasi-generic unifying characteristics. Although this quasi-genre is suffused with Cold War atmospherics, with Cold War ideology forming the background of its plot and message, these films' representational strategy is at some distance from the distinct, cut-and-dried ideological expression that typified most films of that time. And yet, it still succeeded in becoming a primary narrative form of mass entertainment. From 1949, with the shooting and release of *Invisible Fronts* (无形的战线, dir. Yi Ming), New China's first counterespionage film and also one of the foundational films for all new Chinese cinema, and especially with the 1954 release of *The Horse Caravan* (山间铃响马帮来, dir. Wang Weiyi), nearly every film in this quasi-genre has been a huge hit, with enormous popular acclaim.

When I first began to pay attention to this type of film narrative (as well as to a large body of literary works on the same theme from the same period), it was because it was the narrative and film genre with the most salient Cold War imprint, thus my reference to its status as Cold War genre. Moreover, it is the only narrative genre that (mainland) China, positioning itself as a third force alongside the two great Cold War camps, shared with the two other sides. Even though the political and military antagonism between these two camps led to mutual cultural and economic isolation, this particular narrative form nevertheless developed in a parallel fashion. In the West, the James Bond 007 series, one of the most prominent examples of the genre, began in 1953 with Ian Fleming's publication of *Casino Royale*, which was made into a one-hour television program a year later. Beginning with the 1962 release of *Doctor No*, the first film in the series, the Western—indeed the global entertainment—world remained continually fascinated with each 007 film, as well as with the succession of actors who played James Bond of MI6, with his license to kill. This alchemical power produced a series of male action heroes modeled on Bond, and the films' box-office returns made for a remarkably successful brand. From the 1960s onward, James Bond—brave, virile, charming, and romantic, struggling alone against all comers—was the virtual embodiment of the free-world lone hero, synonymous with the superspy.

In a world divided into hostile camps, the Eastern bloc also witnessed, in Soviet literature and film, an even earlier flourishing of the spy/counterspy theme, forming a significant narrative subgenre with deep mass appeal. These works reached their creative apogee somewhat earlier than in the West, in the 1950s, that grim era marking the Cold War's onset. According to my rough estimate, during the relatively brief honeymoon between China and the Soviet Union in the 1950s, of the three hundred official Soviet film imports, there were more than twenty-nine in this genre, which does not include films from other Eastern European countries. Among the more popular imports was the 1947 *Secrets of Counterespionage* (подвиг разведчка, dir. Boris Barnet) and the 1950 *The Greatest Reward* (Высокая награда, dir. Evgeny Schneider).[4] These films provided models for many Chinese films in the genre. However, while acknowledging the Cold War character of these films and recognizing the obvious ideological function they performed in vilifying the enemy and glorifying the heroes, there is a danger that a more subtle function performed by films in this subgenre could be overlooked. In the Cold War West, the spy film, aside from displaying the brave lone hero struggling against multiple foes, was also a display of technological marvels, using a variety of spectacles and special effects to dazzle the eye and ear. In the global context of the Cold War and of Cold War ideology, this doubtless contributes to a Western triumphalist discourse embodying the superiority of the West's material civilization and technology. This also, of course, quite clearly reflects one of the new functional roles of cinema in late-industrial Western society: providing an advertisement for expensive, luxury consumer goods. Once the James Bond 007 series had secured its status as the quintessential film franchise, it became the focus of attention for the transnational market in luxury cars, luxury watches, and weapons, especially for the military. The "Bond Girls," a central dimension of the series' formula, formed a "natural" sexual accompaniment for the advertisement of car brands, watch brands, or weapons brands. By the 1990s, the James Bond films had become the most successful model for product placement of transnational brands, referred to as a form of soft advertising. In the Eastern camp of the Cold War, in Soviet film and literature at least, including those films that concerned World War II, the direct attack on the Western imperialist camp formed the spy genre's primary political content. Interestingly, a recurrent plotline in films of this type in the Eastern bloc, in staging the encounter with antagonistic and destructive Western forces, centered on threats from the military-industrial complex or from industrial programs. A typical object of struggle was the project design engineer or secret blueprints.[5] Thus, with the arms race as background, and a story line stressing the implacable opposition between two social systems, there was also the prominent element of trade war, with national political power at stake. Viewed in retrospect, Soviet films of this type were suffused with a modernization anxiety, giving evidence of a basic existential fact common to all socialist countries, of which the Soviet Union was the prime example: given their status as late modernizers in a deeply threatening world capitalist system, the primary task was not only national security but the rapid development of national industrial capacity.

Returning to the context of Chinese film history, the origin of the spy film—which would become the quasi-genre richest in Cold War symbolism and undoubtedly the most effective vehicle for Cold War ideology—was the 1946 film produced under the Guomindang in the midst of the decisive struggle with the CCP—*Spy Number One* (天字第一号, dir. Tu Guangqi).[6] This film, as soon as it burst upon the scene amid massive attention and clamor, went one-to-one against the 1947 Communist Party/

leftist-backed film *The Spring River Flows East*, parts 1 and 2 (一江春水向东流,上,下, dir. Zheng Junli and Cai Chusheng). The films represented a struggle for the discursive right to represent "New China" and drew distinctive lines between appeals to Confucian ideology and condemnation of government corruption, as well as in the films' appeals to the suffering of the masses. Interestingly, although *The Spring River Flows East* is claimed to have been the film to have "washed away the mighty mountains of the Guomindang in a torrent of tears," it was actually *Spy Number One*, a lesser film by cinematic and film historical standards, that not only inaugurated the spy-film subgenre in Chinese film history but became a generic point of reference: it crossed those strongly fortified Cold War boundaries and was remade or adapted in China, Taiwan, and Hong Kong.[7] In Guomindang-controlled Taiwan, it spun off numerous sequels and remakes, and it was widely imitated and copied in Hong Kong cinema from the 1980s on. It was in fact this film that more or less determined the basic elements of the spy-film subgenre/quasi-genre: a lone hero, against all odds, infiltrates the core of the enemy's territory in disguise; after perils and dangers, with the assistance of an undercover comrade in the same location, he obtains the secret intelligence that guarantees his side's victory and the enemy's defeat. Other tropes that would become standard included a plotline of incessant danger; emotional entanglements, real and false, with a sexy and beguiling bad woman and a simple and honest good woman; scenes of psychological warfare that include sharp, abstruse, double-entendre-filled dialogue; tense moments when friend and enemy are not clearly distinguishable; the painful experience of being misunderstood by a comrade; mysterious and weighty secret-code language; a dramatic rescue scene at a crucial plot point; scenes and tonalities reminiscent of bedroom or interior dramas; and a film noir visual style. After 1949, the Chinese spy film, which although like most film and cultural production of the time generally reflected precedents set in Soviet literature and film, remained largely within the generic tradition established by *Spy Number One*.[8]

The spy-film narrative subgenre is distinctive in being the only type of film, nearly without exception, to cross Cold War boundaries and antagonisms, and it is also the only narrative film type to be continuously produced throughout the period from the 1950s through the 1970s, and even, albeit in a somewhat circuitous manner, up to the present day. This unbroken chain of films, popular among audiences young and old, sophisticated and unsophisticated, included *Invisible Fronts*, *The Horse Caravan*, *The Mysterious Travelling Companion* (神秘的旅伴, dir. Lin Yi and Zhu Wenshun, 1955), *Track the Tiger to Its Lair* (虎穴追踪, dir. Wang Can, 1956), *At Ten O'Clock on the National Day*, *The Lonely Mountain Forest* (寂静的山林, dir. Zhu Wenshun, 1957), *Underground Vanguard* (地下尖兵, dir. Wu Zhaoti, 1957), *Secret Post in Canton* (羊城暗哨, dir. Lu Jue, 1957), *The Case of Xu Qiuying* (徐秋影案件, dir. Yu Yanfu, 1956), *The Intrepid Hero* (英雄虎胆, dir. Yan Qizhou and Hao Guang, 1958), *Guards on the Railway Line* (铁道卫士, dir. Fang Ying, 1960), and *The Secret Map* (秘密图纸, dir. Hao Guang, 1965). In fiction, although novels such as *The Alarm Clock Rings Twice* (双铃马蹄表, Lu Shi, 1952), *The Horse Caravan without Bells* (无铃的马帮, Bai Hua, n.d.), and *The Broken Network* (断线结网, Xie Tingyu, n.d.) could not compete with Soviet counterespionage novels, they won considerable readership.[9] An even more rare distinction is that the spy subgenre persisted through the Cultural Revolution rupture. In the first seven years of the Cultural Revolution, when publications, feature films, and fiction production were relatively stagnant, aspects of the spy subgenre appeared in two of the "Eight Model Theatrical Pieces": *Taking Tiger Mountain by Strategy* (智取威虎山) and *Shajiabang* (沙家浜). In the underground literary scene during the Cultural Revolution, two spy narrative types—infiltrating the enemy and counterespionage—became principal themes in the unofficial fiction that circulated in handwritten copies.[10] This handwritten literature, originating in the big cities but widely circulating in cities and towns throughout the country, included the novels *An Embroidered Shoe* (一只绣花), *The Plum Society* (梅花党), *The Green Corpse* (绿色尸体), and *A Lock of Golden Hair* (一缕金黄色的头发).[11] This body of work constituted a "red" version of the miscellaneous urban fiction from the 1930s that included adventure, horror, and other mass entertainment genres. Differing from Soviet spy literature and film in a crucial respect, Chinese spy narratives rarely touched on the imperialist economic plot or the technological struggle or struggle for technological hegemony plots, focusing more commonly on the political intrigues of the Guomindang/U.S. In my view, rather than illustrating a departure from the modernization anxiety common to late-developing socialist countries, Chinese film and fiction of this kind illustrates the distinctive character of China's particular modernization anxiety. From the 1950s through the 1970s, especially after the severing of Sino-Soviet economic cooperation, China's rapid industrialization and modernization depended most of all on political mobilization and "hurricane"-level mass mobilization; that is to say, it was driven by a substitution of labor for capital.

My interest in this genre lies in its subtle and complex distance from, as well as the connections with, mainstream social and political discourse and ideology in its particular historical period. In labeling it a Cold War narrative type, my aim, referring to the foundational version of this type (and not to the variations on the type that arose in the late Cold War period), is to see in the Manichean, absolute moral and ideological binary of the Cold War the necessary context for sustaining the absolute moral cleavage between the two camps in order to distinguish friend and foe, or good and evil. It also formed the necessary context for demonstrating the enemy's wickedness and treacherousness, and the hero's loyalty and righteousness as he penetrates into the heart of the enemy. For in works of this type in the socialist camp, the most moving elements of the stories are not just in the protagonist's trial by ever-intensifying circles of fire, but in the protagonist's limitless loyalty and dedication. This incorruptible fidelity is not the indefatigable valor of the traditional hero, nor is it the steadfastness of the hero impervious to temptations of power and wealth. Rather, it is that of the hero in disguise who never disgraces his mission, of the hero living within the enemy's camp who remains untainted and uncorrupted by his surroundings. This basic trait is in itself sufficient to explain its persistence throughout the Cold War period in China. In a related manner, many stories about the successful exposure or capture of special agents or undercover plants repeatedly reinforce the language of class struggle and warnings against imperialist subversion, as in the popular phrases "imperialism has not given up its wild ambition to subjugate us"; "the tree may prefer calm but the wind will not subside"; "after the armed enemy has been vanquished, the unarmed enemy remains as before"; the class enemy "is still present, and his aim remains alive"; and finally, "never forget class struggle."

Nevertheless, a discrepancy lies in the fact that works of this narrative type, seemingly so contiguous with national and international class-struggle discourse, are prominent during the 1950s, whereas in the 1960s, when class-struggle discourse became the dominant language of political mobilizations, the genre is less important. Conversely, in the hand-circulated, virtually illegal unofficial literature of the Cultural Revolution, the genre is again prominent. More paradoxically, during the official proclamation of the end of the Cultural Revolution in the late 1970s and early '80s, when history is written anew and class struggle discourse is de-emphasized, the genre has an unexpected resurgence. And again, at the beginning of the twenty-first century, when recent mainstream ideological values of economic pragmatism, developmentalism, and consumerism are consolidated, overcoming many difficulties and obstacles, this narrative form (with deep modification) is once again prominent in mass media, becoming a focal point in the nostalgia craze common to TV serials. One could interpret the correlation in a relatively straightforward way via the theory of reflection between cultural production and historical events, or via a model of shaping public opinion. That this narrative type appears at the birth of new Chinese cinema and flourishes during the 1950s would thus be related to the fact that in this period, the key task of political power was to consolidate itself and to suppress and eliminate destructive or subversive threats to the regime. The great campaigns during the 1950s to suppress counterrevolutionary elements and the protracted campaign from 1955 to 1957 to eliminate counterrevolutionary elements, especially the latter, were aimed conspicuously at eliminating hidden or concealed antirevolutionary elements. This, superficially, would appear to be a fruitful interpretation of the genre's role at that time. But this interpretation doesn't account for the genre's relative lack of prominence in 1960s official culture nor for its prominence in the underground or hand-circulated culture of that time. Nor would it account for its resurgence at the end of the 1970s, with the end of the Cultural Revolution and the concomitant displacement of class-struggle discourse.

In my view, the significance of the spy film quasi-genre in modern Chinese cinema is not directly political in the above sense. In a revealing contrast, in European art and subgenre film from the 1950s through the 1970s, political plot/intrigue films are almost all inverted versions of spy films.[12] Their plots commonly center on dark or corrupt police authorities and how, in the national and international Cold War context, they commit great miscarriages of justice. These include films such as *Z* (dir. Costa-Gavras, France, 1970), *Investigation of a Citizen above Suspicion* (*Indagine su un cittadino al di sopra di ogni sospetto*, dir. Elio Petri, Italy, 1970), *Confessions of a Police Captain* (*Confessione di un commissario di polizia al procuratore della repubblica*, dir. Damiano Damiani, 1971), *The Mattei Affair* (*Il caso Mattei*, dir. Francisco Rosi, 1971), *In the Name of the Italian People* (*In nome del popolo italiano*, dir. Dino Risi, 1971), and *The Lost Honor of Katharina Blum* (*Die verlorene Ehre der Katharina Blum oder: Wie Gewalt entstehen und wohin sie führen kann*, dir. Volker Schlondorff and Margarethe von Trotta, Germany, 1975). At the same time, the great American-English director Hitchcock was creating a new genre, the suspense film, which commonly featured a plotline whereby a common person, having fallen into the middle of a spy plot or political intrigue, manages to save himself by drawing on unexpected reserves of heroism and intelligence.

Leaving aside the details of Žižek's analysis of Hitchcock, suffice it to say that the spy film, aside from being a primary form of entertainment in China during a specific historical period, is also a genre with considerable psychoanalytic interest.[13] *Infernal Affairs* (无间道, 2002), a Hong Kong blockbuster that was a success internationally, is a film that lends itself particularly well to this. On the one hand a classic film of the lone hero penetrating into the enemy's lair, it is also a film about a two-faced hero whose lingering psychological problems correspond to a form of schizophrenia. This doesn't merely refer to the fact that a given subject puts on a disguise and thereby acquires a doubled appearance or a double self, but rather that spy films express a deeper and more hidden actual problem: a genuine anxiety over identity. Given the Cold War context of implacable ideological opposition, it was impossible, in Chinese film, to give direct expression to this subjective anxiety, but it is an anxiety nevertheless, given subtle but deeply resonant expression in the manner in which the hero faces his perilous surroundings. The peril comes not only from the ever-present danger and precariousness that surround the fight within the heart of the enemy camp, but, more importantly, from the many scenes central to the plotline, wherein it becomes difficult to distinguish friend from enemy. To gain the enemy leader's trust, the hero must continually demonstrate his competence and loyalty, all the while dealing with the enemy's probing, suspicious tests. He must repeatedly rely on experience and intuition in order to see through the enemy's traps, or to distinguish which characters are on his side, whether previously implanted agents or contacts. The sword of Damocles is always at hand, with success and failure in perilous balance.

One heartbreaking plot element is that in order to achieve the higher goal or to accomplish a key task, the hero must pretend not to recognize comrades or loved ones and must even remain impassive, hands tied, when they face death. Entrusted with keeping an eternal secret, he is unable to share his exploits or his mission with his loved ones, even when they misunderstand or reject him.[14] On the level of plot, all of this contributes to the flow of hair-raising twists and turns, and, on the level of significance, this illustrates the revolutionary's faithfulness and loyalty. But it can also illustrate a social symptom revealing the deep and secret subjective anguish produced by the great majority of political campaigns and brutal inner struggles—inside the revolutionary camp or "among the people"—that followed the socialist consolidation of power. The tragic character of the confrontation between revolution and authority, between revolt and order, is visible in victims' suffering at the hands of young radicals flying the antirightist flag, or in the trauma and dread that come from group retribution or family disintegration. This narrative type most effectively reveals this sociopolitical unconscious.

When the vigilant and penetrating eyes of the police succeed in the end at ferreting out the hidden class enemy/spy; when the lone hero successfully penetrates the enemy's lair and succeeds in his mission, to return into the bosom of party and people; when the hero, at the point of death, reveals his true identity and intimidates the enemy: all of these final acts make for a happy and harmonious ending, and thus provide an imaginary resolution to an actual political contradiction. This can perhaps explain why this film genre had its golden age in the mid- and late 1950s, and not in the early 1950s or the first half of the 1960s. The late 1950s was the time when the new government, after achieving a preliminary form of political stability, having decisively eliminated its real political enemies, turned for the first time, in a new national and international situation, to mass movements and to struggles within its own political ranks. In the early 1960s, when the Great Famine overran China, society once again entered a period when the economy was foremost, and the spy genre was relatively quiescent. In this period, the only spy film released was *The Secret Map* (秘密图纸, dir. Hao Guang, 1965), which also happens to be the only Chinese spy film with theme and plot directly borrowed from the Soviet spy-film corpus. The film was a minor landmark in two senses. The classic military affairs/trade war problematic illustrated the central problem at the heart of 1960s Chinese society: the national political mobilization to develop national industry. Second, the latent theme of identity confusion presaged a new political maelstrom.

As everyone knows, in the early period of the Cultural Revolution, social contradictions and conflicts burst into the open again, and the social energies thereby unleashed once more rendered ambiguous and indistinct the nature of personal identity "among the people." But soon thereafter, when the earlier sociopolitical targets had either faded away or been pardoned, and conflicts and social cleavages had intensified, this narrative type witnessed an underground and above-ground resurgence. I refer here not only to the flourishing of the hand-circulated underground novels and spy stories mentioned above, but also to films from socialist fraternal countries (those countries who had refused or had drifted away from the Soviet orbit), films that were frequently screened to wide popular appeal: *Guerrilla Unit* (*Njësiti Guerril*, dir. Hysen Hakani, Albania, Chinese release 1969), *The Invisible Line* (看不见的战线, dir. Kim Gil-ho, DPRK, 1965, Chinese release 1971), *Reveal Her True Identity* (原形毕露, dir. Kim Yeong-ho, DPRK, 1964, Chinese release 1974), the *Magnolia* series (木兰花, three parts, dir. Jong Yong-ho, DPRK, 1971, Chinese release 1975), *Oak Tree, Top Emergency* (*Stejar, extrema urgenta*, dir. Dinu Cocea, Romania, 1973), *Walter Defends Sarajevo* (ВАЛТЕР БРАНИ САРАЈЕВО, dir. Hajrudin Krvavac, Yugoslavia, 1972, released in major Chinese cities in 1973 and then widely and officially released in 1977). In *Reveal Her True Identity*, a film that at the time was the talk of the whole country, a South Korean agent working for the American army disguises herself as a former bond servant and current model worker, and surreptitiously enters the DPRK.[15] So once again, we have the spectacle of the same actress simultaneously playing the role of insidious traitor and virtuous innocent, directly portraying the anxiety and tension over personal identity. In *Walter Defends Sarajevo*, the successfully concluded struggle between the true and false Walter foils the enemy's strategy of sowing dissension.

In general, the popular entertainment genre is interestingly and effectively able to symbolically resolve, or at least translate into another level, the principal subjective predicaments within Chinese society. But the multiple contradictions and disjunctures between the standard hero narrative and the historical materialist outlook need not detain us here. Nor is there any need to speculate on the heroic narrative hero's structural lacks: either they, not having sufficiently matured, have not yet reached sufficient heroic status; or, just at the time they are acclaimed as a hero, they disappear into the flood of humanity or, through heroic sacrifice, are sublimated into a pure symbol, an empty placeholder.

More important for my purposes is that when the central agency of authority is identified as either the party or the people, subjective identity is first and exclusively class based, and not gender based. Gender and the actuality of gender are always either a supplementary expression of class or a figure of political rhetoric.[16] For this reason, subjectivity in popular film from the 1950s through the 1970s encounters a fundamental conundrum within its visual system: the absence or illegitimacy of scopic desire in the male subject, which produces ambiguity in both the visual and spatial fields. In this particular historical and cultural context, the spy film again stands apart. This, however, is not due to the appearance of a 007-type hero in worker-peasant-soldier film narrative, but rather due to a common plot element in the subgenre: the protagonist's encounter, after penetrating into the tiger's lair, with the treacherous female enemy agent. The ensuing battle of wits, filled with mutual apprehension, scrutiny, and suspicion, furnished the cinema of the 1950s–70s with a rare instantiation of a complex, crisscross gaze structured by counterfeit emotion and by feigned interest and sympathy. The psychological precondition for this was the requisite decathexis from the gaze on what would under other conditions be the visual image of an alluring and sexually seductive female spy. Interestingly, although the image of the hero is without doubt the master operator of the scene and plot, it is the female spy who is in fact the activator of scopic dynamism. Her double gaze, both treacherous scrutiny and seductive regard, places the protagonist/hero in the position of object of the gaze.

There's no need to explicate at length the difference between this and the presentation of gender in Hollywood or mainstream Chinese film. The internalization of a visual regime of gendered desire was a late arrival in Chinese film, and the subject of the desiring gaze was from the beginning feminine, and vectors of desire often had a symbolic register: the male protagonist was elevated to the position of a corporeal instantiation of the image of the nation.[17] Yet within the particular conventions of the spy subgenre/quasi-genre, while at the same time transmitting and reproducing conventional views of gender, the venomous seductress also inverted the modern power relations of the gendered gaze as rendered most typically in Hollywood cinema. In the pioneering work in this genre, *Spy Number One*, the protagonist was continually subject to the gaze of others—the inscrutable female protagonist, the furtive male servant, the naive yet jealous young woman. These characters all produced a complex and murky network of desirous or suspicious gazes. Our inability to fathom the ultimate motives for these gazes and looks suffuses the film experience with an anonymous and ubiquitous sense of threat and conspiracy.

In films of this type from the 1950s through the 1970s, due to the ideological and political unconscious burdens that film had to bear, the standard position of the male as object of the gaze was obscured; at the very least, the role of sexual desire in these scenes was greatly weakened. This deepened the fissure between the brave lonely hero demanded by this sub-genre and the type of hero in mainstream narrative. The particular Cold War appeal of the spy film in contemporary China lies in the fact that although its expressive structure was determined by the Manichean binary between friend and foe, the ambiguity and tension underlying this binary, as expressed in plot and in filmic representation, was also able to bear the burden of representing deep predicaments within the socialist system and the attendant real tensions over identity. It was precisely this latent politically symbolic capacity that allowed the genre to span different distinct historical periods. It would become once again one of the most prominent film genres in the late 1970s and early 1980s.

With respect to the drifts and reversals amid ideological uncertainty that characterized the late 1970s–early 1980s transition period, the resurgence and then temporary disappearance of the spy film is a significant cultural indicator. The relevant films include *Hunting Number 99* (猎字99号, dir. Yan Qizhou, 1978), *Murder Case 405* (405谋杀案, dir. Shen Yaoting, 1980), *The Blue File* (蓝色档案, dir. Liang Tingduo, 1980), *Dealing with the Devil* (与魔鬼打交道的人, dir. Lin Lan, 1980), and *City of Endless Fog* (雾都茫茫, dir. Wang Bo and Zhang Jin, 1980), as well as the PRC's first TV series, *18 Years in the Enemy Camp* (敌营十八年, dir. Wang Fulin and Du You, 1981). These films were unprecedented in their popularity and became popular topics of conversation. In this period, when the dawning of the new post–Cold War era began to reach China, the resurgence of the spy film doubtless had to do with the fact that it was the only genre, within China's worker-peasant-soldier art of the post-1949 era, with an urban and latent entertainment-commercial character. Almost without exception, the spy films of this era amplified the sumptuous and glamorous atmosphere, filled with fast repartee, that characterized the red spy's interaction with high society. They exaggerated and made even more prominent the doubled character of emotional relationships: a pure and faithful love that could not be revealed versus the exaggerated and public proclamation of hypocritical affection; the confrontation with the real enemy versus a superficial frater-nal affection. But these films' ideological and social symptomatic signifi-cance lies in the fact that under the cover of a genre still structured by Cold War fissures, a subtle transformation of values had begun to manifest itself. In late 1970s and early 1980s filmic narratives, although the plots were more complex and eccentrically varied, the deeper tensions that animated the basic plotline—the difficulty in distinguishing friend and foe, confusion over identity—had become considerably more slack.

In *Dealing with the Devil*, a couple of old colleagues, who also had the required role of long-standing antagonists in Chinese spy films, unexpect-edly at the end of the film were revealed to be underground comrades in arms who did not recognize each other. At that moment, the tension that had built up in the film through the familiar tropes of counterfeit emotion and a feigned interest and sympathy (mentioned above) was resolved in-stantly into humor. Unexpectedly, this narrative trope refers to its origin in *Spy Number One*. Although the latter film hasn't secured a memora-ble place in the history of new Chinese cinema, this plot coincidence has deeper significance. *Spy Number One* is based on a theatrical play, and thus is largely set in interiors. Significantly, the principal villains in the story—the traitors to the Chinese nation—are largely absent from the ac-tion of the film and from its visual field. Of the four main characters in the film—wife, guest (nephew), servant, and daughter—only the daughter, due to her deep love for the male protagonist, has a preestablished identity that awaits confirmation and recognition by the male to whom she is thus sub-ject: is she the daughter of a traitor to the Chinese people or the wife of an underground proletarian? With the other three characters, the transforma-tion of "enemy" into "we" occurs only at the precise moment of utterance of the mysterious secret password ("Which way does the window open?").

The plot's primary antagonism centers on the moment when the old and tender feelings between the wife and the guest reemerge: the climactic point of the exchange of passwords. In fact, the scene flattens out the antagonistic character of the self–enemy struggle, one based on nationalist principles, rendering the scene subordinate to the drama of an old love affair rekindled. When at the last moment the leading lady/wife of the traitor to the Chinese people speaks the password, revealing her identity as the highest leader of the Spy Number One intelligence network, it is clear that in this film, the latent identity anxiety is located in the female lead rather than the male. She humiliates herself and submits herself to serving the enemy, not only sacrificing love but submitting to her husband's hostility, insults, and slights.

I will not discuss here one standardized image of the virtuous heroic female in narrative forms during China's early twentieth-century modernity, symbolized by the prostitute with the brave and generous heart. I will put aside for the moment the fact that this double-sided female protagonist fully corresponds to the discussion of the female image and male anxiety in Laura Mulvey's work.[18] With regard to the socially received psychology and latent ideology of 1947, this film's portrayal of the right wing, of the power of Guomindang culture and society, lies not only in its mobilization of a pro-Confucian ideology of national identification and national unity for an attack on the left wing and on the CCP cultural front tactic of mobilization of class consciousness, but also in the manner by which its image of a female heroine who, in submitting herself to the enemy while concealing deep reserves of patriotism, addresses and consoles the worries and apprehensions felt by those masses of ordinary people living behind enemy lines, precisely by offering them a new mode of identification and reconciliation.

In contrast, the subtle transformations visible in films of this type in the late 1970s and early 1980s, while seemingly reproducing the boundary between friend and enemy and providing a new demarcation of the "inside," in fact erase the various ambiguities and obscurities that structure the earlier demarcations. Though largely lacking the reconciliatory power of films like *Love on Lushan Mountain* (庐山恋, dir. Huang Zumo, 1980), *Dealing with the Devil*, like various other representative versions of the genre, very subtly deploys the absence of the enemy in the final scene in order to decompose the visual imaginary of political antagonism. Spy films of this period actually more explicitly centered the films' dramatic tension on the identity of the protagonist and its doubled representation, but because the antagonist is merely an imaginary enemy, the films' internal divisions and fissures remain intangible and concealed. In *City of*

Endless Fog, the first filmic adaptation of a Cultural Revolution–era hand-circulated text, the classic double-sided female character—the enemy who both desired and threatened the male protagonist, and the accomplice who was the object of the male protagonist's desire—took on some of the characteristics of the Bond Girls in the 007 series. This rebalancing of the male position of subject and object, as well as subject and object of the gaze, was at the same time the subtle beginning of a transformation of the depiction of heroism to something beyond the boundaries fixed in worker-peasant-soldier cultural production. For now it was the individual who would once more emerge from the fissures within the revolutionary heroic narrative artifice. Films such as *The Xi'an Incident* (西安事变, dir. Chen Yin, 1981), *Love on Lushan Mountain*, and *My Memories of Old Beijing* (城南旧事, dir. Wu Yigong, 1983), whose fundamental tendencies and symbolism differed greatly, nevertheless all augured a new social and political order, a unidirectional movement toward reconciliation. But this ideology of reconciliation did not refer to regional political relations, such as those across the Taiwan Straits. Rather they were signs of an internal political reorientation. The spy films produced to great popular acclaim in this period likewise represented a new trajectory in this Cold War genre's struggle between enemy and "us," in its reconfigured depiction of the hero/individual axis, and in its depiction of gender and visuality, thus rendering visible that era's tremendous social transformation.

One might imagine that in contemporary China, this type of cinema, ceasing fairly abruptly after the late 1970s–early '80s flourishing, had disappeared according to a unitary logic: Cold War cultural genres would disappear with the dismantling of the Cold War structure itself. But this sub/quasi-genre in fact continued to resonate, and took on new life, in Europe, the U.S., East Asia, and China. If we can claim that the spy film had at one time represented a wrinkle or fissure in the seemingly monolithic structure of Cold War ideology, the spy films of the post–Cold War era seem to function as a multicomponent prescription for that new abyss which had opened between society and memory. In the era of high-speed globalization, the big screen portrayed a scene of pervasive crisis, a world split with cracks and fissures. The spy film, on the one hand a component of this comprehensive structural integration, thus revealed, in its deeper structural aberrances and tensions, a new global symptom. The Hong Kong film *Infernal Affairs*, as well as its ludicrous Hollywood imitation, gets to the matter at the heart of this sub/quasi-genre.[19] As in Hollywood's *Bourne Identity* franchise, it is without question that the genre's primary narrative object is the question of identity and identification.

One might interpret the spy film's resurgent popularity with reference to the post–Cold War–era context of the intelligence services' struggle for economic information and resources, a struggle that is worsening and intensifying daily, and one which is accompanied by the Western world's determination, in its relentless and unrestrained assertion of its victory and supremacy, to name the enemy. But we should not ignore the fact that this goes hand in hand with the conundrums attendant on the paradoxical and unresolved questions around the basic nature of the nation-state itself, and of personal and national identity. In *Black Book* (*Zwartboek*, dir. Paul Verhoeven, 2006), the Jewish female lead deconstructs and complicates the magnetic attraction of the international antifascist alliance. The loyalty and treachery evinced by the Wang Jiazhi character in *Lust, Caution* provides no clear answers, but rather opens up a labyrinth from which there is no clear exit. In *The Message* (风声, dir. Chen Guofu and Gao Qunfu, 2009), a popular story that unfolds within enclosed interior spaces suffused with sadomasochism, the discernment of real identity is actually so obscure, given the tangled web of the film's logic (which is not confined to plot alone), that the weak and unconvincing mode of postscript had to be deployed in order to explicate the characters' multiple identities: Traitor to the Chinese people? Guomindang spy? Soldier? Communist Party member? This seemingly ambiguous superfluity of identity is in fact a phantom symptom. Recall the opening scenes in all of the Bourne films. Lead character Jason Bourne is lost in amnesia, not knowing what day it is or who he is. "Who am I?" That this is an ancient philosophical question about the nature of being does not obscure the fact that this question also has a contemporary and genuinely practical dimension. The self-knowing individual as pure subject? The self-contained homunculus? This is a comforting but ultimately ineffectual fantasy, especially considering what the history of the twentieth century and the reality of the twenty-first have taught us about the nature of subjectivity. The ongoing work of interpretation and demystification needs to be free of that illusion at least.

CHAPTER 6

In Vogue

Politics and the Nation-State in Lust,

Caution *and the* Lust, Caution *Phenomenon in China*

TRANSLATED BY EREBUS WONG AND LISA ROFEL

I. Premise

The year 2008 may be regarded as special and significant in contemporary China. It was the year of the Olympics in China. The precedents of Japan and Korea had shown that the Olympic games held in a non-Western country mark the extent of the nation's entry into global capitalism and are a harbinger of full-scale economic takeoff. But 2008 also witnessed the devastating earthquake in China's Sichuan Province. This bitter circumstance unexpectedly developed into a heart-warming rendition of national solidarity. In terms of that solidarity, within the one hundred–odd years of the twentieth century and the new millennium, this was nearly the only time in which modern China could be seen as an effective "imagined community" not caused by deliberate mobilization through politics or crisis. In my view, it simultaneously marked the completion, at the turn of the millennium, of a depoliticized political practice dependent on capital. This depoliticized politics involved the erasure of the bloodstains and trauma from the 1989 Tiananmen Square Incident (known as the June Fourth Incident in China). It involved the resolution (or reversal) of the internal contradiction between the legitimacy of a communist regime based on socialist ideological discourse and the reality of class division with China's full turn to capitalism. A "new" cultural hegemony was affirmed.

Nevertheless, here we can discern something very interesting. The opening ceremony of the Beijing Olympics occurred at eight o'clock in the evening on the eighth day of the eighth month (i.e., August) of the year 2008—and I should add that the number eight signifies wealth in Chinese popular thought. This very symbolic opening ceremony was no doubt a maneuver by the state in an absolute sense. However, the ceremony's climactic moment of celebrating Chinese civilization was when former gymnast and Olympic medalist Li Ning, now a successful entrepreneur with his own brand name, Li Ning Sports Clothing, stepped out on the cloud, ran the circumference of the gigantic stadium known as the Bird's Nest, and ignited the Olympic flame. For he had achieved the largest brand-name marketing ever watched by an audience of such an enormous scale. Moreover, he had unintentionally announced a fundamental change in the nature of Chinese society and the role of the state.

Equally striking, with the Sichuan earthquake disaster, the subject who raised the fascinating but fragile banner of national identity was a new social group, namely the new Chinese middle class. What could have been a better time for the new Chinese middle class to appear on the stage? Against the backdrop of natural disaster, we witnessed tears, tenderness, and charity without stint, spontaneous giving as well as volunteers in streams. It was an excellent opportunity for the new middle class, having been formed by consumerism, to achieve, fulfill, and express their international middle-class ethics and values. It also revealed that this new middle class had been constituted out of a new cultural hegemony and served as that hegemony's main support. Compared with the political regime, this new social cohort no doubt stands on a rather unstable base. However, with their enormous consumption power in durable and luxury commodities, they have begun to regulate the Chinese market (including culture), and they dominate the international vision of what China is.

Furthermore, the role they played in the Sichuan earthquake clarified that they now act as a mediating force to integrate society from above and below. This middle class, in terms of percentage of the population, is still relatively small. However, considering China's huge population base, its absolute number is not insignificant. If they constitute what is referred to as China's civil society, then contrary to expectation, right from the beginning of their appearance on the historical stage, they expose the fact that in China, civil society and the state apparatus are two sides of the same coin, only here the state, or China, needs to be redefined.

The year 2008 passed, and 2009 was the sixtieth anniversary of the People's Republic of China. Sixty years is exactly a full cycle in China's old calendar system. Among various scenes of celebration, the most peculiar one was the film, *The Founding of a Republic*, produced as a tribute for National Day. In fact, films of this kind had been part of the conventions of political culture since the founding of the People's Republic. But after the mid-1980s, with the end of the Maoist era, these films were despised by most film critics and neglected by the general public. Yet they remained as officially necessary political propaganda, appreciated by none yet that which no one could renounce. However, 2009 was quite different. This big historical production that meticulously described the formation of the new socialist government was virtually an inventory of the big film stars from the culture and entertainment industry of the new millennium. Not only did it include all kinds of stars from the television and film industries, but it involved actors and directors from art, commercial, and propaganda films, which are supposedly absolutely incompatible with one another. Furthermore, stars from Hong Kong and Taiwan and overseas Chinese were also included. Even the nameless crowd extras in the film were played by celebrated stars. Within cinematic space, such a long and impressive production team list became an interesting and important sign of the "global Chinese." This unprecedented and unimaginable casting successfully drew the audience and achieved a box-office record unseen in the previous two decades for this genre.

The success of *The Founding of a Republic* seemed to reaffirm the identity of an imagined community and the social cohesion manifested in the 2008 Sichuan earthquake and the Olympics. Of course, its true reality does not reside in the deep structure. It can be found right on the surface: at the top of the production team list was the (honorary) director, Han Sanping, the board chairman of China Film Group Corporation. This explained why such an impressive team of actors could be gathered together in the film. As a state-owned monopoly within the film and television world, the company not only controls the lion's share of the film market in terms of production, distribution, and screening but also owns literally all the movie theaters in mainland China and monopolizes the right to import foreign films. In recent years, with its solid capital, the corporation has attempted to get a share of the action in the global film market. Just as with the social and cultural facts surrounding issues such as national imaginary and national identity in China today, the momentum behind this has nothing to do with (Cold War–type) political options but rather with a reality driven by capitalist competition. That in 2008, the manifestation of a new and fairly intense national/racial identity relied on the subjectivity of a new middle class, a social cohort produced by China's economic miracle, should no longer seem peculiar.

The success of *The Founding of a Republic* implied yet another social change. It signaled the end of the most prominent intellectual scene in China since 1995, namely, the confrontation between the so-called liberals and so-called New Left. In a certain sense, neither side had produced a winner. None of their respective demands had gained ground: on the liberal side, free markets and constitutional democracy, and with the New Left, workers' property rights and social equality shared by the majority, including the peasants. To the contrary, the biggest and almost sole winner is an interest bloc composed of state bureaucrats and mega comprador-capitalists, reconstituted through an exchange between power and money. Such a change has forged the dependence of the new middle class on the state regime. At the same time, this characteristic has made the so-called Chinese middle class an enclave within China's social reality. These new middle-class people are well educated and young, concentrated in mega-cities. Their internationalized self-image, orientation, living reality, and structure of feeling have created a huge gap between them and the majority living in the hinterland and rural areas.

At the same time, the mainstream postrevolutionary discourse has insulated the two generations born under the one-child policy from the history and memory of twentieth-century China. While the state bureaucrats/comprador-capitalist interest bloc becomes the sole winner, the new middle class as identified by national statistics is in fact a highly complex spectrum made up of heterogeneous classes and sectors, from private bourgeois entrepreneur whose upward mobility is blocked to the urban "ant tribe" (so-called from the title of a book referring to young college graduates who cannot find stable jobs).[1] Such is the intrinsic, deep reason why this social group is so unstable. Hence, at the end of 2007, *Lust, Caution*, an imported "local" Chinese film, was the prelude to the social changes of 2008–9 and thus is symptomatic of these social changes.

II. The Lust, Caution *Phenomenon*

During the fall and winter of 2007, Ang Lee's *Lust, Caution* became a smash hit, almost a crowd-pandering craze. The film was screened in Taiwan, Hong Kong, and mainland China from September to November and instantly became a box-office miracle and rapidly a fad. A newspaper report that surprised me described the China premiere: when the director, Ang Lee, appeared with the actor Alexander Lee-Hom Wang, the audience gave a huge ovation, shouting, "Long live Ang Lee!"[2] In mainstream media, the most common praise was, "Ang Lee: glory of the Chinese." At the same time, a wave of angry criticism surged up; for example, "China has already stood up but Ang Lee is still kneeling down" (Huang Ji-su) and "*Lust, Caution* glorifies traitors" (Liu Jian-ping).[3] With the condemnation and disputes over Ang Lee and the movie, we find a cultural event unheard of for more than a decade: a film that had become a pop icon was taken up in the social and intellectual field. *Lust, Caution* thereby transcended being about the director, being merely a film, or being just a media circus. It became a social spectacle that caught the attention of the entire Chinese-speaking world. It forged the Ang Lee / *Lust, Caution* phenomenon that has traversed and transcended China, Taiwan, and Hong Kong.

The clamor surrounding this film seems to provide us with various ways to interpret this actually rather simple movie. The numerous interpretations of *Lust, Caution* in the Chinese-speaking world advertently and inadvertently delineate a genealogy of China's new middle class and their international taste. The first of the many debates over *Lust, Caution* discussed its story line through the opposing coordinates of history and the individual. Interestingly, so-called history, especially twentieth-century Chinese history, was thoroughly abstracted and recast based on the last twenty years of depoliticized experience. Thus, the "person" and the "individual" herein became empty yet effective constructs and imaginaries.

The historical background of the story that *Lust, Caution* tells is the Anti-Japanese War in China, during World War II. The inevitable themes of nation-state/identity and loyalty/betrayal, together with the audience's embrace of the film, represent an entangled social, cultural, and psychological symptomaticity. Not surprisingly, discussion over the film revolved around the sexual scenes, which remind us of ancient Chinese erotic paintings. As Prof. H. H. Chang, a Taiwanese scholar, puts it, Ang Lee "has unfolded the pleat in Eileen Chang's words" and "broken the caution of lust."[4] (Eileen Chang wrote the original story on which the film is based.) The existence of two different versions of the film—the mainland version was shorter by nine minutes—ironically increased box-office income.[5] We saw on travel websites on the Internet, "Visit Hong Kong and watch the full version of *Lust, Caution*." We read in the media about a consumer who sued the state-run Radio, Film, and Television Bureau for infringing on consumers' right to see the full version of the film. These phenomena implicitly draw attention to the identity and role of a new middle class (the cinema audience) in contemporary China.

An amateur female spy lured an enemy but in turn got caught by lust and love. This espionage genre cliché was once again replicated to illustrate the [middle-class][6] truisms of human nature/estrangement and individual/ history ("the individual is the hostage of history," "the individual cannot shoulder the guilt of history"). Other interpretations were thus derived, such as "impersonation" ("drama is fake but emotions are real," "life is but a drama"), the Electra complex, and even "women love diamonds."[7]

In Chinese-speaking communities, the popularity of *Lust, Caution* was due to the fact that it was almost like a Russian box (nested boxes within boxes) containing various elements of pop and fad: the super-successful Chinese Ang Lee, and Eileen Chang, the original writer, who managed to capture a politically symptomatic millennial culture, which was global nostalgia and the nostalgia of Chinese communities for a home. That is, she represented old Shanghai, whose dusty historical fragments were once again stirred up by the film. These dusty fragments included Eileen Chang's archetypal characters and situations: Zheng Ping-ru attempting to assassinate Ding Mocun, the head of the secret agents under the puppet government. All of these were wrapped up within one another. Ang Lee could be regarded as the outer box, the innermost being Zheng Ping-ru. Or conversely, Zheng is the outer shell, Ang Lee the inner. In fact when *Lust, Caution* became instantly popular, the long-forgotten Zheng suddenly became famous again. Yet, instead of being a legendary woman and female spy in a great epoch or the spirit of a nation in oblivion, her image was first of all a cover girl on a popular magazine from early twentieth-century Shanghai, driving a sports car traversing the streets, a celebrated belle of Shanghai, one of the countless flat and faded representations of old Shanghai.

In fact, in the popular and cultural-political Russian nested box of *Lust, Caution*, different elements overlapped and became embroiled in a highly complex way: Ang Lee's cinematic writing, the original fiction *Lust, Caution* by Eileen Chang, and Chang's life: the complicated relationship between Chang and Hu Lan-cheng, the probable archetype of the story, and Zheng's attempt to assassinate Ding. Such complexity is rarely found in cinema, including films adapted from novels. A not-so-metaphysical explanation for this peculiar fact could be derived from Ang Lee's introduction. He not only added elements of Eileen Chang's personal life to the heroine's story (Chang's parents got divorced and her father then remarried and left her behind in war-ravaged China); Lee also rounded out the plot with fragments from Hu's memoir, *This Life*. He even let others believe that *Lust, Caution* was actually a reflection of Chang and Hu's relationship: "All of Chang's novels are other people's stories. Only this one is about herself."[8] "I think it seems to be her biography, an emotional work about love."[9] "It is a story about why Chang's love was forfeited."[10] Another factor was two academic books published in 2007, relating to Ang Lee's *Lust, Caution*.[11] By way of academic research, they stamped scholarly authority on the interrelationship and even overlap between Chang/Hu, Zheng/Ding, and the heroine/villain in the film.[12] Yet it was exactly these multiple overlaps of the film, the original fiction, the writer's life, and the historical archetypes that triggered conflicts in the interpretation of the film. To *Lust, Caution* fans, its imbrication with Zheng's assassination could only make the film even more enchanting. Thanks to it, the sweet and graceful face of a young beauty on the magazine cover was once again brought before us. We therefore came to experience another sexual tragedy, just like the urban phantasm of old Shanghai. However, to the castigators it was exactly why Chang and Lee were so outrageous. Borrowing from Chang's traitorous philosophy, Lee tarnished the glory of a heroine, a martyr, Zheng Ping-ru. Or to put it more seriously: "Seducing the audience with sex is but an outfit. The real body is distorting the history to destroy a nation."[13]

Nevertheless, the common identification and overlapping of the film, the original fiction, and the archetype shared by two totally incompatible sides, in my view, are deeply symptomatic of contemporary China.

In fact, Ang Lee's overlaps begin and end with Eileen Chang. He never referred to Zheng Ping-ru / Ding Mo-cun. In a certain sense, Chang was the endpoint of Lee's historical field of vision. In Taiwan during the period of martial law, Eileen Chang was a delicate, ambiguous, and fragile bridge connecting the island and "cultural China." But nowadays, within the Taiwan pro-independence literary discourse, she has become a Chinese Other who has to be exorcised.[14] Finally, for Ang Lee (and today's Chinese cinema audience), Chang appears to be a support for an emotional structure ("Grandma Eileen is calling me").[15] She seems to be a window into the political unconscious, between the sides (Taiwan and mainland China) separated during the Cold War and, in the post–Cold War age, between fragmentation and integration. In the 1990s, art films from Hong Kong and Taiwan (e.g., *Center Stage, Flowers of Shanghai*) applied the same narrative strategy, not by coincidence: taking early twentieth-century Shanghai as the point of intervention into the narrative of "China" to express a cultural identification or political refusal. Ang Lee made use of Chang to stir up a century of dust in China. It fell down once again onto China and floated between the oppositional camps (pro-unification with China and pro-independence) in Taiwan. In the name of the individual, we can bid farewell to the Cold War but also to all the multifaceted realities and dilemmas of identity in the post–Cold War and just stare at the past with a gaze of pathos. For those individuals crucified by historical destiny, a path to redemption in the global age is reopened. It is also the position or perspective opened up for Chinese audiences, which they are pleased to take when confronted with a twentieth-century history that has been abstracted and broken by a depoliticizing, postrevolutionary discourse.

Even more interesting was the crusade against *Lust, Caution* or the tidal wave of nationalism. In China, cinema audiences and netizens are two categories that overlap a great deal. Since its full-scale appearance in China after 1997, the Internet has been an active field of nationalism. Although the first wave of this nationalism on the net was in response to the U.S. bombardment of the Chinese embassy in the former Yugoslavia, the main target has long been Japan: war crimes, the Yasukuni Shrine to fallen Japanese soldiers, the Japanese history textbook controversy, war victim compensation, and so on. However, interestingly, when *Lust, Caution* became a fad and the Utopia Net launched a wave of criticism, there was rarely heated debate on the traitor problem in the film (that is, the Chinese puppet government working for the Japanese).[16] This was due to the success of the film's cultural politics. However, even though the film was framed with historical scenes, what it constructed was actually a floating stage detached from history in an age of globalization. The history in the film, that is, the villain protagonist's social activities, became an absolute lacuna. What we see is merely a pair, a man and a woman, seemingly powerful but in fact helpless because they are under heavy surveillance in a troubled time. What remains but also what is excluded is what has led to *Lust, Caution*'s success: a narrative leading from sex to love, from impersonation to one's "true self." At the same time, "patriotism as the other face" (Ang Lee's words) enabled *Lust, Caution*'s evasion of history and politics.[17] The critics' comment that the movie "glorifies a traitor" was aimed not only at Yi (the villain), but also at the historical reference in the film that rendered this reversal of the good and the bad, that is, the cruelty of the war with Japan. This historical rendering was accomplished exactly through tying *Lust, Caution* the film with the writer's biography, especially with its probable archetype: Zheng's assassination attempt.

For the critics, Zheng was not the sweet smiling face on a magazine cover but a heroine from a heroic family, who epitomized the spirit of a nation in a time of national need. Nevertheless, it was exactly in these critics' angry call for historical memory that an oblivion and rewriting of history appears. The lashing out against *Lust, Caution* stirred up Cold War political memories long forgotten and buried. However, defining Zheng as "our" heroine, a martyr in the struggle against Japan, no doubt demonstrated post–Cold War transcendence or healing (between the enemy camps of that time, the communists and the nationalists). The premise here is that twentieth-century China was a highly continuous and homogeneous nation-state. In order to affirm this premise, it must first of all obliterate, tone down, or forget the grandest politics of the twentieth century, namely the face-off between two camps, two systems, and the life-and-death struggle between two parties, between new and old China in modern history. In Cold War constellation and history (one of the main causes of the separation and face-off across the Taiwan Strait), Zheng being a nationalist spy, her act of assassination through seduction appeared as a lacuna and alterity in contemporary mainland Chinese texts and in mainland Chinese historical memory. In fact, the struggle between two parties, especially its magnification by the Cold War, had from beginning to end intrinsically torn apart the narrative clarity of the Sino-Japanese War. And since the 1990s, a full-scale rewriting of the history of World War II in China by popular cultural producers has had its function, of course, in the political status quo across the strait. But first of all, it was to cover and dislocate the ideological implication of Cold War history and memory. Socialism in the sense of oppositional face-off was replaced by a nation-state in the global capitalist system in order to legitimize a deep and full-fledged capitalization in China. Hence, when the well-known (neo-)Maoist website Utopia launched a protest against *Lust, Caution*, in fact what was a priori accepted was an obliteration of Cold War history: to take "their"/the Nationalists' sex spy as "our" national heroine was to wipe out the once-profound difference and antagonism between capitalism and socialism, Republic of China and People's Republic of China. The oppositional camps in the disputes over *Lust, Caution* clearly expressed different positions, but they implied no real ideological opposition. Both effaced class struggle and opposition in history and reality. The only difference was they picked distinct positions relative, respectively, to worldly humanism and nationalism, positions both located within global capitalism. The nationalist crusade against *Lust, Caution*, not unlike the nationalist wave since the 1990s, was fundamentally a gesture responding to globalization, to capitalism, or to the power hierarchy with "modernization as ideology" as its core.[18] At the lower end of this global power hierarchy, the nation-state became an important substratum to resist nations powerful in reality or imagination, or to pursue the power to stake one's place in the global race. It might also be just an internal difference within a huge and heterogeneous new middle class: those upper-echelon white collars who can afford to fly to Hong Kong on the weekend to watch the full version of *Lust, Caution* (the "international version") identify themselves with the individual in the film who transcends history or floats suspended outside of history, whereas those at the lower echelon of the so-called middle class could hope (sometimes as imaginary fantasy) that the Chinese nation will ascend the global hierarchy.

There was an interesting interlude. Under pressure from the backlash against *Lust, Caution*, Chinese authorities put Tang Wei, the actress, under an interdiction because of her "pornographic performance."[19] However, the director of this "porn," Ang Lee, was invited by the Chinese government to become an honorary consultant for the 2008 Olympics opening ceremony, in place of Steven Spielberg, who resigned because of the Tibet issue.

IV. Espionage Thriller

Among the various discussions about *Lust, Caution*—the original fiction, the archetype, the erotic scenes, the Golden Lion Award it won at the Venice Film Festival, the philosophical talking points about the triumph or failure of humanity—one glaring omission was that the film and the original work belonged to the genre of espionage thriller. In fact, the original English title Eileen Chang gave her novel was *The Spy Ring*.[20] As an espionage thriller, *Lust, Caution* was not an isolated case in world cinema; on the contrary, it was one of the many espionage stories springing up again in world cinema since the beginning of the twenty-first century.

As a Hollywood genre and a subcategory of suspense, the espionage thriller was once a genre commonly shared by the two oppositional camps in the Cold War (i.e., the Soviet Union and the U.S.). However, it did not disappear after the end of the Cold War. On the contrary, it became a new favorite in the post–Cold War age. Perhaps we should look for an answer in the genre itself. In terms of the surface structure of the narrative, the espionage thriller as a Cold War genre was based on the theme of demarcation between the enemy and me, the bad and the good, loyalty proven by wits and courage. Antagonistically oppositional systems of ideologies, beliefs, and values no doubt underpinned this genre. However, further scrutiny would show that the espionage film as a Cold War genre was not so much a direct carrier or duplication of Cold War ideology as an expression of a Cold War political unconscious where we can find a social-cultural symptom. In the espionage film, loyalty to the nation-state, political belief, and value must be proven by successfully impersonating a totally oppositional identity. It must be fulfilled through penetrating the enemy's camp, dancing with the enemy, showing loyalty to the enemy to gain trust. An espionage film usually teems with tension between loyalty and betrayal, truthfulness and pretense, and is packed with dramatic moments of lurking animosity and indeterminacy between friend and enemy. Accordingly, rather than affirming loyalty and identity, the espionage film is instead a revelation of identity ambiguity and anxiety, in an interminable impersonation and identification. Perhaps the true meaning of Cold War espionage films, soul-stirring and heartrending as they were, was actually what was interpreted and revealed by *Infernal Affairs*, a post–Cold War variation. Maybe this is why this very Hong Kong film was immediately purchased and remade by Hollywood and then became an Oscar winner (Martin Scorsese's *The Departed*).

However, in order to understand why the espionage thriller has become popular again, we must contextualize it in a wider international perspective of the post–Cold War/the age of globalism. The end of the Cold War was no doubt a triumph for the West. However, the post-post–Cold War world is not a world in which an overarching hegemony dominates all. On the contrary, boundaries along nation-states are once again highlighted, reallocated, and redrawn. A new round of global competition has been kicked off on various levels: energy, ecology, environmental war, and so on. Regionalization (EU, Mercosur's vision, Asian currency unit discussion, and so on) as globalization's main road but also means of resistance to globalization, has constituted a multifaceted constellation. In the global age, a masterless superpower is once again hanging over the world map. As regionalization—the measurement and resistance to globalization—intensifies, identity tension and anxiety have been pushed once again onto the political agenda by a new war.

At the same time, the most proper match to globalization as rhetoric is the tidal wave of global capitalism that has swept across the former Cold War frontiers to engulf the vast land of the old Eastern camp. Transnational capital and multinational cooperation based on nation-states but transcending territories are more powerful and resourceful than many countries. They are sweeping across the world along with global migration. Well-off immigrants can display an unrestrained and dashing identity of global citizen while underprivileged and illegal immigrants are creating heartrending but horrifying stories every day. These multiple tensions have caused the chasm and drifting apart between the nation and the state within the nation-state, which had originally served as the foundation of community and personal identity.

The fact that the espionage thriller has become popular again is not so much a reflection of a resurgence in a global spy war (economic spy first of all) as an aspect of the global social-cultural crisis in the global age. The espionage thriller as a Cold War genre has been turned inside out. On the narrative surface, the plot fabric is constituted by its political unconscious: manifold indeterminacy of the truth and impersonation and anxiety during identity reaffirmation. However, except for a return to value judgment systems such as individual, family, and humanity, a happy ending is no longer a must (loyalty proven, an anonymous hero praised by a higher power, usually a state). Perhaps it is the international context in which Ang Lee's *Lust, Caution* is located that is also its source of political unconscious. Perhaps it is also a representation (the unconscious) of Ang Lee's identity as part of the Chinese diaspora. Paradoxically, diaspora was supposed to refer to the Jews' loss of national belonging. However, in the global age of great migration, it is redefined as people wandering outside their country or home. In fact, it conceals and reveals the double face of the identity crisis in the era after the post–Cold War: on one hand, we find individual existence outside a nation, in a deep chasm or sliding in the once-solid conjugation between a nation and a state; on the other hand, we have new (statist) nationalism. Ambiguous concepts such as "global Chinese" invoke identity and loyalty on different levels. Maybe it is the predication and paradox haunting us in *Infernal Affairs* (*The Departed*).

In the context of the espionage thriller, two films formed an intertextual proximity to *Lust, Caution*: Steven Soderbergh's *The Good German* and Paul Verhoeven's *Zwartboek*. Each of them contained a reversal of the good and the bad as well as sexual seduction. But to me, the most interesting part was a common cultural return to 1940s cinema, even though in the form of postmodern duplication. For Steven Soderbergh, it was a B movie duplicate; for Paul Verhoeven, it was a parody of the popular European culture in the 1940s and '50s; for Ang Lee, it was a tribute to film noir, Eileen Chang, and Shanghai in the 1930s and '40s. In a certain sense, revisiting the 1940s, the pre–Cold War age, may be a gesture to seal or bid farewell to Cold War memory, a path to touch and dislocate the present reality. But here, revisiting the pre–Cold War age or its representation has unintentionally achieved a suggestion: the arrival of a post-post–Cold War is in fact accompanied by a reemergence of pre–Cold War global problems that had propelled the international communist movement. But this time, things are different. There is no naming of an effective alternative historical agent, no practicable social solution, not even a shared utopian vision. Thus, associated with the discussion of *Lust, Caution* and the *Lust, Caution* phenomenon in China is a reflection not totally irrelevant: the critical theory on which today's film theory and cultural studies rely was mostly a direct or indirect response to the global situation of the Cold War. In the global era after the post–Cold War, have we reached an age "after theory"? If an after-theory age does not imply a return to a pre–critical theory age, then how do we define a new and effective social criticism? How can a new practice of critical representation become possible?

When *Lust, Caution*, a paradoxical prelude, raised the curtain of the great drama of 2008–9 China, the cacophony in a scene of national solidarity was the reradicalization of young students and graduates constituting the lower strata of the so-called middle class. Nevertheless, in alignment with the *Lust, Caution* critics' intrinsic paradox, Huang Ji-su, renowned for the drama *Che Guevara* in 2000, while launching and leading the crusade against *Lust, Caution*, also became one of the contributors to the infamous book *China Is Not Happy*.[21] Leftist or Maoist nationalism? Instead of being an inevitable turning point or choice, it was rather the consequence of an abstract position and poverty of theory (or social imagination).

Lust, Caution has won for Ang Lee cheers and applause, a handsome box-office record, and condemnation. However, between a "traitor movie" and a "sorrowful China," between individual drifting and belonging to a nation-state, a historical stage set and the real bloodstain, "the rise of China" and the crisis in China as well as in the world, there lies a reality far more complex and heavy. Beyond the text, history has not ended.[22]

History, Memory, and the Politics of Representation

TRANSLATED BY REBECCA E. KARL

The underlying logic of the renewed emergence at the turn of the twenty-first century of the theme of history and memory does not just recall the bloodiness of the disasters and massacres of the twentieth century. Even if modern civilization of the twentieth century was in fact catastrophic and genocidal—genuinely calling into being one trauma of witnessing after the next and thus rendering history and memory into a shocking thematic—nevertheless, this theme cannot be said to constitute the entirety of the century's practice of cultural politics.[1]

The conjunctural moment of the 1980s and '90s saw the curtains drop on the Cold War as the short twentieth century came to a close.[2] Since then and repeatedly, "verifying" memory so as to rewrite the historical real has become a common and embedded global cultural practice and reality. Yet what is illustrated here is not merely the general logic of victors writing history. Rather, in some sense, this practice demonstrates the cultural logic of the last half of the twentieth century, when one of the most important arenas taken up by post-structuralism, deconstruction, postmodernism, and the whole gamut of critical theories was precisely the relations among history, memory, and historical writing. Hence, we could perhaps see the whole last half of the twentieth century as akin to a long-exposure photograph.

An alternative historical perspective, established upon the basis of historical materialism and class theory, emerged in Russia after the 1917 revolution and particularly within the socialist bloc after World War II to serve socialist ideology and its cultural construction; its self-conscious rewriting and revising of the cultural practice of history not coincidentally exposed the political imbrication of historical writing with structures of power. At the same time, from the beginning of the Cold War era, and particularly at the front lines of the confrontation on both sides of the divide, the same history appeared in ways utterly different from and even completely opposite to each other. Not only did these proximate "photographic exposures" result in a certain muting of the sacred aura of the historical, but they also demonstrated history to be the result of certain narrative practices. A comparison of the two clearly reveals the function of history as a screen to project and conceal.

Another important historical transformation of the last half of the twentieth century: the establishment of independent nations in previously colonized areas and the breaking apart of colonialism. At the same time as this process led to the revisionism of third-world national histories and the consequent re-visioning of general history, it also exposed the fact that all historical writings have at their base a certain global capitalism or Eurocentrism. For this reason, when the Cold War ended, the Western world—or, that is, capitalist logic—which supposedly triumphed without a battle, began to resume its hegemonic hold on all history writing. And yet this mode of writing itself inevitably encountered waves of obstacles and barriers put in its path by the above-named critical theories.

What is truly ironic is that, as the 1970s French philosopher Michel Foucault once noted, the mainstream postwar Western European strategy for elaborating the theme of history and mass memory came to deploy history so as to conceal and suppress mass memory, deconstructing the mass imaginary to call into question its critique of the present and of history. At the turn of the [twenty-first] century, particularly at the very beginning of this new century, the victors' version of history rewrote the twentieth-century experience of history in the borrowed idiom of that revolutionary and activist era of individual memory of trauma.[3] Naturally, the old canards that "the individual is the hostage of history" or "the individual cannot be responsible for historical crimes," at the same time as absolving the individual nevertheless also successfully rendered judgment on the logic of those who failed. As for that old mass cultural industrial product—film—in 1987, [Bernardo] Bertolucci's Hollywood-style Chinese film, *The Last Emperor* (末代皇帝), unexpectedly became the initiator of evil; and by 1994, the globally popular *Forrest Gump* (阿甘正传) used memory to begin the historically necessary mechanism for forgetting "truth."

Just as in that brief scene in the film when the visible shadow of a feather floats across Gump's life horizon, then Gump, with an IQ of 74 and his ever closely cropped hair, traverses the whole of postwar American history, and at each crucial moment, with the use of his limited and predefined individual revisionist memory, he orally transmits the torrid historical process. Besides *Gump*, of course, particularly significant is the emergence of the post-unification German narratives of history and memory, where the two Germanys were slowly reconnected through discussions surrounding films such as *The Lives of Others* [*Das Leben der Anderen*] (窃听风暴), *The Reader* (朗读者), *Downfall* [*Der Untergang*] (帝国毁灭), *A Woman in Berlin* [*Anonyma—Eine Frau in Berlin*] (柏林女人), and so on. Each of these proceeds through the memoryscape of one person's recollections or an individual's story so as to construct anew an absolutely required but always impossible political reconciliation and grand unity.

As for turn-of-the-century China, the representation of history and memory is even more complex and fraught. In actuality, one of the trajectories of the rapid political-cultural movements of the 1980s was precisely the self-conscious rewriting of history. Whether filled with primarily tragic accounts that recalled the tortured words of the former president Liu Shaoqi ("It is a good thing that history is written by the people") or, whether mobilizing the words of Hu Shi, then newly again in fashion ("History is a young woman dressed up at will by the appointed people"), there was not a single political critique or cultural reconstruction that participated in the movement to rethink history and culture that did not reflect an extensive and deep awareness of the significance of the politics of history and culture.[4] The transition from the 1970s to the 1980s produced some fundamentally specific characteristics: the era's most representative sociopolitical behavior in rewriting history was precisely encoded in the moves to rehabilitate intellectuals by "filling in the blanks of" and "rediscovering" [the stories of those who had been purged during the Maoist period]. It doesn't matter whether the significance of filling in the blanks or rediscovering resided in the reflection of older lacunae in historical narratives or in systems of deletion for, by disrupting existing strands of logic so as to expose gaps and blanks, the parameters and coordinates of revisionist narratives of history were deeply embedded in the process of rewriting.

First, as a modern nation-state, China had clearly defined its historical perspectives and their narrative framework so as to replace the parameters of a previous era: the May Fourth period's (or what Lu Xun called the "kindlers'") recognition and concern for the world's oppressed; the antifascist solidarity of the World War II era and the deep influence of the third world; the internationalism of the post-1949 period and the third-world perspectives of the 1970s—all of these were soon incorporated into narratives of the global capitalist system.[5] Modernization as a new edition of the logical form of catching up pushed aside the global revolutionary imaginary of communist ideals.

Second, in the return to the use of the special types of documents called "reversing cases" (*fan'an wenzhang*) often deployed in the 1950s and onward, the historical materialist narrative logic was rapidly erased.[6] Even more important, its fundamental parameters were lost: class—even if this class concept and especially its proletarian and bourgeois referents had never been strictly defined—as a social analytic and Marxist conceptual category most often came to be deployed reductively in a revisionist sense as a mere descriptive for "the exploited, the oppressed." Once upon a time, not only was this alternative version of historical analytic logic used to supplement and foreground the peasant rebellions in the dynastic period, but class analysis also had emphasized that the history that had been reversed would in turn be reversed again, to demonstrate that "it is the people, and only the people who are the motive force of world history."[7] And yet, the turn of the 1970s–80s saw the reversal of the reversal, during which history recovered its "original" aspect; indeed, it wouldn't be too much to say that historical narrative restored the mainstream logic of the modern world. However, China—this effective experiment in political culture—simultaneously also formed and exhibited a specific sociopolitical and cultural difficulty: that is, along with the continuation of the party-state and its rule there is the political and economic rupture with the past. The former demands the extension of existing ideology and its linked articulations of political legitimacy, whereas the latter seeks new bases for legitimacy, all the while demanding the reversal of older ideological constructs. Yet the latter directly demonstrates the spontaneous alternative logic of historical writing by suturing the inherent gaps and conflicts as well as the narrative disruptions it occasions, even while not being able to actually substantiate any original relevant or extant twentieth-century narrative. However, of course, everyone knows that a piece of logic that extends into history is always the product of some mainstream ideology deployed to fulfill some required conditions.

In the last two decades of the twentieth century, a huge division opened in history (*lishi*) between experience (*li*) and the past (*shi*): certain resultant blanks perhaps required skipping particular years to become some sort of premise for the grounding of the past as history. At the same time, in the last two decades of the twentieth century, the particular position occupied by China in the world only strengthened this paradox between historical writing and articulations of ideology. At the turn of the 1970s and '80s, China's "new era" commenced; or it is perhaps more accurate to say that it was the 1972 Joint Communiqué of the United States of America and the People's Republic of China that actually cast China into the global Cold War system as a post–Cold War polity and culture. It was with the 1970s and '80s that the Cold War was concluded; the West triumphed without fighting a war, and China remained the last large socialist country standing, thus drawing to it every Cold War treatment summoned by the post–Cold War world. This further dislocation, as a form of delirium or aphasia, only strengthens the destructiveness, tragedy, and cynicism of contemporary historical narrative.

Meanwhile, one cultural strategy silently making its way in certain social circles is a form of historical narrative montage. At the same time, like cutting alternative episodes of contemporary history, such montage attempts to bypass difficulties by constructing a new hegemonic logic. However, when what needs to be cut is not merely certain years but rather major swaths of contemporary history—the 1950s–70s, or even the 1940s–70s—such a strategy not only has to leap over a huge temporal abyss, but, because of the multiple heterogeneities and the pattern of the logic, it also exudes a certain narrative and cultural fogginess. Moreover, because of the absenting of important contemporary historical moments, it directly or indirectly leads to a crisis in its own legitimacy. Another narrative strategy that perhaps derives from the drive to substitute a multiplicity of politics for ideology is of some interest, or, at least, it speaks volumes. If we say that "history" was a key term of politics and culture in the 1980s, then what paraded under the name of history to denote cultural and political experience largely had nothing but ahistorical characteristics. If we take the distorted echoes produced by the new fabulation of the May Fourth period, once again a history in which certain years are absented—where the real expression of history becomes counterhistorical—then the new woven chain of cause and effect thereby chronicled is consulted and turned upside down.

Meanwhile, the contemplation of history all of a sudden produced a superstable structure of Chinese history, which, similar to root seeking or to *River Elegy* (河殇, 1988),[8] allowed Chinese history (including contemporary history) to reemerge from the ignorant and seemingly already dead folk fables of yore as a circular or viciously circular spatiality without time or linear progress.[9] At the same time, during the moment of the rise of new Chinese cinema, many works of the directors of the so-called fifth generation followed the indications about which years to include or not, as well as the disputes over concrete and abstract episodes. In the first part of the 1980s, this arena became the site of huge conflict between the cultural power of film and the state offices of management and censorship. In actuality, this also became the characteristic signature of the fifth generation's cinematic culture. That is, space and models suppressed time and narrative, and folk customs, rituals, costumes, and objects came to construct a formal aesthetic style that became the site where history or history's "array of nothingness" (in Lu Xun's term) resided. In some sense, the ahistorical history writing of the 1980s exhibited the social utility of the two-sidedness of culture. We might say that the May Fourth era's narrative subject is that a history that does not account for its past and that nevertheless becomes truth or the place where truth might reside directly contends with periodized history (chronicles and state narratives) and thus represents a radically transformed choice and attitude toward the historical. If this is correct, then at this point the ahistoricized result attained by this type of historical narrative at the same time takes up a hugely different social burden: when some kind of elementary Chinese historical narrative depicts twentieth-century China—the very century that witnessed so many of human history's revolutionary experiments—as revealing an unchanged or unchangeable homogeneous prospect, this perversion undoubtedly gets us to a different, apolitical political experience that translates into radical judgment and a so-called "farewell to revolution."

Meanwhile, the history writing that goes under the name of "the individual" or "memory" is yet another very effective strategy because, from beginning to end, it becomes a logical displacement and a new mainstream structure for the concomitant writing of history as contemporary history.

Perhaps we could say that in the 1980s, the emergence of the "individual" and "memory" was part of an effort to pit the individual against class and the collective, to pit memory against the almost-collapsed state mode of historical narration of the time. At the same time and perhaps even more important, in the name of memory, the individual could peel himself or herself away from history or that reality just passed. If, in the name of memory, memory is avoided, even when society is seeking to restore normality from the weight and explanation of history after the great eras—especially those great eras filled with complexity and rancor—then perhaps what needs to be raised is the fact that the individual of the 1970s and '80s is the collective name for an imaginary figure, while memory approaches most closely to naming a compensatory daydream. The individual becomes the enclave for history, perhaps even its redemption, or the blank slate upon which the future can be written. For this reason, saying that "scar," or "rethinking," or "fourth-generation" cultural writing successfully unearthed forgotten mechanisms in the name of memory allows a new mainstream logic and historical narrative to gradually insinuate themselves. If this forgotten memory, so called, is the result of the replacement of ideology by politics at the turn of the 1970s–80s, then the 1987 Hollywood-style Chinese-themed movie *The Last Emperor*, shot by a major European director, at the same time served, not coincidentally, to present individual memory and mainstream history writing with a model for Chinese film, although perhaps not only for film. In the director Bernardo Bertolucci's world, the individual, albeit honored as king of his domain, is nevertheless merely a reed in the gale-force winds of history; he is kidnapped and bound by the violence of history, in the face of which he can only be either cynical or stubborn. He has no ground upon which to traverse the historical space of the great eras. In his ritual ascension to the throne, the last emperor, Pu Yi (or should we say the future Manchukuo emperor), is like a three-year-old's toy or a puppet, undoubtedly becoming the best simile Bertolucci could muster for the human condition. Maybe the particularity of Bertolucci's story is not, after all, in the fact that his historical perspective is completely defined by the individual, which is almost universal in modern Western storytelling; rather, it resides in the fact that, relative to the individual, history has no main theme other than its incessantly changing scenery. This is used as a stage for the performance of the son's story—his mother fixation, patricidal desires, and even the religious initiation ceremony, all of which allow him to take on the name of the father. Similar to psychoanalytical theory, the most basic disorder is not merely highly predictable, it is also ahistorical or antihistorical. What Bertolucci's history accomplishes is precisely the personal tragedy of historical confusion. For this reason, *The Last Emperor* seemingly emanates from an individual's memory—the original basis is Pu Yi's memoir *The First Half of My Life* (which is without a doubt highly politicized, a form of witnessed and chronicled history from a particular perspective)—but in Bertolucci's staging, whether of the Qing court's big celebrations or of the Red Guards' "red character dancing," we could say that for him, it is the details truthfully rendered that compose the stuff of history, all of which has little to do with China as such, but also has nothing really to do with the historical either. What thereby emerges is thus merely another Bertolucci-style individual: one who is tossed about under the father's coercion and who is infantilized by or through his mother fixation as the son/child emperor. For this reason, no matter whether it is about Europe's stormy passages at the turn of the last century in the film *1900*, or modern China's shining full-dress costume drama in *The Last Emperor*, or even the land war in Europe of World War II in *The Conformist* (随波逐流的人), or the Paris-centered 1960s' "last revolution in Europe" of *The Puppetmaster* (戏梦人生)—in all these stories related to selfishness or self-defense, the invasion of privacy or frailty of Bertolucci's individual, because historical space can provide no means of securing an escape, history is therefore undifferentiated.

Of course, it is said that once Chinese people saw Bertolucci, they learned from him the mainstream strategies and techniques of cinematic storytelling, which is like saying that Chinese film people awakened to how to erase history in their stories of China through Bertolucci's "China story." This is because at this time and place, the name of history is precisely the present shape of contemporary politics. Perhaps it is just coincidental that it was in 1987 that *The Last Emperor* was shot in China and in that same year, Zhang Yimou's debut film, *Red Sorghum* (红高粱), received a major prize at the Berlin International Film Festival, demonstrating that the films of the fourth and fifth generations of directors that had led the new trends in Chinese film, or perhaps the new tide of Chinese film, had crested and now possessed a certain finality. For it is precisely in this film [*Red Sorghum*] that the first half of the action is situated out of place and out of time—or, that is, outside of historical space altogether—even if it is said in a very light aside, "So they say the Japanese devils had come, and so they had; if you turned your head, you could see the road had been paved to Qingshakou." This has the effect of bringing into the same frame a timeless history and a history with time, thus demonstrating and bringing to fruition a radical critique of the (anti)historical rendering of eras. In the 1990s, Chinese film not only won the vocal approval of the world but also won great box-office success. *Farewell My Concubine* (霸王别姬), *To Live* (活着)—all of them deployed a Bertolucci-like storytelling mode. At the beginning of the story, the protagonist's or a family's fate is situated in the midst of modern and contemporary Chinese history, but this history is depicted as a panorama of scenes: savage and saber-rattling, historical change is almost completely undifferentiated and has no explanation. Never mind everything that surrounds China in the 1990s or the cultural incidents that exhibit the Cold War aspects of the post–Cold War; and never mind the essentialism of the Euro-American world as encoded in its "oriental despotic" imaginary: in the cinematic worlds of *Farewell My Concubine* and *To Live*, history is always the antithesis of the individual (in the large or small sense).

Here, the interesting exception to the cultural-political logic of inscribing ahistoricity into historical writing can be found in the two decades around the turn of the new century in the sequence of films by Jia Zhangke that came to represent Chinese cinema or cinema art. In the work that gained him his international voice and stature, *Platform* (站台), Jia Zhangke established his representative mode of writing about the individual and fate: that is, it is a story about a nobody who tenaciously survives in an era of storminess rippling through rapidly changing social space. Because his works always take up the lives of subalterns, his protagonists' marginal identities and the filmmaker's recognition of those identities combine to take on a distinctive yet charismatic aspect. However, once Jia Zhangke's films and stories reencounter history, they become an exceptionality that once again can be seized by the conventional. Jia Zhangke's two linked films at the beginning of the twenty-first century, *24 City* (二十四城记) and *I Wish I Knew* (海上传奇), both deploy documentary-like techniques, or perhaps we should say they deploy the shape of a documentary-flavored technique. At this point, the story is about an individual (a nobody or a somebody) who is all alone in the world traversing history; and it is here that Jia successfully recapitulates the results achieved by mainstream history writing and its ahistorical mode. Concerning the story of several generations of workers in a large state-owned factory, *24 City* actually recalls a peripheral episode of the history of the republic. In this span, no matter whether it is the 1950s, a period that, for large state-owned factory workers, is said to have been "a red-hot era"; or the 1980s, the era in which social strata in China began to redivide; or the huge transformations of the 1990s, the era of the decline of the proletariat as a class; or the twenty-first century, when alienation between labor and capital is complete: the reality of the radically transformed and anonymous society of labor in the film is depicted as a seemingly undifferentiated, predestined force.

As for the other urban memory—*I Wish I Knew*—the burden of twentieth-century history is displayed more clearly, replete with all its necessary cultural-political syndromes. This near-documentary takes place on the eve of the Communist Party's military occupation of Shanghai [in 1949] and tells the story of an underground Communist Party operative, Wang Xiaohe, who has been caught and sentenced to execution by the special tribunal" of the Guomindang [Nationalist Party]. At the level of the encounter and intermingling of Wang's story with the stories of the thousands of Guomindang military officials fleeing the mainland for Taiwan, there is a coincidental intermingling with two other stories: the narrative of a female worker in a cotton factory, Huang Baomei, who has been granted an audience with the main leader of her factory; and the cinematic shooting of a romantic scene of the movie *Spring in a Small Village* (小城之春) by the actress Yuan Weiwei. These coincidences are entirely undifferentiated. As such, in the blink of an eye and freakishly, everything becomes just a matter of the vicissitudes of life that create different people. Although everything is designed to be sneered at as a cynical joke, the undifferentiated nature of everything abstracts the individual's identifications and sympathies, turning buried memories of historical violence into a second death. Here, what is demonstrated is not only the so-called postmodern flattening of history, but also the conscious or unconscious erasure in twentieth-century history, especially the dissipation of the depth of Cold War history, of the first time in modern history—and perhaps also the grandest era—of a globalized utopian experience, which was the attempt to search for an alternative to capitalism; the erasure, that is, of all the historical suffering that that radical special difference occasioned as well as all of the suffering that that history itself created. Similar to world and European art films, the critical social role Chinese art films shoulder, or intend to shoulder, has already begun to dissolve; the writing of the cultural elite already bears little dissimilarity from the mainstream choices made by political and economic elites, thus tending ever further toward the ahistoricity or antihistoricity of mass culture.

In reality, the most important and essential fact about China's 1990s is that the mass culture industry and mass media took over the state and elite cultural functions of the past. It has become a substitute ideological mechanism, making up for crises and prohibitions, while at the same time also functioning as the inevitable result of neoliberal globalization. If we take only narrative culture and mass visual culture, then it is evident that TV series have replaced movies and started to serve as the ideological voice of mass culture. Television series underwent the crazed beginnings of consumerist culture, the intensity and warmth of shared joy and the voyeuristic participation in troubles, the aftermath of the miscellaneous and arbitrary rewritings of red classics. In many aspects of historical narration or historical storytelling, TV series have demonstrated their signifying capacity to cut through discursive barriers and to reinforce mainstream values. It is true that historical costume drama series, especially those occasional excessive Qing court dramas exemplified by the place of the narrative subject of *Yongzheng Dynasty* (雍正王朝), represent a transformation in the Chinese imaginary of themselves and of symbolic gender roles. *The Years of Burning Passion* (激情燃烧的岁月) begins with the passions of the previous century so as to enter into the reclamation, rewriting, and reorganization of the cultural trajectory of contemporary history. It represents the attempted establishment of a new cultural hegemonic structure and its successful implementation. The historical heroic tales *The Drawn Sword* (亮剑) and *My Chief and My Regiment* (我的团长我的团); the high tide of spy and war series such as *The Plot* (暗算) and *Lurking* (潜伏); or family drama series such as *Guandong Adventure* (闯关东), *Desert Mother* (沙漠母亲), and so on; plus all the new army stories such as *Shocktroops* (士兵突击): these have been extremely successful in forcefully pushing a new set of mainstream values and the state consensus. With the final development of this new historical return and predominant path in Chinese films on the big screen, the formal establishment of a hegemonic structure put in place by the stimulus of the new political economics can be specified. For, if we take vulgar narrative art and TV series as the contemporary exemplars of an efficient mass culture, then cinema—especially big-ticket films made by the large studios—still functions as another layer of mass cultural mainstream values, as a direct display window for hegemonic structures. Or, perhaps, in discussing cultural hegemonic structures, TV series can be said to be similar to "B" movies of cinema's golden age, more like the site of multiple social forces or verbal expressions of subjective game theories, or, even a space for (sociopolitical) negotiation and reconciliation. This can be compared to "A" films, which are more like the demonstrated self-expression of an already accepted common hegemony, the arena for confirmed verbal expression. For this reason, the examples of the huge costume dramas starting with *Hero* (英雄) in 2002 and extending through *Curse of the Golden Flower* (满城尽带黄金甲) in 2006, using empty but colorful modes of expression, serve historical narration as a means once again to situate the throne above kneeling slaves—even if the latter continue to pose a danger to the absolute power of adulation, thus suggesting a certain attitude toward contemporary rulers. But all of these dramas combine to construct an absurdist expression of neoliberalism, paradoxically placed as part of the establishment of the new cultural political mainstream.

As a social and political nodal point, in 2007 a war film—or we could say the reinstallation in film of modern and contemporary history—appeared: *Assembly* (集结号). *Assembly* not only cleaned up at the box office but, in the opinions of most common viewers as well, it exemplified the mainstream cultural narration of history. It exemplified how the difficulties of official political culture could break out of encirclement in visual and verbal form, and how mass culture could finally displace the writing of the subject [of history]. The film provided evidence that the new cultural hegemony had attained an intricate if not yet stably consolidated place. In *Assembly*, the individual yet again has an encounter with and a relationship to history: the emotional and significant Gu Zidi (played by Zhang Hanyu), the commander of the Ninth Company [of the People's Liberation Army] stands alone in the face of a monumental historical turning point, a resolute and stubborn man, almost bigoted in his attitude toward what history demands of the names and situation of individuals, and of the power of memory. He faces the memorial to the anonymous martyr and eulogizes: "A mother and a father gave a name to their son. How have you become an anonymous son and orphaned child?" This theme appears as a repetition of the cultural rethinking of the 1980s. Here, the director, Feng Xiaogang, courageously deploys pioneering and experimental camera language and techniques: he has Gu Zidi in a nightscape, in the midst of a fiery exchange, turn his head to the lens. In a short moment, he interrupts the film's enclosed frame, allowing the character to directly address the director and audience in the theater, as if he were leaping across both historical space and the gap created by the screen to meet the puzzled queries of those sacrificed and kidnapped by history. Yet afterward, in a classical cinematic coincidence, Gu Zidi completes his impossible task: he regains the code designation for the Ninth Company; he releases the names of those disappeared by history; and, in the name of those disappeared, he regains the position and honor they would have deserved. What is interesting is that in the film, the emergence of this cinematic coincidence comes through an effective dissolution of the cultural thematic: the loss and recovery of the individual's name and position is precisely the sequence through which the historical narrative and its significance are restored. Subsequently, the only episodic refrain [of this cinematic coincidence] is when a soldier of the Ninth Company rushes up to the front in the middle of the night. Gu Zidi looks into the camera. And yet as this scene comes to a close, the episode and the camera lens once again flash back to a long shot, and with a reverse shot, or, say, with a calm view, the narrative semantic is reconstituted: through the mist of the night and history, Gu Zidi looks at us, the audience, and then once more turns around and runs to catch up with the troops entering into the depth of the cinematic frame, fading into the distance, into the night mist and thus into the profundity of historical time. The inquiry into history, in the end, is once more historical reconstruction; and, in the name of memory, history ultimately becomes about the name of the individual, who is once again sacrificed for history. And yet, especially as the film titles move back and forth, once the story has achieved its "great unity" denouement, history has also quietly completed its displacement: the history to which we've been returned is no longer the history with which the story began. The history that had been was one symbolized by rupture, one symbolized by the complete heterogeneity of the new historical temporality, when the anonymous martyr in its midst indicated the "tens of thousands of revolutionary martyrs who preceded him," "those who courageously were sacrificed, who dared to teach us how to exchange our old lives for a new day." Yet the history that displaces this signifies the conclusion to a materialist and class-analytical global imaginary perspective and, in terms of national-state history, the dead now appear as those who heroically met with their own demise; and in the historical place of the dead is now a name. The value and importance in the narrative signifying modern China's winding progress toward modernization has now been rechristened and has now returned to its namelessness and anonymity. The new gravestones of the Ninth Company in reality now become the new memorials to anonymous martyrs, except that this time they precisely become the foundation stones as well as the symbolics for the beginnings of the history of the nation-state.

As an indicator of the establishment of new mainstream values, *Assembly* not only achieved unprecedented box-office success in the cinematic marketplace, but, even more importantly, it unexpectedly became a metaphor for a hegemonic narrative: it successfully enlists and twists the themes and motivations of the historical rethinkings and critiques of the 1980s, while at the same time absorbing and dissolving the critical narrative of the 1990s that was posed in opposition. That is, it successfully absorbs the so-called liberal rejection and repudiation of social history while also deploying the so-called New Left mode of defending the achieved industrialization of the 1950s–70s. In terms of the zig-zagging path of modernization of the China century, it retrieves important fragments of contemporary history so as to reconstruct the homogeneity of twentieth-century Chinese history, thus creating a narrative of historical continuity.

Perhaps we could say that the success of the space of *Assembly* in some sense became the overture to 2008, China's Olympic year. The same year the global financial crisis at the imperial center began and made its way through Euro-America to spread the world over, infecting all with a financial virus and from its bottomless breadth and depth, it became quite clear that a new world subject had to be established: the rise of China. With the rapidity of this rise as measured in GDP, China has become the second-largest economy in the world, the largest consumer of the world's luxury goods, the biggest spender on tourism in the world, and the life support for capitalism. At the same time that it began to transform and reorganize the global political-economic scene, it also revised the parameters of social culture and the writing of politics and history. If we say that the global transformation of the first decade of the twenty-first century marks the beginning of the "after the postwar" era, then what appears as the position of the state is undoubtedly the strengthened intensification of the continued logic of modernization and the coherence of the Chinese historical narrative. For this reason, the subject thematic of Chinese culture has been pushed to the forefront. However, it is precisely because of the establishment of this new mainstream that in mass culture—especially as exemplified in visual culture—there have sprung up presentations of modern and contemporary Chinese history that, once more, represent the subject and the subject position of the ancient court in a contrastive light, which only exacerbates cultural difficulties and social symptomaticity.

As for the self-identification and self-representation of the Chinese cultural subject, ultimately the most prominent problem is a very strong vacuum of self-consciousness and values. I have discussed in a different essay the fact that the point of departure of Chinese culture in the banner slogans of the May Fourth period—anti-imperialism, antifeudalism—has already changed shape to become the hole at the heart of this subject.[10] This is because anti-imperialism as a cultural subject inherently calls forth the resistance of national or nativist culture. Yet solving the problem of the subject of antifeudalism requires that the premodern dynastic court culture, along with its traditions, is not allowed to rise like a phoenix from the soil in which it died—as if the reborn young China had never risen from the ashes of the court. Yet, within modernist Chinese culture, there is one side that banishes the self in the cultural depths, and another side that sharply defines the I/other modernist subject construction. This latter takes the Western powers, their military and naval might, and modern science and technology as the other, giving birth to a history of redemption, with callow youth and a blank slate being the "I." In this schema, the other provides the mirror of my future, which then is only the path to Westernization and modernization. Perhaps we could for a moment put in abeyance our outline history of modernity and capitalism: at its origins, capitalism was always already tending toward a global expansion. Not only did it begin in this fashion, but it understood the whole world as its resource, labor, and market domain, and through direct war and violent invasion, it coerced the whole world into joining the modern historical trajectory.

If this is so, then the significance of twentieth-century Chinese history resides in the fact that any attempt to reproduce the Western logic of desire never produced a successful reproduction in reality. Indeed, the turns of modern history stubbornly refuse to produce similar performative scenes. That is, modern culture was designed as a mode of others looking upon ourselves; therefore "ugly" Chinese culture needs to be thoroughly abandoned. Yet the beautiful other also happens to be the relentlessly savage foe, rendering modern Chinese culture from its very origins conscious of the Western path without ever being able to turn it into a royal road to success. This is precisely the demonstrative and indicative significance for China of the "October Revolution's shot heard around the world" or the Russian Revolution. This is also the internal reason and derivation of the Chinese social structure debates of the 1920s and '30s. This also helped to indicate the direction taken by the massive transformations of post-1949 China.

That is to say, if we take the zig-zagging path of modernization as our guide, twentieth-century Chinese history—this history that incorporates such a multitude of heterogeneous tensions, replete with contradictions, punctuated by moments of determinism—forged a path whose logic was dissimilar from that of modern Euro-America, where the cultural self and the subject position were filled with historical memories of difference. For this reason, at the beginning of the twenty-first century, in the era after the post–Cold War, the resumption of the thematic of China has once again exhibited the hollowness of the Chinese cultural self. This is not another sideswipe through the May Fourth cultural great rift in the historical firmament, but rather the result of yet one more attempt at a cultural reconstruction and ideological experimentation at the turn of a century.

If we look back at *Assembly*, a representative work of mass culture, it is not hard to see that the parameters and logic of history completed in the narrative successfully displace one another, while at the same time it once again describes a process of the historical subject finding itself (or we could say that this historical subject finds itself through its mass cultural exhibition). Particularly when we speak of cinema, Feng Xiaogang's major success is his restoration of the most exhilarating and socially grounded narrative modes of 1950s–70s Chinese film found in movies with revolutionary themes. The direct path to his success in breathing new life into this hoary old cinematic genre leads from more recent American war films such as *Saving Private Ryan* (拯救大兵瑞恩) and *Band of Brothers* (兄弟连) as well as the Korean film *Tae Guk Gi: The Brotherhood of War* (太极旗飘扬). The cutting and pasting from these genre films turns war once again into a spectacle. In order to achieve this goal, the director (along with the scriptwriter, Liu Hong) designed some necessary bridges and reversals into the scenes, allowing the Ninth Company not only to deploy its enemy's techniques—here, the Guomindang's American-made military materiel—but also its enemy's German-made uniforms. At the same time, the naming convention of "brothers" is switched to "comrades" or "battle mates," even while the absolute starring role of the courageous, upstanding, ever-moral company commander and military affairs officer is replaced by the impeccably disciplined, compassionate father-figure-like role model of a political instructor and political commissar. And yet, once the war of liberation, or that is to say the 1947–49 civil war period, is over and the PLA [People's Liberation Army]/communist soldiers need to be globalized in the after-postwar era, as the image of military officers appears on Chinese screens, the history of this war and the history that this war symbolizes, the history that this war inaugurates, at the same time gradually is emptied out and displaced. Just as *Assembly* successfully achieves its globalization, this is precisely when the Cold War goes beyond a war film spectacle and approaches a form of black magic: its premise is to disappear the different reasons for the history of this [civil] war. In historical discourse, or at least in the mainstream historical narrative of the past, this civil war is not only a common modern civilized historical occurrence, but it is also a determining moment in China's future historical path. It not only is a military confrontation with international geopolitical and geo-economic forces in the background; it is also a morale-building exercise for the Chinese people, a war in which the weak become strong. In historical perspective, what allowed the Communists and the Communist Party's army to win this war was primarily the deep and total mobilization of society/peasants through the realization of land reform and the consequent politicization of military affairs: "the party commands the gun," "headquarters come to the level of the company"—all of which became common Marxist teachings in the military's efforts to eliminate illiteracy. And yet, all of this is completely absent in the schema of the film *Assembly*. By comparison, the superficial characteristic of the Ninth Company is a total lack of politics or historical differentiation between military brotherhoods, between the incapacitation of the political commissar and political officers, between the courage of soldiers and officers and the problem of illiteracy. In this sense, the success of *Assembly* is in how the story touches people's emotions even as it completes an apparently fresh set of Cold War memories in which the historical political subject is eliminated. In this way, it succeeds in rewriting memory and reconstructing history.

Yet the self-erasure of the political subject of twentieth-century Chinese history has forced a simultaneous erasure of the difference of twentieth-century Chinese history. It signifies a repudiation of the process through which a cultural self was established, and it exhibits once more the hollow process of the creation of any new subject. Prominent examples can be found not only in how, in the large-scale historical dramas from *Hero* to *The Promise* (无极), the narrative logic of those elements that reside outside the spheres of great power is weakened and neglected. They can be found not only in how, in the renarration of the classic *The Orphan of Zhao* (赵氏孤儿), the behavioral logic in the story and of the characters becomes unintelligible and freakish. It is also in the self-conscious absence and expressive difficulties of the subject in modern Chinese historical narrative. Here, two large-scale experimental films—*Nanjing! Nanjing!* (南京！南京！) and *The Flowers of War* (金陵十三钗)—used historical memory to explain the Nanjing Massacre to global audiences. Their surprising symbolic narrative choices exemplify this cultural contagion. As regards this episode in modern Chinese history as a horrifying historical incident, the directors, Lu Chuan and Zhang Yimou respectively, significantly chose, at the same time and not coincidentally, to narrate this historical moment from the perspective of the other. Lu Chuan elected to deploy the perspectival narrative voice of a young Japanese officer who is part of the invading army; Zhang Yimou selects an American mercenary as his story's protagonist. If we say that borrowing others' eyes to see into the depths of our own memories is a necessary internal cultural marker of banishing the familiar, then the manner in which these two films design the image of the Chinese soldier as the extension of the self is also not coincidental: within the first third of Lu Chuan's film, the Chinese soldier "correctly" disappears, thus implying the exemplification of a profound cultural difficulty. In *Nanjing! Nanjing!*, the Chinese soldier Lu Jianxiong is originally one of two protagonists in the script and yet his narrative logic is impossible to sustain, so he is ultimately abandoned. *The Flowers of War* exhibits an even more perfect and prudent narrative. That is, because the film is set in an old church under the protection of the Red Cross, and because practically all the most important scenes are witnessed or are being witnessed through the perspective of the round stained glass window (religiously symbolizing the eye of God), not only does this directly indicate the absenting of the Chinese subject but, even more, it successfully evaporates the special historical narrative and vision of the Nanjing Massacre as an event.

It turns out that representations of politics are not only linked to history and memory but, at the beginning of the twenty-first century, they also represent an extremely prominent theme within politics. That is, in today's China, history and memory are not only about the past but are intimately connected to the contemporary moment and help indicate a certain future. After all, all history is contemporary history, and what is always suppressed is its recovery from the future.

INTERVIEW WITH DAI JINHUA, JULY 2014

This brief interview was in response to my query that Dai Jinhua explain how she developed her theoretical apparatus.

My generation began with very simple lives. I come from a very "common" background, "common" in two senses: my family was not of the previously wealthy classes [prior to the socialist revolution] and my generation shared similar experiences and outlook on life.[1] But still there were problems. On the one hand, in terms of the overall context, women and men were treated equally. I was a student cadre and leader of the group that went together to the countryside during the Cultural Revolution. I never had questions or suspicions.

But I had my own experiences growing up that didn't have an explanation. For example, that one's menstrual period got in the way of labor. Or the fact that I am very tall and that was seen as a problem. My relatives said I would never be able to get married. So I had contradictory experiences: there was no standardized experience but I was sometimes baffled and painfully confused. It seemed an individual experience with no way to talk about it. The very beginning was here.

I started college in 1978, with the beginning of economic reform. It was a period in which masculinity and power came together. The criticism of Maoism was from a masculinist perspective. That was very clear: the marriage pressures on men and the lack of individual power. It was all from a masculinist perspective. The social culture was to ridicule women as iron girls. I was nineteen years old when I started college. I had conflicts with this male power. "What use are female PhDs?" "What use are talented women?" "Marriage should be your only business." Su Qing [the writer] once said, "I bought the nails with my own money but what is the point?

Men take care of women—that is natural." Since I studied literature, these came to my attention.

Because of these unhappy experiences, I began to ask, "What is a woman?" I read Western novels and traditional Chinese novels, but I couldn't identify with them. My idols were all male figures, so one starts to doubt oneself. I began to feel a sense of alienation. I concluded that I am not a woman. I don't understand what it means to be a woman. I resisted [that prescription]. In my third year at university, we passed around a book among a group of women students: Simone de Beauvoir's *Second Sex*. It had a huge influence on me. She explained my life's aporia, why I don't resemble a woman. I also read the American author Betty Friedan, who addressed the "mystery" of women. What she wrote had no relation to my life, but I thought our problem was also that it was a "problem that could not be named." These two books had a big influence on me. But I still didn't know this term "feminism."

When I graduated, I wanted to write a book about Chinese women authors. I went to teach at the Beijing Film Academy; I wanted to study film. Christian Metz was very important to me, but it was hard to understand theory after structuralism. I wanted to understand postwar film theory. I encountered Laura Mulvey and discovered that feminist theory was very important in film theory. Mine was not a linear path through Western feminist theory. I went against the grain. From Mulvey, I read Lacan. From Beauvoir, I read Western novels.

Then it became clearer to me. I read a lot of feminist theory. The biggest questions in feminist theory then were socially oriented, but for China the questions were individual. It [feminist theory] spoke to me personally. We didn't have the same social structure; it became instead a way for us to understand our individual lives. It also became very fundamental to my analysis of film. It uncovered my own self-doubts, my own feelings of inferiority: I am tall, and I speak fast. I am aggressive, like a man. It helped me to understand patriarchal society. And I could also see how men are oppressed by other men, how the patriarchy also oppresses men.

I could also see the performative aspect of gender. This allowed me not to hate masculinity or men, but to understand their problems also. In the 1980s, many men introduced feminist theory because they wanted to introduce Western theory. All the way until the 1995 UN Women's Conference [held in Beijing], men said women were not strong enough to do this introduction of theory. But an object of analysis was not clear. Then Meng Yue and I published *Emerging on the Horizon of History*. Meng Yue wrote about modern women authors and I wrote about contemporary women authors. This book is considered to be the first feminist analysis of literature in post-Mao China. I used film theory to analyze these novels. Meng Yue brought in some twentieth-century theory. But we didn't think of this as really a full feminist text, though we were analyzing women authors. Today, there is some critique of its feminist aspects, but we didn't think we were doing that, although we had a feminist consciousness.

As soon as we finished, then Tiananmen happened. We published it after that. Suddenly it felt as if culture was empty, and society was silent. If the book had appeared before Tiananmen, there would have been a lot of discussion. But because of Tiananmen, there was no discussion. It was discussed a lot outside of China. Certain male theorists thought we were thinking about problems too narrowly. There was a group in the U.S. of comparative literature students from China. They loved it. There were actually three factors affecting the reception of that book: Tiananmen, gender discrimination, and the commercialization of culture.

But our book had a strange fate. They loved it in the U.S. and they came to China and talked about it. Their students looked for it but couldn't find it because it was published by an old-fashioned press. But in China, the word did not spread, until the UN Women's Conference, or at least until 1993 when they began preparing for this conference, with UNESCO and several NGOs [nongovernmental organizations].

International NGOs have influenced the shape of feminism in China. But they don't trust mainland Chinese women, so they are always bringing in overseas scholars of Chinese descent. This is the NGOization of China. Of course, they also spread the ideas of gender and also women's studies. In the 1980s in China, everyone was studying literature. But the result of the NGOization was that those who had studied literature now became like sociologists because of NGO funding. This first book we wrote was seen as either a vanguard for the new feminism or was an object of critique for using "men's" theory. Then it was read widely. And women students used our language from the book, recognizing this language as feminist language.

I went to Beijing University [as a faculty member] during the commercialization of literature. The patriarchal attacks became more direct during this period, which was the beginning of the 1990s. Men came up and attacked my ideas and also personalized my political stance by saying I must have been harmed by men. At this time, I stood up and said I am a feminist. For me, that meant "gender consciousness" (*nüxing zhuyi*) and not "women's rights" (*nüquan zhuyi*). They really just wanted to undermine my position. On the other hand, students said I was not willing to stand up and say I am a feminist!

Feminism as in nüxing zhuyi is not the same as feminism as in nüquan zhuyi. Both are feminist. The former incorporates the latter, though not the other way around. Women's rights are not our biggest problem; gender ideology is the biggest problem. We had never considered how the PRC's women's liberation had shaped us. We took it for granted. The problem was that it was not enough. When feminism started to be discussed in socialist countries such as China, they emphasized difference, in contrast to the emphasis on sameness of socialism. But it was built on the basis of the equality of women, legally and ideologically in China. That is why I emphasized ideology. We were not aware of gender discrimination, so we didn't expect what came along with economic reform. The changes to the constitution were all retreating from previous laws. For example, women's position was very high in socialist law, compared to other countries. Other countries used to look to China's law for examples of laws that gave rights to women. That was the first stage.

Then I went to the United States, after 1995. I wasn't in China for a whole year. It seemed like another world. After I returned, the difference between rich and poor was increasingly clear. I was shocked by these changes. Gender became society's rhetoric but it also became a cover-up. Everyone called the situation a "gender problem," thereby making the problems seem small. It was a new kind of violence, redistributing the wealth and also sacrificing women in the process. The government said there was no pressure on women. But the Women's Federation showed there was pressure because they made women step down [from their jobs] more than men. They were exploiting women's labor power. Young women from the countryside became the labor force. Twenty years ago, in the fires that killed so many women, actually those women workers were still not even of age to work.[2] I then realized that talking about gender meant talking about class problems. This is the way the two were linked at that time. At the same time, there were a lot of women's studies programs, but they used theory about middle-class women from Euro-America. There was no way to use that

theory to analyze these women workers. That theory was for women bene-
fiting from the reforms, not these women who were exploited.

So I then began to reanalyze class. There was no way then to talk about
class, although there was a lot of violence involving class. They refused to
use the term "class" (*jieji*), not just intellectuals but also [urban] workers
who had been laid off (*xiagang*). The truth is that this theory of class was
exactly what we needed to discuss what was going on. But everyone had rejected this kind of language and theory. So I went back and reread Marxist
theory. But then I realized that some of this class theory also had problems.
It was not just a problem of grand narrative. Class is not just something
you describe but something Marx created as a way to interpret what was
going on with capitalism. But perhaps it still is effective for people to use to
recognize what is going on in their lives. Then I asked, what is the relation
between these two grand narratives, gender and class?

We can't talk about "women" as a homogeneous group, but this kind of
division by class can also hide the conflict between the countryside and the
city or between different regions of the country. Now middle-class women
could have domestic servants and displace their own oppression onto these
women. There is also the problem of age: they made all women retire at
forty-five years old in the factories. So even middle-aged women are dis-
criminated against.

Marxism doesn't resolve all these problems. I found myself still thinking through the relation between gender and class and their differences. I
didn't want to be a kind of feminist who left out these other problems, who
did "only" feminism. It had become a middle-class thing. I left off this kind
of feminism.

I decided not to be a feminist specialist. But it is intrinsic, so there is
always a feminist center to my thinking, but there is also a class analysis. I
began to participate in different class-based women's activism. It was the
first time I had participated in this kind of activism since I had started
teaching. I was a volunteer, not a leader. I just helped out and did things
according to what they wanted me to do, in these local small organizations
that addressed women's problems. It has been a very satisfying experience.
They understood me, when I lectured, even though I have often been criticized for using language difficult to understand. They understood, even as
I changed some of my language, though not my analysis. It gave them some
kind of satisfaction. I am aware that I sympathize with these lower class

women who are exploited but I am a middle-class woman. I sometimes ask what use is all that I do for society.

And still, there was an aporia in my theory. But I also saw it in academic life in China. I began third-world investigations and participated in the World Social Forum. I participated in the environmental movement, in the rural reconstruction movement, which encourages collectives and ecological awareness.

Theoretically, what kind of thinking is possible in this moment? I find three levels in my work. The first is theoretical: do we need a new historical subject (*zhuti*)? How do we avoid a grand narrative? How do we avoid using historical subjects such as proletariat but how do we still think about capitalists? And do we need utopia? The second level is the cultural battleground, the media. I want to put my voice out there. I want to interact with the mainstream, but I don't want to become mainstream. The third level is volunteer work, helping the lower classes to recover their collectivity, their communities. Then they can be stronger to develop answers to their problems. Then we can respond to the exploitation of capitalists. We have to feel about for the problem form. I have suspicions about microfinance. I have suspicions about this form of collectivity because it pulls women into a capitalist way of life. But there are other kinds of organizations where women in the countryside organize themselves. They don't want NGOs involved or this kind of microcredit stuff. I want to keep these three levels separate. I don't want to use my volunteer work to write another book. I don't want to have a sense of moral righteousness.

We can use feminist theory to analyze women's lives, but we can actually use it to analyze the most important social problems: to respond to the violence and exploitation of society, to recognize difference. This is the last utopia of the twentieth century that is still left. The others have already been discarded. As Derrida said, Marxism is already a ghost, a ghost of capitalism. But feminism is still something people dream of reaching, even as there are still contradictions in this dream.

NOTES

Series Editor's Preface

1 For a detailed examination of historical and contemporary understandings of the term *tianxia*, see Wang, *Chinese Visions of World Order.*
2 Borges, "On Exactitude in Science," 325.

Editor's Introduction

1 See Zhou, "Rethinking the Cultural History of Chinese Film," 235–63; and Wan, "The Island of the Day Before," 16–17.
2 The phrase "history experienced reconstruction" is Zhou Yaqin's. See Zhou, "Rethinking the Cultural History of Chinese Film," 239.
3 Harney and Moten, *The Undercommons.*
4 For a brief biography of Dai in English, see Jing Wang and Tani E. Barlow, "Introduction."
5 See Zhong, *Masculinity Besieged?*
6 Dai uses quotation marks around the geopolitical entity of "China" to emphasize the competing and historically shifting narratives about how to define this entity. Is it a sick victim of colonialism or an anticolonial fighter? Is it a leader of the third world? Is it a powerful new entity that has left the socialist past far behind, or does the socialist past continue to haunt this place called China? Is it a homogeneous culture or one riven by various conflictual differences?

Introduction

1 [By "the other side," Dai refers to the West.—Ed.]
2 Hardt and Negri, *Multitude.*
3 Amin, *Eurocentrism*, 8.
4 Marcos, "The Fourth World Has Begun."
5 The three principles are that the party must always represent the requirements for developing China's advanced productive forces, the orientation of

China's advanced culture, and the fundamental interests of the overwhelming majority of the Chinese people.

6 Perhaps I should mention a 2003 episode that seems insignificant at first glance: rural land policy abolished the regulation of distributing land on the basis of minimal per capita entitlement to a certain amount of land. This means that, in an urban-rural dual system, the urban-born children of peasants working in cities, or second-generation migrant workers, will become China's potentially landless peasants.

7 Fei, *Xiangtu Zhongguo*.

8 [The May Fourth Movement is viewed as a founding moment of Chinese nationalism and modernization. Begun on May 4, 1919, to protest the Treaty of Versailles that allowed Japanese takeover of Chinese territory, the movement sparked an anticolonial, nationalist movement that also attacked Chinese tradition. Chinese urban intellectuals articulated their criticism of traditional cultural values, especially those from Confucianism, and called for radical Westernization of Chinese culture in order to modernize the country. One of the key components of the movement was the vernacularization of written Chinese, what the author is calling classical Chinese.—Ed.]

Chapter 1. I Want to Be Human

1 After the Japanese army seized the Chinese capital, Nanjing, it carried out murder, torture, rape, and looting on a massive scale. The horror of this massacre was exacerbated by the fact that many murders were committed in a most primitive manner, using daggers or knives as weapons or burying and burning the victims alive. This incident also involved gang rapes and tortures of men and women as well as the dissection of the bodies of the dead, many cases of which were carried out in Chinese homes in the presence of the elderly and children.

2 For descriptions of how the director sought approval from the central government, see Wang, "Lu Chuan." [Lu Chuan's earlier works include *Missing Gun* (2002) and *Mountain Patrol: Kekexili* (2004). *Missing Gun* is a black comedy about a small-town policeman searching for his gun. *Mountain Patrol* tells the story of the heroic efforts of a small group of mountain patrollers to stop the illegal poaching of Tibetan antelopes in Kekexili, a region near Tibet. The film presents a realistic depiction of an existing social issue in a suspenseful and melodramatic style.—Trans.] The phrase "Chinese style of resistance" comes from an interview with the director by Liu Wei, Wang Nannan, and Wang Xuguang. The director also states in this interview, "One reason that made me want to make this movie is that in all existing historical representations of the Nanjing Massacre, the Chinese have been portrayed as passive and nonexistent. It is not that they truly did not exist, but their existence as individual and collectivity has been neglected and erased. I have

tried to restore the historical existence of the Chinese through this movie." The headline on this movie's poster is "We are still alive, because we have been resisting." See Liu, Wang, and Wang, "Lu Chuan fangtan."

3 Lu, "A Madman's Diary," 10.

4 Lu Xun describes the slide show incident in the following paragraph: "I don't know what advanced methods are now used to teach microbiology, but at that time lantern slides were used to show the microbes, and if the lecture ended early, the instructor might show slides of natural scenery or news to fill up the time. This was during the Russo-Japanese War, so there were many war films, and I had to join in the clapping and cheering in the lecture hall along with the other students. It was a long time since I had seen any compatriots, but one day I saw a film showing some Chinese, one of whom was bound, while many others stood around him. They were all strong fellows but appeared completely apathetic. According to the commentary, the one with his hands bound was a spy working for the Russians, who was to have his head cut off by the Japanese military as a warning to others, while the Chinese beside him had come to enjoy the spectacle" (Lu, preface to "A Madman's Diary," 4).

5 Lu, "A Madman's Diary."

6 [The discourse of "Chinese national character" refers to a series of discussions among Chinese intellectuals starting in the late 1910s about the flaws of Chinese culture and people. Although the aim of these discussions was to seek self-improvement through self-criticism, this discourse bears complex connections with the orientalist representations of Chinese people by missionary writers and risks essentializing Chinese culture. For further reading on this subject, see Liu, *Translingual Practice*.—Trans.]

7 [This line comes from *Bai Mao Nu* (*The White-Haired Girl*, dir. Wang Bin and Shui Hua, 1951), a film that depicts the liberation of a slave girl by the Communist Party. The film was adapted from an opera of the same time by He Jingzhi and Ting Yi.—Trans.]

8 "Scar literature" or "literature of the wounded" refers to a literary genre of the late 1970s that portrays the sufferings of intellectuals during the Cultural Revolution.

9 Zong, "Wo shi shui," 88–99.

10 [The film script *Ku lian* (*Bitter Love*) was published in the literary magazine *Shi Yue* (October) in March 1979. Director Peng Ning made the film *Tai yang yu ren* (*The Sun and the Human*) based on this script in 1980, produced by Changchun Film Studio. On April 20, 1981, *Jiefangjun Bao* (the People's Liberation Army daily) published an editorial titled "Sixiang jiben yuanze bu yong weifan: Ping dianying wenxue juben 'Ku lian'" (We cannot tolerate any violation of the four basic principles: On the film script "Bitter Love") by the newspaper's Special Commentator. After that, a series of critical articles from official sources was published. This criticism of *Bitter Love* is often regarded as the beginning of a new movement of cultural discipline and political per-

secution in the era of the Reform. It even caused social unrest, which was quickly suppressed.—Trans.]

11 [The June 4 incident refers to the Tiananmen protest and crackdown in 1989, when protesters gathered in Tiananmen Square demanding political reform and democracy. This movement was repressed on June 4, 1989.—Trans.]

12 Lu used the phrase "a love story in the style of *Titanic*" in a television interview. He Dong, interview with Lu Chuan, *Fenghuang Feichang Dao*.

13 See the article on the movie's official website, titled "Nanjing! Nanjing! Ba da miankong: Renxing de huanyuan."

14 Lu, "Duihua Lu Chuan."

15 It needs to be mentioned that these acts of violence were widely publicized and severely condemned by Chinese citizens from various social sectors and by international society even as they were being carried out.

16 Rabe, *La Bei Riji*; Wickert, *The Good Man of Nanking*.

17 Wang, Bai, and Chang, "Lu Chuan."

18 One scene of the movie shows a Japanese soldier, Ida, murdering a girl by hurling her out the window.

19 The film's emphasis on interiority can also be observed in its depiction of Ida, a foil of Kadokawa, whose hardened exterior and insanely sadistic psychology contrast with Kadokawa's healthy but sensitive constitution. Ida's sadism leads him not so much to torture Chinese civilians as to torment their souls. For instance, he tries to destroy Jiang's Christian faith and take advantage of Tang, an assistant to Rabe, who desires to protect his family. The implication of this emphasis on the psychological is that it humanizes the murderer. Not only does Kadokawa redeem his humanity in his tormented act of saving the beautiful Jiang by shooting her, but Ida appears to be more humane when he is shown to be having a man-to-man, or human-to-human, talk with Tang after Tang has decided to sacrifice his life for others. He cannot help but wear a lonely and sad expression after he has given the order to execute Tang.

20 The historical figure Rabe has another function, in addition to serving as a direct allusion to the Nanjing Massacre: his presence enables the movie's focus to fall onto the refugee camp, a historically verifiable detail from *La Bei Riji* (The diaries of Rabe). The movie manages to depict this massacre by shuttling between two symbolic settings of Nanjing: in one setting, we see a panoramic representation of the city, where siege, resistance, murder, rape inside the comfort station, and celebration of the seizure of Nanjing take place; in the other setting (the refugee camp), we see mostly the drama of the Chinese characters and no mass murder or rape. The refugee camp as a zone of exceptionality provides a logical justification for the absence of scenes of mass murder and underwrites the humanism of this movie. We can say that the internal struggles of the Japanese soldier and the setting of the refugee camp both frame the movie's historical representation, turning it into a story about humanism, not mass murder and the collapse of humanism.

21 [The first Sino-Japanese War was fought between Qing dynasty China and Meiji Japan from 1894 to 1895. The second Sino-Japanese War took place between 1937 and 1945.—Trans.]

22 Yuan, "Dianyingju fujuzhang."

23 *Daguo Jueqi* (The rise of the great nations) is a twelve-episode television documentary made by Channel 2 of Chinese Central TV in 2006. It depicts the successive rise of great nations, including Portugal, Spain, Holland, England, France, Germany, Russia, Japan, and the United States. Song et al., *Zhongguo bu gaoxing.*

24 Foucault, *Society Must Be Defended*, 8.

25 See He Dong, interview with Lu Chuan.

26 Wu and Jin, "Lu Chuan."

Chapter 2. Hero *and the Invisible* Tianxia

1 Fan, *Yueyang Pavilion.*

2 [In other words, the film does not have the logic of the ancient tales of swordsmen wandering the world, which would be "self-cultivation." That logic means that self-cultivation leads to family harmony, proper state governance, and world peace. Instead, the film has a modern logic of wanting to be with one's girlfriend.—Ed.]

3 [These phrases are usually invoked to describe Western cowboy films. Dai Jinhua is deliberately playing with those tropes here to describe Chinese films.—Ed.]

4 [The Hong Kong writer Jin Yong (or Louis Cha) and the Taiwanese author Gu Long are two of the most famous martial arts novelists in the modern Sinophone world, whose works have been perennial best-sellers and adapted for TV and film in the greater China region.—Ed.]

5 [These are classical phrases to describe earlier periods of Chinese history, especially the period known as the Warring States (475–221 BCE), when smaller kingdoms vied for control over one another. The Qin kingdom eventually won, bringing the various kingdoms into one unified empire. These phrases have also been used to describe the period known as the Three Kingdoms (220–280 CE), when the unified Han dynasty (206 BCE—220 CE) was divided into three states. The third of these phrases, "grand ambitions vie for supremacy" (逐鹿问鼎), is based on the original phrase, 逐鹿中原, from Sima Qian's (司马迁) *Records of the Grand Historian* (史记), the chapter titled "Ranked Biography of Marquise Huaiyin" (淮阴侯列传), written during the Han dynasty and then later revised to refer to the Warring States and the Three Kingdoms' battles for supremacy and control over tianxia.—Ed.]

6 [Jianghu literally means rivers and lakes. In contrast to tianxia, which refers to a world order legitimized through the state, jianghu refers to nongovernmental or, better to say, antigovernmental space, such as the world of

martial heroes and the modern-day world of gangsters and criminal secret societies.—Ed.]

7 [Majia, which literally means "vest," is popular cyber lingo in China, referring to an online ID registered by an existing member of an online community for the purpose of deception or anonymity. It is similar to what is called a sock puppet in the U.S.—Trans.]

8 [The novelists and film directors who called themselves a new school of martial arts literary and cinematic production include Jing Yong, Liang Yusheng (novelists), Hu Jingquan (King Hu), and Chang Che (film directors).—Trans.]

9 [*Shuihu zhuan*, or *Outlaws of the Marsh*, attributed to Shi Nai'an (施耐庵), is a popular classic novel about a peasant uprising during the Northern Song dynasty (960–1127). This phrase comes from chapter nineteen of the novel. Here, the Zhao royal family is the ruling family of the Song.—Ed.]

10 [The term Jiuzhou (Nine Provinces or Nine Regions) first appears in *Yugong*—a text accepted as the earliest geographical document in the Confucian canon—to refer to territorial divisions during the Xia (a quasi-legendary dynasty) and Shang (1766–1122 BCE) dynasties, and has now come to symbolically represent China.—Ed.]

11 [Jiangnan refers to the area in China south of the Yangtze River. This author, who was named the richest writer in China in 2013, has clearly chosen this term as his pen name.—Ed.]

12 [Tianxia, as a concept about the universe, is a key component in Confucianism by which the tributary system was rationalized and explained in premodern China. More than the natural world or a geographical notion of the globe, tianxia was also the moral Confucian concept by which the political order was universally defined; whereas Zhongguo, literally the Middle Kingdom or the central state, was used to refer to the center of the extended Chinese world (tianxia). In the late nineteenth and early twentieth centuries, when the Western idea of an international order of nation-states challenged the Chinese notion of tianxia, the term Zhongguo began to take on a statist sense to denote China as a nation-state. At the same time, shijie, adopted from Japanese, became a neologism in modern China to refer to the Western concept of the world.—Ed.]

13 For an explanation of the May Fourth Movement, see author's introduction, note 8.

14 [Dai uses Deleuze's concept of the fold to emphasize that the seeming interior of a phenomenon, concept, or practice always already contains its exterior. See Deleuze, *The Fold*.—Ed.]

15 ["Middle Kingdom" is the literal translation of the characters used for what we today call China—itself a term from the Latin *Sina*.—Ed.]

16 See Hobsbawm, *Nation and Nationalism since 1780*.

17 [The name the Qin king chose to be called after unification, Shihuang, literally translates as "first emperor."—Ed.]

18 Dai, "Screening the Celebration," 181.

19 In 2003, the CCP changed its self-designation from revolutionary party to ruling party (*zhizheng dang*). A new goal—to protect private property—was put into the Chinese constitution; the CCP encouraged private entrepreneurs to become party members; and the party-state decided there would no longer be continuous reassessments and redivisions of rural land, depending on changing sizes of households. This decision meant that younger generations would no longer necessarily inherit land in the countryside.

20 Victors decide history, even as memories have been eviscerated.

21 Dai, *Gender China*, 162–65.

22 [Written by the Han historian Sima Qian (ca. 145–90 BCE), *Shiji*, or *Records of the Grand Historian*, is a masterpiece of historical writing about China and the world from ancient times to his contemporary period. Finished around 109 BCE, it is divided into "Annals," "Treatises," "Biographies," and so on, a form that was adopted in the twenty-four "Dynastic Histories"—the official accounts compiled to cover all the dynasties from the time of Sima Qian.—Ed.]

23 [This phrase apparently comes from a letter written by Mao Zedong to his wife Jiang Qing. This famous quote can be found in many places. See Jin Chongji, "The Cultural Revolution's Ten Years of Chaos."—Ed.]

24 [Written by Tang poet Luo Binwang, *Tao Wu Zhao Xi* (Denunciation of Empress Wu) is a denunciation of the usurpation by the empress Wu Zetian (624–705) during the Tang dynasty. Supporting Li Jingye's rebellion against Wu Zetian, Luo Binwang drafted this denunciation, the formal title of which is *Dai Li Jingye Chuan Xi Tianxia Wen* (Declaration of war against Wu Zhao on behalf of Li Jingye).—Ed.]

25 Li, *The History of the Southern Dynasties*, vol. 5, 1473.

26 The war to liberate all humanity.

Chapter 3. Temporality, Nature Morte

1 [As explained later in the essay, Shen Hong came to the Three Gorges dam to look for her long-absent husband, who has been working there.—Ed.]

2 [Words in square brackets have been added by the editor.—Ed.]

3 Xiao Ma is one of Han Sanming's coworkers.

4 [For a brief description of the May Fourth Movement, see author's introduction, note 8.—Ed.]

5 Mao, "Water Song: Swimming," 1; Mao, "Reply to Comrade Guo Moro."

6 This is from a popular Cultural Revolution song, derived from a folk song of Ankang, Shaanxi province, called "I Am Here" (我来了). It first appeared during the Great Leap Forward.

7 The quote is from Mao, "On Coalition Government," a report he made at the CCP's seventh national congress meeting.

8   [By "new person," Dai refers to the figure prominent in presocialist literature of the first half of the twentieth century.—Ed.]

9   The phrase "sent-down youth" refers to urban youth who were sent to the countryside during the Cultural Revolution to learn from the peasants.

10 Wu Yusen (吴宇森), English name John Woo (Ng Yu-Sum), Chinese-born Hong Kong film director, writer, and producer. He is a major influence on the action genre. He has directed several notable Hong Kong action films: *A Better Tomorrow* (英雄本色, 1986), *The Killers* (喋血双雄, 1989), *Hard Boiled* (辣手神探, 1992). His Hollywood credits include action films *Hard Target* (1993) and *Broken Arrow* (1996), sci-fi action thriller *Face/Off* (1997), and action spy film *Mission: Impossible 2* (2000).

11 His "name," Xiao Ma, just means Little Ma, Ma being the surname. No one ever calls him by his first name.

12 What Han Sanming would have to pay his wife's brother to get him to desist from selling her to a labor boss.

13 [Dai is arguing that although psychoanalytical theory would have us treat the abuser and the abused as a pair, namely, the exploiter and the exploited, even in this sense they are not "harmoniously" matched. Dai is further playing on the Chinese government slogan emphasizing a "harmonious society."—Ed.]

14 Wu, Hong, and Boyi Feng curated *Micro-narratives: Zhang Xiaotao and Li Yifan's Social Graphics*, exhibition at Beijing 798 Iberian Art Gallery, August 2008 [微观叙事: 张小涛+李一凡的社会图像 2008年8月, 在北京798伊比利亚当代艺术中心].

Chapter 4. The Piano in a Factory

1   [This is the literal translation of the Chinese title of the film.—Ed.]

2   This was the film's advertising catchphrase.

3   Zhao, "A Lost Social Class."

4   Chen Kaige, lecture.

5   Li, "Between Reality and Absurdity," 26.

6   Yi, "Zhang Meng Uses Absurdity to Illuminate Reality."

7   [In Chinese funeral rituals, the deceased are accompanied in their journey to heaven by various paper objects and figures, including paper money and paper servants, among other things.—Ed.]

8   [Shuzhen is one of the laid-off workers.—Ed.]

9   Du, "500-Character Poem," 2265. [Du Fu was a Tang dynasty poet who lived 712–770.—Ed.]

10 Liu, presentation at "Representations: History and Memory."

11 Wang Gong, or Engineer Wang, is a retired engineer who studied in the Soviet Union. He is invited by Chen Guilin to offer technical support for his piano-making project. He is viewed by Chen Guilin and his former cowork-

ers as better educated—an "intellectual"—and equipped with better knowledge of machine making.

12 [A mockumentary by Jia Zhangke, *24 City* portrays a former industrial factory being turned into a middle-class condominium building. The café and art gallery space now known as 798 is an actual large, former industrial factory space in northeastern Beijing.

13 Jiang, "'I Don't Make Guns, I Only Make a Steel Piano.'"

14 "Zhang Meng Explains *The Piano in a Factory*."

15 Jiang, "'I Don't Make Guns, I Only Make a Steel Piano.'" Zhang Meng saw a piano that workers had made during the Cultural Revolution. This is the origin of the film's plotline.

16 Liu, presentation at "Representations: History and Memory."

17 Zhao, "A Lost Social Class."

18 [Wang Shuo is a well-known contemporary novelist who relies on deep irony to tell his stories. His writings are social commentaries, full of biting humor, on contemporary life in China.—Ed.]

19 An interesting reference point is Wang Bing's (王兵) *West of the Tracks* (铁西区), part 2, which portrays adolescent lives in factory districts in a manner remarkably similar to works from the 1960s British New Wave. Rather than any real intertextual references, this is due far more to similar realities in different countries and historical periods.

20 Xue, "Special Interview with Director Zhang Meng," 6.

21 In fact, postwar East Germany remained the most industrialized country in the entire Soviet socialist camp. Perhaps this is why *The Piano in a Factory* chose mostly East German music.

22 Wu, "The Melancholia of the Chinese Working Class."

23 Li, "Between Reality and Absurdity."

24 Li, "Between Reality and Absurdity." ["Iron rice bowl" is a term popularized at the beginning of economic reform in the 1980s to disparage the system of a guaranteed lifetime job with benefits.—Ed.]

25 Xue, "Special Interview with Director Zhang Meng."

26 [*The Twilight Samurai* (2002) is a Japanese historical drama about the trials and tribulations of a low-ranking samurai.—Ed.]

Chapter 5. The Spy-Film Legacy

[The first phrase in the Chinese title of this article, 谍影重重, which literally means "layers and layers of spy films," is also the mainland Chinese title for the films in the Jason Bourne series, the latest of which is *The Bourne Legacy*.—Trans.]

1 [The term "quasi-genre" (准类型) is a coinage by the author, who contends that unlike the generic or subgeneric divisions of Hollywood film, Chinese

film does not divide into distinct genres and subgenres. The spy film is a partial exception to this, hence the designation "quasi-genre." This qualification should be kept in mind in all her uses of "genre," "subgenre," and "quasi-genre" (personal communication with the author).—Trans.]

2 This was a common way to describe these narratives at the time.

3 See Luo, "Shijiande baoli / jiyide zhengzhi."

4 *Secrets of Counterespionage*, also titled in English *Secret Agent*, was directed by Boris Barnet for the Kiev Film Studios in 1947, and released in translation in 1950 by the Dongbei Studios. *The Greatest Reward* was directed in 1938 by Evgeny Schneider for the Soviet Children's Film Studio. The film was released in China in 1953 by the Changchun Film Studios.

5 Films include *The Greatest Reward*, *Spy-Catching on the Ocean Floor* (тайна двух океанов, dir. Konstantine Pipinashvili, 1955), *In Times of Peace* (в мирные дин, dir. Vladimir Braun, 1951), and others.

6 Actors included Oyang Shafei, Zhou Chu, and Dong Shumin.

7 "Washed away . . ." was a common joke among Taiwan scholars.

8 See Zhao, "Manchangde lu, jianxinde lu."

9 In the early 1950s, Soviet "counterespionage" novels were translated and published in great numbers in China. Although they were fairly crude and were rarely taken seriously as literature, they were one literary form that effectively substituted for the mass popular urban literature of the 1930s and '40s. *The Destruction of the Bandit Lair* (匪巢覆灭记, original by Boris Vasiliev, no Russian title), one example of the genre, was reprinted six times between 1953 and 1954.

10 See Yang, *Wenge shiqide dixia wenxue*.

11 See Bai, *Anliu*; Zhang, *Yizhi Xiuhuaxie, Meihuadang, Lüse shiti*.

12 This refers to the films from the late 1960s through the middle 1970s that took political affairs as their primary subject matter, which were also referred to as "political films." They depicted real political events and political movements and individual characters' relationship to these events and movements, as reflected in their actions and their fates. These films originated in France and later spread to western Europe, northern Europe, Latin America, Japan, and the United States. Italian political films were especially important.

13 Žižek, "Alfred Hitchcock, or, The Form and Its Historical Mediation."

14 *The Eternal Secret* (Yongyuande mimi) was another translation of the title of the Soviet film *Secrets of Counterespionage*. See note 4.

15 [In the socialist era, and perhaps most prominently in China, the government often chose "model workers," "model soldiers," "model households," "model villages," "model communes," and so on. They would be lauded in the media and given medals.—Ed.]

16 For a related discussion, see my essay "Cong shehui xiangzheng dao zhengzhi shenhua," 116–18.

17 In my view, this transformation and its mode of visual presentation first matures in Sun Yu's silent film *The Big Road* (大路, 1934). It differed from the representation of women in early advertising and as "calendar girls" in that the image of the woman was made to serve as symbol of the "nation" or "New China."

18 See Mulvey, "Visual Pleasure and Narrative Cinema," 6–18.

19 [The Hollywood imitation of *Infernal Affairs* is Martin Scorsese's *The Departed* (2006).—Ed.]

Chapter 6. In Vogue

1 [The term is taken from Lian, *Ant Tribe*. It refers to those young college graduates seeking opportunities in the cities, having no stable jobs and no social security.—Ed.]

2 Feng, "At *Lust, Caution* Premiere, Fans Shouting 'Long Live Ang Lee Movie!'"

3 Huang, "China Has Already Stood Up but Ang Lee Is Still Kneeling Down"; Liu, "*Lust, Caution* Glorifies Traitors." [The essays were widely linked and posted.—Ed.]

4 Chang, "Break the Caution of Lust."

5 In fact, there were more than two versions around the globe.

6 [Words in square brackets have been added by the translators.—Ed.]

7 These were mainstream media themes at the time.

8 Gu and Wei, "Crisscrossing Fates."

9 Ma, "Ang Lee's *Lust and Caution*."

10 Yu, "Ang Lee."

11 Xia, *Lust, Caution*; Cai, *Eileen Chang's Lust Caution*.

12 Eileen Chang was eager to explain the archetype of her stories. Yet she strongly refused to relate *Lust, Caution* to the Zheng affair. However, how she came to know the details of the incident remains a mystery.

13 Huang Ji-su, interview, *New York Times*, November 20, 2007.

14 Chen, "Eileen Chang and the Historiography of Taiwan Literature"; Qiu, "From Eileen Chang to the Making of Taiwan Female Literature Tradition."

15 Jiang Yong, interview with Ang Lee, "For the Thousand Generations to Come, It Is Nothing to Drive a Few to Death."

16 [Utopia Net is a website, http://www.wyzxwk.com/, that has since closed.—Ed.]

17 Abeel, "IndieWire Interview, 'Lust, Caution' Director Ang Lee."

18 Latham, *Modernization as Ideology*.

19 [No film or advertising content featuring Tang Wei was allowed to be shown in mainland China under this ban. The ban was lifted only three years later, in 2010.—Ed.]

20 Fu, "Spy Ring, Cinema Circle."

21 Song et al., *Zhongguo bu gaoxing*.

22 Qiu, "*Lust, Caution* in Taiwan."

1   [The "trauma of witnessing" is a concept Dai borrows from the literature on the Holocaust; it can also be rendered "crisis of witnessing." See Felman and Laub, *Testimony.*—Trans.]

2   [The "short twentieth century" refers, by contrast, to Arrighi's notion of the "long twentieth century." See Arrighi, *The Long Twentieth Century.* Here it refers to the century of revolution bounded by 1911–89 or 1917–89.—Trans.]

3   [Words in square brackets throughout this essay have been added by the translator.—Ed.]

4   Huang, *Wang Guangmei Discusses Liu Shaoqi's Last Years*, 1–13. [Wang Guangmei was a Chinese politician and first lady, Liu Shaoqi's spouse. Liu Shaoqi was president of the PRC 1959–68—Ed.] Hu, *On Pragmatism*, 208–48.

5   Lu, "Postscript," 209. [Lu Xun was one of the most famous leftist writers of the early twentieth century.—Ed.] The interesting part is that those whom Lu Xun had labeled "the weak peoples"—Eastern Europeans—were precisely where Europe and the world encountered one another and where the "third world" actually resided.

6   [*Fan'an wenzhang* (翻案文章) means the overturning of cases in which individuals were labeled counter-revolutionaries.—Ed.]

7   Letter from Mao Zedong to Yang Shaoyi and Ye Yanming of January 9, 1944. The original text reads, "History is made by the people, and yet on the old stage (those literary and cultural works that are not of the people), the people were rendered irrelevant: the platform ruled by the gentry gentlemen, ladies, young misters and misses, these were reversed by you, and now you need to reverse it all again in order to restore the original face of history. We need to open a new phase of history based upon this old version, so we need to celebrate it." In Chinese Communist Party Editorial Group, *Mao Zedong Shuxin xuanji*, 222.

8   [*River Elegy* was a collectively produced six-part documentary aired on China Central Television that portrayed traditional Chinese culture as stagnant and the cause of China's seeming weakness in relation to the West, especially, as posited by the series, China's supposed refusal to embrace overseas expansion. After the 1989 Tiananmen demonstrations, some of the filmmakers were arrested while others fled the country.—Ed.]

9   As for China's "superstable structure" of feudal society, this is Jin Guantao's and Liu Qingfeng's early 1980s perspective. It had a huge social and intellectual influence at the time. Jin and Liu, *Zhongguo fengjian shehui*, 2. This was later published as a book: Jin and Liu, *Lishi de Chensi.* It was then developed into another book: Jin and Liu, *Xingsheng yu weiji.* "Root seeking" or "root-seeking literature" was one of the most important trends and schools in China at the beginning and through the middle of the 1980s. The name

comes from a short essay by Han Shaogong, "Wenxue de 'gen.'" Representative authors of this trend or school are Han Shaogong, Ah Cheng, Mo Yan, Zheng Yi, Wang Anyi, and Li Rui.

10 Dai, "May Fourth and Film."

Interview with Dai Jinhua

1 Words in square brackets have been added by the editor.
2 Over twenty years ago, the country was shaken by two major factory fires that were early forerunners of how China was becoming the sweatshop of the world. Most of those killed were rural migrant women. One was the 1993 toy factory fire in Shenzhen that killed eighty-one women; the other was a Fujian textile factory, with six women killed.

SELECTED WORKS OF DAI JINHUA

Meng Yue and Dai Jinhua. *Emerging from the Horizon of History: The Study of Modern Women's Literature* [浮出历史地表: 现代妇女文学研究]. Zhengzhou: Henan People, 1989.

Dai Jinhua. *Film Theory and Handbook of Criticism* [电影理论与批评手册]. Beijing: Scientific and Technical Documentation Press, 1993.

Dai Jinhua. *Breaking Out of Encirclement in the Mirror City: A Collection of Essays* [镜城突围: 女性·电影·文学]. Beijing: China Writers, 1995.

Dai Jinhua. *Mirror and Secular Myth: Eighteen Examples of Close Film Reading* [镜与世俗神话: 影片精读18例]. Beijing: China Radio and Television Press, 1995. Reprint, Beijing: China Renmin University Press, 2004.

Dai Jinhua. *Invisible Writing: Chinese Cultural Studies of the 1990s* [隐形书写: 90年代中国文化研究]. Nanjing: Jiangsu People's Press, 1999. Also published as *The Cultural Typography of the Mirror City: Chinese Culture Studies of the 1990s* [戴錦華. 鏡城地形圖: 九十年代中國文化研究]. Taipei: Unitas, 1999; *Hidden Narrative: Reading of 1990s Chinese Culture* [숨겨진 서사: 1990년대 중국 대중문화 읽기]. Seoul: Sookmyung Women's University Press, 2006.

Dai Jinhua. *Piece Together: A Collection of Essays* [拼图游戏]. Jinan: Shandong Taishan, 1999.

Dai Jinhua. *Still in the Mirror: Interviews with Dai Jinhua* [犹在镜中: 戴锦华访谈录]. Beijing: China Knowledge, 1999.

Dai Jinhua. *Scenery in the Fog: Chinese Cinema Culture 1978–1998* [雾中风景: 中国电影文化1978–1998]. Beijing: Peking University Press, 2000. Also published as *Look Over from the Leaning Tower: Chinese Cinema Culture 1978–1998* [戴錦華. 斜塔瞭望: 中國電影文化1978–1998]. Taipei: Yuan-Liou, 1999; *Scenery in the Fog: Chinese Movie and Culture 1978–1998* [무중풍경: 중국영화문화 1978–1998]. Pusan: Sanjini, 2007.

Dai Jinhua. *Writing Cultural Heroes: Cultural Studies at the Turn of the Century* [书写文化英雄: 世纪之交的文化研究]. Nanjing: Jiangsu People, 2000.

Dai Jinhua. *Cinema and Desire: Feminist Marxism and Cultural Politics in the Work of Dai Jinhua*. Edited by Jing Wang and Tani E. Barlow. New York: Verso, 2002.

Dai Jinhua. *The Fording Boat: Female Writing and Female Culture in Reform Era*

China [涉渡之舟：新时期中国女性写作与女性文化]. Xi'an: Shanxi People's Education Press, 2002.

Dai Jinhua. *Imprint* [印痕]. Shijiazhuang: Hebei Education, 2002.

Dai Jinhua. *Film Criticism* [电影批评]. Beijing: Peking University Press, 2004.

Dai Jinhua. *Gender China: The Gender Scene in 100 Years of Chinese Cinema* [性別中國：共同鋪演中國電影百年的性別風景]. Taipei: Rye Field, 2006. Also published as *The Gender Politics of Chinese Cinema: Cultural Politics of Post–Cold War Era* [戴錦華.中国映画のジェンダー・ポリティクス：ポスト冷戦時代の文化政治. Tokyo: Ochanomizushobo, 2006; *Gender China: Chinese Movie and Gender Rhetoric* [성별중국: 중국영화와 젠더수사학]. Seoul: Yeoiyeon, 2009.

Dai Jinhua and Liu Jianzhi, trans. and eds. *The Masked Knight: Selected Works of Subcomandante Marcos* [蒙面骑士：墨西哥副司令马科斯文集]. Shanghai: Shanghai People, 2006.

Dai Jinhua. *The Trace of Sandglass* [沙漏之痕]. Jinan: Shandong Friendship, 2006.

Dai Jinhua. *Film Theory and Criticism* [电影理论与批评]. Beijing: Peking University Press, 2007.

Dai Jinhua, ed. *Interspace of Light and Shadow: Film Workshop 2010* [光影之隙：电影工作坊2010]. Beijing: Peking University Press, 2011.

Dai Jinhua, ed. *Reminiscences of Light and Shadow: Film Workshop 2011* [光影之忆：电影工作坊2011]. Beijing: Peking University Press, 2012.

Dai Jinhua, ed. *Traces of Light and Shadow: Film Workshop 2012* [光影之痕：电影工作坊2012]. Beijing: Peking University Press, 2013.

Dai Jinhua and Sun Bai. *The Cinematic Chronicle of "Hamlet"* [‹‹哈姆雷特››的影舞编年]. Shanghai: Shanghai People's Press, 2014.

Dai Jinhua and Teng Wei. *The Cinematic Reincarnation of Jane Eyre* [‹‹简·爱››的光影转世]. Shanghai: Shanghai People's Press, 2014.

Dai Jinhua. *The Island of the Day Before: Self-Selected Film Critique of Dai Jinhua* [昨日之岛：戴锦华电影文章自选集]. Beijing: Peking University Press, 2015.

Dai Jinhua. *A Key with No Name* [未名之匙]. Shanghai: Fudan University Press, 2015.

BIBLIOGRAPHY

Abeel, Erica. "IndieWire Interview, 'Lust, Caution' Director Ang Lee." *IndieWire*, September 26, 2007. http://www.indiewire.com/2007/09/indiewire -interview-lust-caution-director-ang-lee-73818/.

Amin, Samir. *Eurocentrism: Modernity, Religion and Democracy.* Translated by Russell Moore and James Membrez. New York: Monthly Review Press, [1988] 2009.

Arrighi, Giovanni. *Adam Smith in Beijing: Lineages of the Twenty-First Century.* New York: Verso, 2007.

Arrighi, Giovanni. *The Long Twentieth Century: Money, Power and the Origins of Our Times.* New York: Verso, 1994.

Badiou, Alain. *Hypothèse Communiste.* Paris: Éditions Lignes. Published in English as *The Communist Hypothesis*, translated by David Macy and Steve Corcoran. New York: Verso, 2010.

Bai Shihong, ed. *Anliu: Wenge shouchao wencun* [Undercurrent: A collection of Cultural Revolution handwritten literature]. Beijing: Wenyi chubanshe, 2001.

Borges, Jorge Luis. "On Exactitude in Science." In *Collected Fictions*, translated by Andrew Hurley, 325. London: Penguin, 1999.

Cai Dengshan. *Eileen Chang's Lust Caution* [张爱玲《色·戒》]. Beijing: Writer Press, 2007.

Chang Hsiao-hung. "Break the Caution of Lust." *China Times* (Taiwan), September 28–29, 2007.

Chang, Iris. *The Rape of Nanking: The Forgotten Holocaust of World War II.* New York: Basic Books, 1997.

Chen Fang-ming. "Eileen Chang and the Historiography of Taiwan Literature" [张爱玲与台湾文学史编撰]. In *Reading Eileen Chang* [阅读张爱玲], ed. Yang Ze. Taipei: Rye Field, 1999.

Chen Kaige. Lecture presented at Beijing Film Academy [北京电影学院], Beijing, September 1984.

Chinese Communist Party Editorial Group, ed. *Mao Zedong Shuxin xuanji* [The collected letters of Mao Zedong]. Beijing: Renmin chubanshe, 1983.

Dai Jinhua. *Cinema and Desire: Feminist Marxism and Cultural Politics in the*

Work of Dai Jinhua. Edited by Jing Wang and Tani E. Barlow. New York: Verso, 2002.

Dai Jinhua. "Cong shehui xiangzheng dao zhengzhi shenhua: cuiwei yishu shijie yiyu" [From social symbolism to political mythology: From the margins of high art]. In *Dianying lilun yu piping shouce* [Handbook of film theory and criticism], 116–18. Beijing: Kexue jishu wenxian chubanshe, 1993.

Dai Jinhua. *Gender China: The Gender Scene in 100 Years of Chinese Cinema* [性別中國：共同鋪演中國電影百年的性別風景]. Taipei: Rye Field, 2006.

Dai Jinhua. "May Fourth and Film" [五·四与电影]. *Film Art* [电影艺术], no. 3 (2007): 34–37.

Dai Jinhua. "Screening the Celebration: Chinese Film in the New Millennium." In *The Island of the Day Before: Dai Jinhua's Selected Film Essays.* Beijing: Beijing University Press, 2015.

Deleuze, Gilles. *The Fold: Leibniz and the Baroque.* Translated by Tom Conley. Minneapolis: University of Minnesota Press, 1993.

Du Fu. "500-Character Poem: A Reflection on the Road from the Capital to Feng Xian Town" [自京赴奉先县咏怀五百字]. In *A Complete Collection of Tang Dynasty Poems* [全唐诗], vol. 7, 2265. Beijing: Zhonghua Shuju, 1980.

Fan Zhongyan. *Yueyang Pavilion* [岳阳楼记]. In *Guwen Guanzhi* [古文观止], vol. 9, 419–21. Beijing: Zhonghua Shuju, 1959.

Fei Xiaotong. *Xiangtu Zhongguo.* Shanghai: Guancha, 1948. Published in English as *From the Soil: The Foundations of Chinese Society.* Translated by Gary G. Hamilton and Wang Zheng. Berkeley: University of California Press, 1992.

Felman, Shoshana, and Dori Laub. *Testimony: Crises of Witnessing in Literature, Psychoanalysis, and History.* New York: Routledge, 1991.

Feng Ze. "At *Lust, Caution* Premiere, Fans Shouting 'Long Live Ang Lee Movie!'" *Metro Express,* January 11, 2007.

Foucault, Michel. *Society Must Be Defended.* New York: Picador, 2003.

Fu Zhongli. "Spy Ring, Cinema Circle: The *Lust, Caution* Story by Stephen Soong and Edward Yang" [间谍圈 电影圈, 宋琪和杨德昌的色·戒故事]. *INK Literary Monthly,* August 2007.

Gu Dongting and Wei Yiping. "Crisscrossing Fates: Shanghai, Eileen Chang and Zhang Ping-ru." *Life Weekly,* September 18, 2007.

Han Shaogong. "Wenxue de 'gen'" [The "roots" of literature]. *Changchun* 4 (1985).

Hardt, Michael, and Antonio Negri. *Empire.* Cambridge, MA: Harvard University Press, 2000.

Hardt, Michael, and Antonio Negri. *Multitude: War and Democracy in the Age of Empire.* New York: Penguin, 2004.

Harney, Stefano, and Fred Moten. *The Undercommons: Fugitive Planning and Black Study.* Port Watson: Minor Compositions, 2013.

He Dong. Interview with Lu Chuan. *Fenghuang Feichang Dao,* April 14, 2009. http://ent.ifeng.com/feichangdao/200904/0423_5223_1122829_8.shtml.

Hobsbawm, E. J. *Nation and Nationalism since 1780: Programme, Myth, Reality.* Cambridge: Cambridge University Press, 1990.

Hu Shi. *On Pragmatism* [实验主义]. In *The Collected Works of Hu Shi*, vol. 2 [胡适文集第二册], 208–48. Beijing: Beijing University Press, 1998.

Huang Ji-su. "China Has Already Stood Up but Ang Lee Is Still Kneeling Down." 2008. https://baike.baidu.com/item/黄纪苏.

Huang Zheng. *Wang Guangmei Discusses Liu Shaoqi's Last Years* [王光美谈刘少奇的最后岁月]. Beijing: JiuZhou, 2012.

Jiang Hong. "'I Don't Make Guns, I Only Make a Steel Piano'—Three Northeasterners Made *The Piano in a Factory*" ["我不造猎枪, 我只造钢的琴"— 三个东北人 弄出《钢的琴》]. *Nanfang zhoumo*, July 14, 2011.

Jiang Yong interview with Ang Lee. "For the Thousand Generations to Come, It Is Nothing to Drive a Few to Death" [记者访谈《李安: 为了千秋万代 逼死几个人不算什么》]. *Southern Metropolis Daily*, August 1, 2007.

Jin Chongji. "The Cultural Revolution's Ten Years of Chaos" [文化大革命"的十年动]. In *Outline of China's Twentieth Century History* [二十世纪中国史纲], 906–20. Beijing: Social Sciences Documentation Press, 2009.

Jin Guantao and Liu Qingfeng. *Lishi de Chensi: Zhongguo fengjian shehui ji qi changqi yanxu yuanyin shentao* [Contemplating history: China's feudal society and the reasons for its endurance, a discussion]. Beijing: Sanlian shudian, 1981.

Jin Guantao and Liu Qingfeng. *Xingsheng yu weiji: lun Zhongguo fengjian shehui de chaowending jiegou* [Flourishing and crisis: On the superstable structure of China's feudal society]. Changsha: Hunan Renmin chubanshe, 1984.

Jin Guantao and Liu Qingfeng. *Zhongguo fengjian shehui: Yige chaowending xitong* [China's feudal society: A superstable system]. Guizhou: Guizhou shifan daxueyuan xuebao, 1980.

Latham, Michael. *Modernization as Ideology: American Social Science and "Nation Building" in the Kennedy Era.* New Cold War History. Chapel Hill: University of North Carolina Press, 2000.

Li Dongran. "Between Reality and Absurdity: A Piano out of Steel" [现实与荒诞之间, 一架"钢的琴"]. *Sanlian Shenghuo Zhoukan*, 2011.

Li Yanshou. *The History of the Southern Dynasties* [南史], vol. 5. Beijing: Zhonghua, 1975.

Lian Si, ed. *Ant Tribe: An Account of the University Graduates Ghetto* [蚁族: 大学毕业生聚居村实录]. Guangxi: Guangxi Normal University Press, 2009.

Liu Jianping. "*Lust, Caution* Glorifies Traitors." *Global Times*, November 9, 2007.

Liu, Lydia. *Translingual Practice: Literature, National Culture, Translated Modernity, China, 1900–1937.* Stanford, CA: Stanford University Press, 1995.

Liu Wei, Wang Nannan, and Wang Xuguang. "Lu Chuan fangtan: Yi shiyi yu aiqing lai pai Nanjing" [Interview with Lu Chuan: Depicting Nanjing with poetry and love.] *Liaowang News Weekly*, April 22, 2009.

Liu Yan. Presentation at "Representations: History and Memory" [再现: 历史与

记忆]. Beijing University, Center for Cinema and Cultural Studies, October 28–30, 2011.

Lu Chuan. "Duihua Lu Chuan: Shi guanzhong jiu le Nanjing! Nanjing!" [A dialogue with Lu Chuan: The audience saved *Nanjing! Nanjing!*]. Sina.com, April 30, 2009. http://ent.sina.com.cn/m/c/p/2009-04-30/06542498213.shtml.

Lu Xun. "A Madman's Diary" [狂人日記] (1918), translated by Yang Xianyi and Gladys Yang. In *The Columbia Anthology of Modern Chinese Literature*, 2nd ed., edited by Joseph S. M. Lau and Howard Goldblatt. New York: Columbia University Press, 2007.

Lu Xun. "Postscript: Soviet Art and Culture Policies" [苏俄文艺政策]. In *Lu Xun's Collected Writings* [鲁迅全集], vol. 4. Beijing: Renmin Press, 1981.

Luo Yongsheng. "Shijiande baoli/jiyide zhengzhi: Wujiandao xiliede yuyan jiedu" [The violence of time and the politics of memory: An allegorical interpretation of the *Infernal Affairs* series]. *Zihua*, no. 2 (2006).

Ma Rongrong. "Ang Lee's *Lust and Caution*." *Life Weekly*, September 18, 2007.

Mao Zedong. "On Coalition Government" [论联合政府]. Report presented at the Chinese Communist Party's seventh national congress meeting, April 24, 1945.

Mao Zedong. "Reply to Comrade Guo Moro" [满江红·和郭沫若同志]. In *Chairman Mao's Poems* [毛主席诗词]. Beijing: Renmin Wenxue, 1963.

Mao Zedong. "Water Song: Swimming" [水调歌头·游泳]. *Poetry Review* [诗刊], 1957, 1.

Marcos, Subcomandante. "The Fourth World Has Begun." Translated by Nathalie de Broglio. *Nepantla: Views from the South* 2, no. 3 (2001): 559–72.

Meng Yue and Dai Jinhua. *Emerging from the Horizon of History: A Study of Modern Women's Literature* [浮出历史地表：现代妇女文学研究]. Zhengzhou: Henan Renmin, 1989.

Mulvey, Laura. "Visual Pleasure and Narrative Cinema." *Screen* 16, no. 3 (autumn 1975): 6–18.

"Nanjing! Nanjing! Ba da miankong: Renxing de huanyuan" [The eight faces of *Nanjing! Nanjing!*: Kadokawa's recuperation of humanity]. Sina.com, 2009. http://ent.sina.com.cn/m/2009-04-13/ba2469496.shtml.

Qiu Gui-fen. "From Eileen Chang to the Making of Taiwan Female Literature Tradition." In *Reading Eileen Chang*, edited by Yang Ze. Taipei: Rye Field, 1999.

Qiu Liben. "*Lust, Caution* in Taiwan: Return to History by a Sorrowful China" [«色·戒»在台湾：以中国悲情还原历史]. *Southern Metropolis Daily*, October 4, 2007.

Rabe, John. *La Bei Riji* [The diaries of Rabe]. Translated by Translation Team. Nanjing: Jiangsu Renmin Chubanshe, 1997.

Shi Nai'an and Luo Guanzhong. *Shuihu zhuan* [Outlaws of the marsh]. Beijing: Renmin Wenxue Chubanshe, 1997.

Sima Qian. *Records of the Grand Historian* [史记]. Beijing: China Economics Press, 2010.

Song Xiaojun, Wang Xiaodong, Song Qiang, Huang Jisu, and Liu Yang. *Zhongguo bu gaoxing: Da shidai, da mubiao, ji women de neiyou waihuan* [China is not pleased: Big times, big goals, our anxieties and challenges]. Nanjing: Jiangsu Renmin Chubanshe, 2009.

Special Commentator. "Sixiang jiben yuanze bu yong weifan: Ping dianying wenxue juben 'Ku lian'" [We cannot tolerate any violation of the four basic principles: On the film script "Bitter Love"]. *Jiefangjun Bao* [People's Liberation Army Daily], April 20, 1981.

Wan Yan. "The Island of the Day Before: Film, Scholarship and Me" [昨日 之岛: 电影, 学术与我] (an interview with Dai Jinhua). In Dai Jinhua, *The Island of the Day Before: Film Critique of Dai Jinhua* [昨日之岛 : 戴锦华电影文章自选集]. Beijing: Beijing University Press, 2015.

Wang, Ban, ed. *Chinese Visions of World Order: Tianxia, Culture, and World Politics*. Durham, NC: Duke University Press, 2017.

Wang, Jing, and Tani E. Barlow. "Introduction." In *Cinema and Desire: Feminist Marxism and Cultural Politics in the Work of Dai Jinhua*, edited by Jing Wang and Tani E. Barlow, 1–12. New York: Verso, 2002.

Wang Wenshuo, Bai Ying, and Chang Ailing. "Lu Chuan: Paishe 'Nanjing' shi yige qu fuhaohua de guocheng" [Lu Chuan: Making "Nanjing" is a process of de-stereotyping]. Xinhua News Agency, April 24, 2009. http://view.qq.com/a/20090426/000020.htm.

Wang Xiaofeng. "Lu Chuan: Wo xiang pai yige zhanzheng benxing de dongxi" [Lu Chuan: I want to make a movie that shows the true face of war]. *Sanlian Shenghuo Zhoukan*, November 2009.

Wickert, Erwin, ed. *The Good Man of Nanking: The Diaries of John Rabe*. New York: Knopf, 1998.

Wu Hongfei and Jin Lehao. "Lu Chuan: Pai chu zhongguoren de Kangzheng" [Lu Chuan: A depiction of Chinese resistance]. *Nanfang Renwu Weekly*, May 27, 2009.

Wu Xiaobo. "The Melancholia of the Chinese Working Class" [中国工人阶级的忧伤]. *Financial Times* (Chinese edition), July 20, 2011.

Xia Shiqing. *Lust, Caution: Eileen Chang and Hu Lan-cheng* [色·戒 : 张爱玲与胡兰成的前世今生]. Linfen, Shanxi: Shanxi Normal University Press, 2007.

Xue Feng. "Special Interview with Director Zhang Meng: Persist as Much as You Can" [导演张猛专访 : 能坚持,就再坚持一下]. *Film World* [电影世界] 6 (2011).

Yang Jian. *Wenge shiqide dixia wenxue* [Underground literature of the Cultural Revolution]. Beijing: Chaohua chubanshe, 1993.

Yi Dongfang. "Zhang Meng Uses Absurdity to Illuminate Reality" [张猛用荒诞照亮现实]. *Jinghua shibao* [京华时报], July 18, 2011.

Yu Qi. "Ang Lee: It Is Hard to Live in Eileen Chang's World." *Dongfang Zaobao* [东方早报], August 28, 2007.

Yuan Lei. "Dianyingju fuzhuzhang: 'Nanjing! Nanjing!' Jingdezhu lishi he xianshi kaoyan" [Interview with the deputy director of the film bureau: *Nanjing! Nanjing!* can stand the test of historical and contemporary realism]. *Nanfang Zhoumo*, April 29, 2009.

Zhang Baorui. *Yizhi Xiuhuaxie, Meihuadang, Lüse shiti* [An embroidered shoe, a plum painting, the green corpse]. Beijing: Dazhong wenyi chubanshe, 2005.

"Zhang Meng Explains *The Piano in a Factory*: Moving between Reality and Absurdity" [张猛解密《钢的琴》, 感动在现实与荒诞之间]. June 30, 2011. http://ent.163.com/11/0630/11/77PTLSJL000300B1.html.

Zhao Hanmo. "A Lost Social Class" [失落的阶级]. *China Youth Daily* [中国青年报], August 3, 2011.

Zhao Ming. "Manchangde lu, jianxinde lu: You kan dianying dao xie dianying" [The long and arduous road: From watching movies to writing movies]. Zhonghua renmin gongheguo gonganbu [Public Security Bureau, People's Republic of China], 2007.

Zhong, Xueping. *Masculinity Besieged? Issues of Modernity and Male Subjectivity in Chinese Literature of the Late Twentieth Century.* Durham, NC: Duke University Press, 2000.

Zhou, Yaqin. "Rethinking the Cultural History of Chinese Film" (an interview with Dai Jinhua), translated by Lau Kin Chi. In *Cinema and Desire: Feminist Marxism and Cultural Politics in the Work of Dai Jinhua*, edited by Jing Wang and Tani E. Barlow, 235–63. New York: Verso, 2002.

Žižek, Slavoj. "Alfred Hitchcock, or, The Form and Its Historical Mediation." In *Everything You Always Wanted to Know about Lacan but Were Afraid to Ask Hitchcock.* New York: Verso, 1992. Chinese translation by Mu Qing, Shanghai: Renmin Chubanshe, 2007.

Zong Pu. "Wo shi shui" [Who am I?]. In *Zong Pu Daibiao Zuo* [Zuo Pu's representative works], 88–99. Zhengzhou: Huanghe Wenyi Chubanshe, 1987.

TRANSLATORS' BIOGRAPHIES

CHRISTOPHER CONNERY is visiting professor of cultural studies at Shanghai University and professor of literature and cultural studies at the University of California, Santa Cruz. He is also a member of the Shanghai-based Chinese-language Grass Stage Theater (Caotaiban). He has published on early imperial textual culture (*Empire of the Text: Writing and Authority in Early Imperial China*, 1998) and global cultural studies (*The Worlding Project: Doing Cultural Studies in the Era of Globalization*, 2007), and has published many articles on oceanic ideologies in capitalism, the global 1960s, and contemporary Chinese intellectual politics.

LENNET DAIGLE is a translator and PhD candidate at the University of California, Santa Cruz. His dissertation, "Ethical Exemplarity and Historical Hermeneutics in Early PRC Literary Criticism," analyzes the controversies concerning historical fiction that preceded the Cultural Revolution.

REBECCA E. KARL is professor of history at New York University. Her most recent book is *The Magic of Concepts: History and the Economic in Twentieth-Century China* (Duke University Press, 2017). She is the cotranslator, with Xueping Zhong, of Cai Xiang's *Revolution and Its Narratives* (Duke University Press, 2016), and coeditor/cotranslator, with Lydia Liu and Dorothy Ko, of *The Birth of Chinese Feminism: Essential Texts in Transnational Theory* (2013). She is currently the recipient of a multiyear Institute for New Economic Thinking fellowship that supports her newest project, tentatively titled "The Worlds of Economic Thinking in China's Twentieth Century."

JIE LI is assistant professor of East Asian languages and civilizations at Harvard, with research interests in modern Chinese literature, film, media, and cultural history. She is the author of *Shanghai Homes: Palimpsests of Private Life* (2014) and coeditor of *Red Legacies in China: Cultural Afterlives of the Communist Revolution* (2016). Her published articles include "A National Cinema for a Puppet State: The Manchurian Motion Picture Association" and "From Landlord Manor to Red Memorabilia: Reincarnations of a Chinese Museum Town." She is completing two books: *Utopian Ruins: A Memorial Museum of the Mao Era* and *Cinema at the Grassroots: The Exhibition and Reception of Cinema in Socialist China*.

YAJUN MO is assistant professor of Chinese history at Boston College. She is currently at work on two projects—a book tracing the development of modern Chinese tourism and diverse experiences of travel in modern China, and a study of Zhuang Xueben, one of the first ethnographic photographers in modern China.

LISA ROFEL is professor of anthropology and codirector of the Center for Emerging Worlds at the University of California, Santa Cruz. She is the author of *Other Modernities: Gendered Yearnings in China after Socialism* (1999) and *Desiring China: Experiments in Neoliberalism, Sexuality, and Public Culture* (Duke University Press, 2007). She has completed a collaborative book (with Sylvia J. Yanagisako) titled *Fabricating Transnational Capitalism: A Collaborative Ethnography of Italian-Chinese Global Fashion* (Duke University Press, 2018).

SHUANG SHEN is associate professor of comparative literature and Asian studies at Pennsylvania State University. She is the author of *Cosmopolitan Publics: Anglophone Print Culture in Semicolonial Shanghai* (2009) and coeditor of a special issue of *Social Text* on "China and the Human" (2011 and 2012) and a special issue of *Verge* on "Asian Urbanisms" (2015). She has published articles and essays in *Comparative Literature*, MLQ, *Modern China*, MCLC, PMLA, *Xinmin Weekly* (in Chinese), and *Wanxiang* (in Chinese). She was the recipient of a Fulbright U.S. Scholar grant and a Chiang Ching-Kuo Foundation Scholar Grant in 2015–16. She was also a senior research fellow at the Asia Research Institute at the National University of Singapore in 2015. She is currently working on a book that studies trans-Pacific circulation of Sinophone literature during the Cold War period.

EREBUS WONG currently works as a researcher in the Kwan Fong Cultural Research and Development Programme, Lingnan University, Hong Kong.

INDEX

Abusers and the Abused, The (photo series), 88–89
adventure (genre), 111, 115
advertising, 113, 128, 177n17
alcohol, 80, 83, 85
amnesia, ix, xxi, 39, 41, 110, 126. *See also* erasure
Anderson, Sherwood, 85
antifeudalism, 18, 28, 155
anti-imperialism, 18, 27–28, 40, 155
"ant tribe," 130, 177n1
architecture, 1–2, 10
arms race, 113
art films, 41, 75, 89, 91, 94, 150–51; in Chinese film industry, 43–44, 129; vs. commercial films, 69, 72; from Hong Kong and Taiwan, 70, 134; non-Western, 68–70; vs. spy films, 117
assassins, 59–60, 132–33, 135
Assembly (film), 19, 152–54, 156–57
At Ten O'Clock on the National Day (film), 110
auteur theory, 68, 79
authoritarianism, 9, 17, 20

Becker, Wolfgang, 104
Before the Flood (documentary), 85, 87, 90
Beginning of the Great Revival (film), 20
Beijing Olympics, xv, 9, 42, 45, 58, 127–29, 154; Ang Lee as consultant for, 136
Bertolucci, Bernardo, xiv, xxiii, 142, 147–49
Bing Ai (documentary), 85–87

Bitter Love (film script), 29–30, 169n10
Black Book (film), 126, 139
"B" movies, 91, 152; spy-films as, 109, 139
Bourne Identity (franchise), 126, 175n

camera: invention of, 68; perspective of, 77, 79, 94, 97
candy, 82–83, 85
capitalism, xiv, xviii, 155; and art films, 69; and China, xvi, 3, 6–7, 14, 127, 154; and cosmopolitanism, 40; crisis of, 22; disappearance of alternatives to, 5, 13, 16, 18, 20, 54, 63, 87, 90, 139; and history writing, 142; and money, 85; and the nation-state, 138
castration, 50, 100
Chang, Eileen, 132–34, 137, 139, 177n12
Chang, Iris, 35–37
Chen Kaige, 60, 67, 92
China: and alternative futures, 18, 20, 22, 55, 63; defined in relation to the West, 4, 16, 18–19, 27–28, 33, 37, 155, 172n12; empty signifiers of, 51, 55, 58; history of, 171n5, 172n10; as international creditor, 11, 17; narrative construction of, xix, 30, 40–41, 43, 56–57, 59, 79, 143–44, 167n6; "rise of," xvi, xviii, 10, 14, 17–18, 42, 45, 58, 78, 140, 154; Sino-Japanese relations, 34–35, 40, 44, 171n21; Sino-Soviet relations, xv, 3, 62, 112, 115–16; and the third world, xv–xvi, 3, 62. *See also* People's Republic of China

China Film Group Corporation, 129
Chinese Civil War, 14, 19, 157
Chinese Communist Party (CCP): in *Assembly*, 19; films promoted by, 20, 113–14, 129; in *I Wish I Knew*, 150; and liberals, 7–8; military success of, 157; regime continuity in capitalist China, xxii–xxiii, 6, 30–31, 127, 144; in spy films, 110; struggles within, 119; transition from revolutionary to ruling party, 12, 167n5, 173n19
Chinese language: classical vs. vernacular, 54–55; standardization of writing system, ix–x, 56–57
Chinese model, 17–20
Chinese national character (*guominxing*), 28, 169n6
Christianity, xix, 38–39, 44, 88, 158, 170n19
Chronicle of the Misty Realm (novels), 53–54
chronotope, 100
City of Endless Fog (film), 122, 124–25
City of Life and Death (film), xiv, xix, 25–26, 31–33, 35, 37–46, 158, 170nn19–20; global audience for, 44–45; reception of, 41, 43; supported by Chinese government, 41–42, 168n2
civil society, 43, 128
class: avoided by Chinese scholars, 2; background of Dai Jinhua, 160; consciousness, 42, 124; and gender, xvii, 82, 99–100, 121, 163–65; identity, 80–81, 100–101; vs. individual, 147; Marxist vs. revisionist meaning of, 144; polarization, 6–7, 98, 127; struggle, 22, 28–29, 116–17. *See also* new Chinese middle class; working class
Class (neighborhood in Wangjing), 1
coal mining, 73, 80, 83–84
Cold War, 2; art films in, 68–69; in *Assembly*, 157; China's position in, xv, 3, 14, 40, 58, 62, 145; end of, xv, 4–5, 17,

104–5, 122, 141; and historical narrative, 142; history erased, 135–36, 150; and Nanjing Massacre, 35; post–Cold War, 6–8, 13, 19, 30, 63, 90, 126; socialism in, 76–77; and spy films, xxii, 109–14, 116–18, 123, 125, 137; Taiwan in, 134. *See also* post-post–Cold War era
comfort women, 39
communism. *See* Chinese Communist Party; Marxism; socialism
Communist Manifesto, The, 3
Confucianism, 26, 114, 124, 168n8; *tianxia* as key concept in, 172n12
consumerism, 10, 13–15, 42, 45, 52, 59, 113, 117, 128, 151, 154
cosmopolitanism, xxiii, 30, 36, 40, 52; vs. nationalism, 41
critical theory, 139–41
Crouching Tiger, Hidden Dragon (film), 51
Cultural Revolution, 59–62, 120; Dai Jinhua in, xvi, 160; language reform in, 54–55; and the spy genre, 115–17; transition out of, 28–29
cultural self-awareness, 18, 20, 70

Dai Jinhua, xiii–xviii, 160–65
danwei (work unit), 100–101
Dealing with the Devil (film), 123–24
de Beauvoir, Simone, 161
deindustrialization, 92–93, 99–100
Deleuze, Gilles, 40
democracy, 7, 9, 14, 21, 130
Democratic People's Republic of Korea, 120
demolition, 71–74, 80, 99–100
Deng Xiaoping, 4, 70
development. *See* modernization
diaspora, 45, 139
Ding Mocun, 132–34
dreams, 45

economic reform, xxi, xxiii, 76; and closure of state-run enterprises, xxi, 92, 99; effect on women, 163–64; and growth, 10; inaugurating post–Cold War era, 4

Emperor and the Assassin, The (film), 48, 60

entertainment film, 43–44

erasure: of alternative noncapitalist futures, 20; of communist-nationalist struggles, xxii, 19, 157; of history, xiv–xv, xix, xxiii, 17, 45, 48, 145–46, 148, 150, 154; of Nanjing Massacre, 34–35, 39–41, 158–59; of nonaligned movement, 62–63; of socialist and revolutionary past in China, xx–xxi, xxiii, 13–14, 46, 130, 136, 144, 157–58; of Tiananmen massacre, 127

espionage. *See* spy films and literature

Eurocentrism: in history writing, 142; of international film festivals, 69

European Union, 5, 9, 14, 16–17, 138

famine, 16, 119

fantasy, 47–48, 53; and the camera's eye, 68; fantastical realism, 97; in *Still Life*, 82

Farewell My Concubine (film), 149

femininity, 160–61; in legacy of Zheng Ping-ru, 132; in spy films, 113–14, 121–24

feminism, xvi–xvii, 161, 164–65; and international NGOs, 162; and new middle class, xvii; *nüxing zhuyi* vs. *nüquan zhuyi*, 163

Feng Xiaogang, 19, 43, 152–53, 156

Feng Yan, 87

fifth-generation Chinese filmmakers, xxiii, 45, 67, 77, 79, 148; aesthetic of, 47, 58, 75, 146; and May Fourth Movement, 75–76; raised in Mao era, 59; and representation of suffering, 92

film festivals, 91; awards granted to Chinese filmmakers, 43, 45, 67, 90, 137, 148; and non-Western filmmakers, 68–70

film noir, 109, 114, 139

financial crisis of 2008, xv, 3, 9–11, 14–15, 98, 154

Flowers of War, The (film), 158

fold (Deleuzian concept), xvi, 40, 55, 57, 172n14

Forrest Gump (film), 142–43

Foucault, Michel, 44, 142

Founding of a Republic, The (film), 129

Friedan, Betty, 161

gangster films, 82, 102–3

gaze: cinematic, 77, 79, 89, 97; gendered, 121–22, 125; global, xix; of pathos, 134; Western, xviii

gender, xxii, 74, 78; and class, xvii, 82, 99–100, 121, 163–65; in historical costume dramas, 151; and human trafficking, 84; and Maoism, xvi, 160; performativity, 161–62; and reception of Iris Chang, 36; in spy films, 113–14, 121–25, 177n17; and Zheng Ping-ru, 132–33

General Motors, 16

genre: adventure, 111; in Chinese film industry, 43–44; cinema as, 50; in mass entertainment, 115; political intrigue, 117, 176n12; propaganda, 43, 20, 129; quasi-, 109, 175n1; revolutionary, 156; spy, xxi–xxii, 109–26, 132, 137; suspense, 118; tragedy vs. tragicomedy, 98; western, 171n3

Germany: auteurs in, 68; East German music, 104, 175n21; and the Holocaust, 34–35; postunification historical narratives of, 143

"global Chinese," 129, 139

globalization, xiv–xv, xxiii, 4; in *Assembly*, 157; and disappearance of second world, 85; and humanism, 30–31; imbricated in the local, xviii, 11, 52, 130, 139; and international capital flows, 5, 14–15; and the Olympics, 127; opposition to, 8, 20, 90; and regionalization, 138; and *tianxia*, 63; and U.S. war on terror, xv, 8–9

Good Bye Lenin! (film), 104–5
Good German, The (film), 139
Good Man of Nanking, The (book), 35–40
Great Chinese Famine, 119
Guomindang, 150; in spy films, 110, 114–15, 124
guominxing (Chinese national character), 28, 169n6

hand-circulated literature, 116–17, 120, 125
hegemony: admiration for, 40; American, 8–9; of capitalism, xiv, 142; of class-struggle ideology, 28; competition for, 12, 58, 115; cultural, 13–15, 127–28, 145, 151–52, 154; vs. regionalization, 138; and *tianxia*, xx, 52–54, 56
Hero (film), xx, 19, 47–50, 53, 55–58, 152, 158; domestic vs. international audience for, 51, 58; links to Mao era, 59–61
historical materialism, 60, 76, 120, 141, 144
history: ahistorical, xxiii, 145–46, 148–49; apolitical, 52; and the individual, 132, 134, 142, 147–48, 152–53; "MacGuffinication" of, 48, 55; made by the people, 76–77, 143–44, 178n7; and memory, xiv, xxiii, 141–43, 146–47, 159; politics of, 142–43; subject of, xix, 21, 76–77, 139, 144, 152, 157, 165; Western vs. Chinese, 4, 13, 15, 36, 76, 156. *See also* erasure
Hitchcock, Alfred, 118
Hollywood: and auteur theory, 68; distribution network, 47; films, 16, 19, 37, 91, 98, 109, 126, 138, 147; representation of gender in, 121–22
Holocaust, 33–34
Hong Kong: celebrities of, 129; cinema of, 47, 70, 80, 118, 134; gangster films, 82, 102, 111, 138; *Lust, Caution* screened in, 132; popular culture of, 48, 171n4; translation of "nostalgia" in, 8

Horse Caravan, The (film), 111
Huang Ji-su, 131, 140
humanism: and Christianity, 38–39, 44; in *City of Life and Death*, xix, 25–26, 40, 170nn19–20; "the human writ large," 29–31, 41, 44; and reception of *Lust, Caution*, 136; in twentieth-century China, 26–31, 37

identity: class, 42, 80–81, 100–101, 121, 124, 128, 132; confusion in spy genre, xxi–xxii, 118–20, 122–24, 126, 137; cultural, 18; national, 10, 14, 27–28, 30, 36–37, 42, 45, 124, 126–31; of "the people," 120; in post–Cold War era, 134, 138–39
imagined community, 28, 127, 129
imperialism, 12, 27; anti-, 18, 27–28, 155; Chinese, 56–58; Japanese, xxiii, 40; monetary, 83; in spy films, 113, 116; Western, 86; of United States, 8–9
individual: heroic, 125; and history, xiv, xxiii, 132, 134, 142, 146–47, 152–53; in *The Last Emperor*, 147–48; and the nation, 139–40; vs. "the people," 77; as pure subject, 126; in *Still Life*, 78–79
industrialization, 10, 92, 119–20; defended by Chinese New Left, 154; Soviet, 113
Infernal Affairs (film), 118, 125, 137, 139
Internet literature, 48, 53–54
Invisible Fronts (film), 111
iron rice bowl, 105, 175n24
I Wish I Knew (film), 149–50

James Bond franchise, 109, 112, 125; advertising in, 113
Japan: in global 1960s, 87; "Japanese devils," 38, 40, 45, 149; as leading capitalist country, 9, 11, 127; occupation of China, xxii–xxiii, 131, 135; reluctant to acknowledge Nanjing Massacre, xix, 33–34; Sino-Japanese relations, 14, 28, 34–35, 40, 44, 134, 168n8, 171n21; sym-

bol of humanity, xix, 32–33, 38–40, 43; symbol of modernity, 27, 40–41

jianghu (outlaw world), 52, 171n6

Jiang Zemin, 12, 70

Jia Zhangke, xx–xxi, 67–68, 70, 72, 74–75, 77, 79, 83–84, 89–90, 149, 175n12

Jiuzhou (publisher), 53, 172n10

June Fourth Incident. *See* Tiananmen Square

Kuimen, 83–84

Kusturica, Emir, 104–5

La Bei Riji (book), 35–40

labor. *See* working class

land reform, 19, 157, 168n6, 173n19

language reform, 54–55

Last Emperor, The, xxiii, 142, 147–48

Law Archive (art installation), 88–90

Lee, Ang, xxii, 109, 132; consultant for Beijing Olympics, 136; controversy surrounding, 131, 133–36, 140; and Eileen Chang, 133–34; part of Chinese diaspora, 139

liberals in China, 7–8; and the New Left, xv, 14, 130; reject social history, 154. *See also* neoliberalism

Li Ning, 128

Liu Shaoqi, 143, 178n4

Li Yifan, 87–89

love: for America, 11; in *City of Life and Death*, 31; in Eileen Chang's life, 133; for homeland, 30, 57, 87; in *Lust, Caution*, 135; and money, 83–84; in *Piano in a Factory*, 95; in spy films, 119, 123–24, 132; in *Still Life*, 75, 79, 81; and *tianxia*, 49

Lu Chuan, xiv, xix, 25, 32, 38, 41, 44–45, 158, 168n2

Lust, Caution (film), xxii–xxiii, 109, 126, 130–37, 139–40; censorship of, 132, 136, 177n19; controversy around, 131, 133, 135–36, 140; reception in Taiwan, 134

Lu Xun, 26–27, 144, 146, 169n4, 178n5

luxury goods, 10, 15, 82, 99, 113, 128, 154

MacGuffin (plot device), 48, 55

"Madman's Diary, A" (story), 26, 169n4

majia phenomenon, 52, 172n7

major-theme movie, 43–44, 46

Mao Zedong: era, 29, 76–78, 129, 143; global influence of, xv, 3; images of, 70, 85; language reforms of, ix; masculinist critique of, xvi, 160; nostalgia for, 8; and Qin Shihuang, 59–60; rejection of, xiv, xvii; slogans of, 102, 116; third-world doctrine of, 62; and Three Gorges project, 76; and *tianxia*, xx, 61

martial arts films and literature, 47–48, 52, 171n4

Marxism: concept of class in, 144; contemporary significance of, 3, 21, 164; of Dai Jinhua, xiii; as ghost of capitalism, 165; and humanism, 28–29; lacunae of, xvii; material traces of, xiv, 2, 85; in the People's Liberation Army, 157; and political violence, 20; subject of history in, 76; temporality of, 4. *See also* socialism

masculinity: and critique of Maoism, xvi, 160; and patriarchy, 161–63; and scopic desire, xxii, 121–22; and working-class identity, xxi, 99–100

mass culture, 155–56; hegemonic, 13, 151–52; and history, 142; spy genre as part of, 109, 111, 115, 117, 176n9

May Fourth Movement, 18–19, 55, 76, 78, 144–46, 155–56, 168n8

memory: of the Cold War, 136, 139, 157; collective vs. individual, xxii–xxiii, 125, 147–48; of historical atrocities, xix, 34–35, 44, 158–59; and history, xiv, 13, 135, 141–43, 146–47, 152–53; vs. mourning, 21; in *Piano in a Factory*, 96, 104; politics of, 37–41; of Mao era, 59–61, 78, 100–101; in *Still Life*, 84; of twentieth-century China, 46, 130

Meng Yue, xiii, 162

Message, The, 109, 126

middle class. *See* new Chinese middle class

Middle Kingdom, 56, 172n12, 172n15

migration, 5; and globalization, 138–39; and land policy, 168n6; migrant workers, 1, 84, 101, 179n2; and Three Gorges project, xxi, 71, 73–74

mirror stage, 18, 41

modernism (art), 68–69

modernity: capitalist, xxiii, 155; Chinese discourses of, 26–28, 48; critique of, 55, 63, 69, 75; vs. tradition, 18; in *Yellow Earth,* 76

modernization, 10–11, 71; anxiety, 113, 115–16; destructiveness of, xxi, 18, 72, 87, 89; displaces revolutionary imaginary, 144, 153–54; glorification of, xxi; as ideology, 136; legitimates Chinese regime, 13; prehistory of, 75; and primitive accumulation, 100; socialist route to, 3, 16, 154; temporalities of, 4, 75; and Three Gorges project, 70–71, 86; and Westernization, xv, 8–9, 19, 28, 54–55, 76, 87, 144, 155–56, 168n8

money, 14–15, 85, 92; in Chinese funerals, 174n7; materiality of, 83; symbolism of, 84

montage: in historical narrative, 13, 145; in *Piano in a Factory,* 96–98, 103

Mulvey, Laura, 124, 161

name of the father, 99–100, 148

Nanjing Massacre, xix, 25–26, 29, 31–33, 43, 158–59, 168nn1–2, 170n20; and Chinese self-image, 40–41; nonrecognition of, 34–35, 39; and other historical atrocities, 36–37; publicized, 170n15; and refugee camps, 38–39; Sino-Japanese relations affected by, 44

Nanjing! Nanjing! (film). See *City of Life and Death*

nationalism, xx, 14, 28, 36; and anti-Japanese sentiment, 40–41; and glo-

balization, 139; in Guomindang ideology, 124; in interpretation of Chinese history, 56–57; of May Fourth Movement, 168n8; and new middle class, 42, 45–46; in responses to *Lust, Caution,* 134–36

nation-state: after communism, 21, 136; China's emergence as, 3–4, 28, 127, 129, 172n12; and globalization, 16, 46, 138; and the individual, 139–40; as lens for Chinese history, 13, 56–57, 135, 153–54; in *Lust, Caution,* 131, 140; middle-class identification with, 14, 128; and modernization, 76; and spy films, xxii, 126, 137

neoliberalism, xiv–xvi, 4–5, 40, 98; cultural impacts of, 68–69, 151–52; and global hierarchy, 40, 54; and nostalgia for 1930s, 7–8

new Chinese middle class, xv, xviii; and Chinese national identity, xx, 14, 42–46, 136; cosmopolitanism of, xxiii, 15, 45–46, 130–32; emergence of, 9–10, 128; feminism appropriated by, xvii, 164; humanism of, 26

New Left, 7–8; and art films, 68–69; and Chinese liberals, xv, 14, 130, 154

new media, 41, 48, 52–53

New Wave cinema, 68, 70

North Korea, 120

nostalgia, 7–8, 21, 105, 117; for old Shanghai, 132, 139

nüquan zhuyi (women's rights), xvi–xvii, 163

nüxing zhuyi (gender ideology), xvi–xvii, 163

Occupy Wall Street, 21–22

October Revolution, 141, 156

one-child policy, 130

orientalism, xviii, 17, 149, 155–56, 169n6; and authority of white Europeans, 36

Orphan of Zhao, The (play), 158

Oscar (Academy Award), 47, 51, 138

patriarchy, xvii, 161–63

peasants, 130, 168n6; communist mobilization of, 157; rebellions, 144, 172n9

people, the, 78, 102; history made by, 76–77, 143–44, 178n7; vs. the human, 28; identity of, 120–21

People's Republic of China: founding of, 4, 28, 42; vs. Republic of China, 136; sixtieth anniversary of, 128–29; women's liberation in, 163

Piano in a Factory, The (film), xxi, 91–105; black humor in, 93; cinematography of, 93–97; music and dance in, 97–98, 103–4; reception of, 104–5; rejects tragedy, 98–99, 103

Platform (film), 67, 149

political intrigue (genre), 117, 176n12

political unconscious, xvi, xviii, 39, 119, 122, 134, 137–39

popular culture. *See* mass culture

pornography, 136

postmodernism, 47, 82, 84–85, 105, 139, 141; in architecture, 10; cynicism of, 110; and flattening of history, 150

post–post–Cold War era, xv, xix, 11–12, 19, 87, 154–56; communism in, 20; the nation in, 129–30, 138; and neoliberalism, 40; vs. pre–Cold War era, 139; and rise of China, 14–16; and U.S. imperialism, 9; utopian imagination in, 21

post-structuralism, xiii, 141, 161

primitive accumulation, 10, 17, 100

product placement, 16, 113

proletariat. *See* working class

propaganda film, 20, 27, 40, 43, 46, 129

prostitution, 74, 85, 124

psychoanalysis, xiii, 44, 50, 89, 99, 118, 148, 174n13; inadequate for political analysis, 100

Pu Yi, xxiii, 147–48

Qing dynasty, 27, 57; in popular media, xxiii, 148, 151

Qin Shihuang, xx, 47, 58, 172n17;

achievements of, 56; in popular culture, 57; revisionist histories of, 59, 61, 63

Rabe, John, 26, 35–40, 170nn19–20

Rape of Nanking, The (book), 26, 35–37, 44

realism, 47, 85, 96; magical, 97

Records of the Grand Historian (book), 171n5, 173n22

Red Guards, 61–62, 148

Red Sorghum (film), 148–49

regionalization, 138

renminbi (RMB), 15, 83

Reveal Her True Identity (film), 120

reversing cases (*fan'an wenzhang*), 144

revolution: and alternative futures, 21; as a cause of suffering, 119; and the CCP, 12; in Chinese history, xx, 59; and "counterrevolutionary elements," 117; Cuban, 9; culture of, xviii; erased from history, xx–xxi, xxiii, 13–14, 46, 130; and folk culture, 78; global, 62, 144; justice of, 60; of 1911, 4; post-, 54, 63, 130, 146; vs. reform, 90; and resistance, 87; and revisionist history, 142; Russian, 141, 156; temporality of, 153–54. *See also* Cultural Revolution, The

"root-seeking" literature, 146, 178n9

Rousseau, Jean-Jacques, 88–89

"scar" novels and films, 29, 147, 169n8

Schindler's List (film), 37, 44

scopic desire, xxii, 121–22

Second Sex, The (book), 161

Secret Map, The (film), 119–20

September 11 attacks, 8–9, 11, 51, 89

sexuality, 81, 84–85; in *Lust, Caution*, 131–33, 135–36; in spy films, 113–14, 121–22, 139

Shanghai, 15; Communist Party occupation of, 150; migration to, 70, 74; of the 1930s, 8, 13, 132–34, 139

Shanxi coal mines, 73, 84

58–59; in the Cultural Revolution, 61–62; idealism of, 49–50, 57; and May Fourth Movement, 55; in popular culture, 52–54; translation of, 51, 58; vs. Zhongguo, 55, 172n12

Tibet, 42, 136

time. *See* temporality

tobacco, 80, 83, 85

To Live (film), 149

tracking shots, 93–97

trade war, 113, 119

traditional Chinese culture, 18, 20, 28, 48, 55, 63, 81, 87, 178n8; May Fourth Movement opposition to, 168n8

tragedy: and fifth-generation filmmakers, 92; politics of, 98; staged as comedy, 93

trauma: at decline of Chinese empire, 27; individual, xiv, 142; of Nanjing Massacre, xix, 25, 31, 34–35, 39–41; of revolution, 119; of Tiananmen Square, 127; of twentieth century, 44, 92; of witnessing, 141, 178n1; of working class, 103

24 City (film), 150–51, 175n12

Underground (film), 104–5

underground cinema, 67, 85

underground literature, 116–17, 120

unemployment, 74, 103; as global phenomenon, 98; and market reforms, 92–93, 99, 101, 104

United Nations, 62; Women's Conference of 1995, 161–62

United States: and capitalist imaginary, 14; in Chinese spy films, 110; dollars, 83; empire, 8–9; indebted to China, 11; 1972 Joint Communiqué, 145; reception of *Rape of Nanking* in, 35, 37

utopia, xiv, xix, 21, 95, 150, 165; communist, 4, 20; discarded by capitalist globalization, 63, 139; and human-

ism, 27, 29–30; endlessly deferred, 16; neo-Maoist website, 134, 136

Verhoeven, Paul, 126, 139

Village Archive (documentary), 88

Walter Defends Sarajevo (film), 120

Wangjing, 1

war on terror, xv, 8–9, 89

Wenchuan earthquake, xv, 9–10, 42, 127–28

Westernization, xv, 8–9, 19, 28, 54–55, 76, 87, 144, 155–56, 168n8

West of the Tracks (documentary), 101, 175n22

"Who Am I" (story), 29

worker-peasant-soldier art and film, 109, 111, 121–22, 125

working class, xviii, 72, 82–83, 89–92; dignity of, xxi, 96–97, 102; fraternal solidarity among, 103; as historical subject, xix, 76–77, 97, 165; marginalization of, 95, 150; and masculinity, 99; migrant workers, 1, 73–74, 84, 101, 168n6, 179n2; old vs. new, 100–101

Xinhai Revolution, 4

Years of Burning Passion, The (TV series), 151

Yellow Earth (film), 67, 77–78

Zhang Meng, xx–xxi, 92–94, 97, 99–101, 103–5

Zhang Yimou, xx, 19, 37, 43, 47, 50, 58, 67, 92, 148, 158

Zheng Ping-ru, 132–35, 177n12

Zhongguo (China), 55, 172n12

Žižek, Slavoj, 55, 100, 118

Zong Pu, 29

Zwartboek (film), 126, 139